ALONSO NÚÑEZ DE REINOSO:
The Lament of a Sixteenth-Century Exile

ALONSO NÚÑEZ DE REINOSO:

The Lament
of a Sixteenth-Century Exile

Constance Hubbard Rose

Rutherford • Madison • Teaneck
Fairleigh Dickinson University Press

Associated University Presses, Inc.
Cranbury, New Jersey 08512

ISBN: 0-8386-7612-X
Printed in the United States of America

CONTENTS

ACKNOWLEDGMENTS

I should like to express my sincere appreciation to Stephen Gilman, Raimundo Lida, and Francisco Márquez Villanueva for their inspiration and guidance, to the late Antonio Rodríguez Moñino for his innumerable bibliographical suggestions, to Marcel Bataillon for showing the way, to Frank Casa for his excellent advice, to Richard Lowell Rubenstein for checking the theological argument for consistency, and to Louise G. Cohen and Henry W. Sullivan for their assistance and their faith.

The author also wishes to thank Professor Benzion Netanyahu, for permission to quote from his book *The Marranos of Spain from the Late XIVth to the Early XVth Century According to Contemporary Hebrew Sources*, New York: Kraus Reprint Corp., 1966. Reprinted by permission.

INTRODUCTION

Y esparcirte ha Jehová por todos
los pueblos desde el un cabo de
la tierra hasta el otro cabo de
la tierra . . . Y ni aun en las
mismas gentes reposarás, ni la
planta de tu pie tendrá reposo.
Deuteronomy 28 : 64, 65[1]

Ando assi de sierra en sierra
. . . .
De una tierra en otra tierra
Como si fuese gitano
Peregrino.
. . . .
. . . ya no espero
Salir de tierras agenas.
Núñez de Reinoso

To the droves of Peninsular Jews and *conversos* of
the sixteenth century, the victims of the Second Diaspora,
the Biblical prophecy of castigation once more became
a reality. The historical events that precipitated this
were: in Spain, the establishment of the Office of the
Inquisition in 1478 and the Expulsion Order of 1492;

---

1. *La Santa Biblia,* versión de Cipriano de Valera. Revisada y corregida, Nueva York, 1881.

9

in Portugal, the influx of refugees from Spain, the forced
conversions of 1499, and the eventual installation of the
long-resisted Office of the Inquisition in 1547. By the mid-
sixteenth century, there was in the Peninsula a sizable
portion of the citizenry faced with the prospect either
of the vicissitudes of compulsory migration or the anxiety
of living in a land that might, at any moment, reject them.

Among these hapless people, thus cognizant of being
creatures of circumstance, was born a feeling of group
identity. There was generated a desire to communicate
the experience. Recognizing their lives as circumscribed
by history, as subject to its forces, men sought means
to affirm the bond of consciousness of their mutually
shared plight. This, in turn, led to the development of
new modes of literary expression by which *converso*
authors could relate the historical predicament in which
they and their potential readers found themselves en-
trapped. The rediscovery and vogue for the Byzantine
novel among intellectuals may be interpreted, in part,
as a means of expressing enforced exile, with the con-
comitant of endless wandering and travail; while the
growth of the pastoral, as expressing the desire to discover a tranquil land immune from the mutability of
fortune and the slings and arrows of quotidian existence.
The first mode refers to the historical situation, which,
temporally and geographically links the Second Diaspora
with the First as a cyclical repetition of events. The
second mode proposes a timeless or ahistorical situation
where past misfortunes are not only recounted but pal-
liated, a pastoral world recreating some Golden Age that
antedates that of Virgil, an imaginary, prehistoric period
in the Land of Canaan before the children of Israel
sinned and bowed to the sentence of a vengeful God.

In one man's recorded response to his personal experience, it is possible to observe both of these literary reactions: the Byzantine as a diagnosis of the sickness of the times, and the pastoral as the yearned-for anodyne. Núñez de Reinoso's novel, *La historia de los amores de Clareo y Florisea y de los trabajos de la sin ventura Isea*, is a Byzantine-chivalric *phantasia* with Arcadian introduction and coda; the appended poems serve both to illuminate the fictional events and explain the author's life. For Reinoso's "historia" is a true history; his fiction is not three steps removed from truth, but truth's very essence adorned—"veritatem rerum pulchris velaminibus adornare"; it is the story of his life, and his hopes, struggles, and despair.

Description of the volume

The volume published in Venice by the Gabriel Giolito de Ferrari press in 1552 consisted of a novel and poetry. Each part is separately paginated, and each bears its own dedication and laudatory sonnet. Both novel and poetry are dedicated to Juan Micas, the first in the form of a letter that carries the date January 24, 1552. Of the two sonnets, one is anonymous, "De un caballero cuyo nombre se encubre para mayores cosas," and the other is by Lodovico Dolce, a well-known author in his own right, as well as editor for the Giolito press and translator of the Latin fragment of Tatius' work that served as the basis for the first half of Reinoso's novel.[2] At the conclusion of the novel is a letter to Juan Hurtado de

---

2. *Amorosi Ragionamenti. Dialogo nel quale si racconta un compassionevole amore di due amanti, tradotto per M. Ludovico Dolce, dal fragmento d'uno antico Scrittor Greco* . . . , Vinegia, Gabriel Giolito de Ferrari, 1546.

Mendoza, señor de Fresno de Torote, dated March 1, 1552. The second dedication precedes the poems, which are seventeen in number. They can be summarized as follows:

1. Esta primera hablando con una señora su prima desculpa los yerros de sus obras.

A frankly autobiographical poem, in *décimas*,[3] in which he complains about life in Italy and divulges details about his former existence in Spain.

2. Carta a la señora donna Maria de Guzman.

Another autobiographical poem, in *décimas*. The setting is Italy.

3. Otras glosando este: Villancico.

As the title says, a *villancico* that expands the ideas presented in the second poem. The principal topic is nostalgia, "soledad de España," as suggested in the *estribillo*:

> *Pues que bivo en tierra agena*
> *Muy lexos de do nasçí*
> *Quien aura dolor de mí?*

4. Muerte de Lágrimas y de Diana.

A pastoral, written in *décimas* and set in Portugal.

---

3. In this study, the word *décima* is employed to describe a ten-line, eight-syllable poem composed of two *quintillas*. This is not the interlocking *décima espinela* of the seventeenth century. It is otherwise known as the *copla real* in Spain, but since no such term is used in Portugal, I have employed the more generic designation as it is applicable to both Spanish and Portuguese poetry.

5. Comiença la egloga de los dos pastores Baltheo y Argasto.

A pastoral dialogue in which old friends meet and relate their unhappy states. Description and remarks by "Autor" are in *décimas*; dialogue is in *estrofa manriqueña*; there is one song, a *villancico*. There is much autobiographical and topical material; the setting is Portugal.

6. Untitled.

An elegy, in which the death of Darinel is mourned by his fellow shepherds. A *villancico* whose *estribillo* reads:

> *Por Delia si hermosa cruel*
> *Murio el pastor Darinel.*

7. Untitled.

In *décimas*, the topic is typical of *cancionero* love poems. The first lines are:

> *Pues vuestra graçia perdi*
> *Por querer lo que quereis*
> *Desacordado de mi.*

8. Untitled.

A *villancico*, a typical *cancionero* love poem. The *estribillo* reads:

> *Prometieron me los ojos*
> *Mi señora de no os ver,*
> *No lo quieren mantener.*

9. Untitled.

A *villancico* in which he complains of how trying it is to deal with stupid people. The *estribillo* reads:

De los males el mayor
Que en el mundo puede ser
Él con neçios entender.

10. Untitled.

A "perqué de amores".[4] The poem consists of series of quartets, composed of octosyllabic lines. The first quartet reads:

Por qué ventura me tiene
Con un dolor tan llagado?
Porque la causa do viene
Satisfaze a mi cuydado.

11. Al sennor Alonso Nunnez de Reynoso un su amigo y servidor.

In *décimas*, supposedly by "Thomas Gomez," in which he asks Núñez de Reinoso to stop complaining and enjoy life in Italy or to return to Spain. He further asks the reason for Reinoso's exile.

12. Alonso Nunnez de Reynoso al sennor Thomas Gomez: Respuesta.

Also in *décimas*. The poet reexamines his life and reveals his state of mind, but does not answer the question.

13. Siguese un romance.

A *romance* on the same subject. The first lines are:

El que nasçio sin ventura
Solo va sin compañía.

---

4. The *perqué de amores* was a favorite poetic exercise of *cancionero* writers who wished to display their "virtuoso" ability. This linguistic *tour de force* consisted of a series of questions introduced each time by "Por qué" and answers introduced by "Porque."

14. Comienza la glosa deste romance.

As announced, a gloss on the same subject, in which each *décima* concludes with two lines from the *romance*.

15. Alonso Nunnez de Reynoso al sennor Feliciano de Silva.

A Horatian epistle in *terza rima,* in which he laments his life in Italy and praises his friend. This is the first example of Italian verse form among his poems.

16. Al sennor don Lope de Guzman.

Another Horatian epistle in *terza rima* in which he complains about life and praises his friend's poetic ability.

17. Stancias de Rugier, nuevamente glosadas.

The most impersonal of his poems, a translation of Stanzas 61 and 62, Canto XLIV of Ariosto's *Orlando furioso,* followed by a *glosa* which, like its model, is in *octava real.*[5]

---

5. Cf. his translation of stanza 61 to the original Italian:
   Rugier qual siẽpre fui tal ser yo quiero,
   Hasta la muerte y mas ser pudiere,
   O sea amor manso o cruel guerrero,
   O la fortuna de lo que quisiere,
   Que peñasco muy firme ser yo espero,
   Al qual la Mar con fieros vientos hiere,
   Con bonança jamas o con tempestad,
   No mudare querer ni mi voluntad.

   Ruggier, qual sempre fui, tal esser voglio
   fin alla morte, e più se più si puote.
   O siami Amor benigno o m'usi orgoglio
   o me Fortuna in alto o in basso ruote,
   immobil son di vera sede scoglio
   che d'ogn'intorno il vento e il mar percuote:
   né già mai per bonaccia né per verno
   luogo mutai, né muterò in eterno.

Of the seventeen poems, only two were ever reprinted; they are included in volume sixteen of the BAE
series, the *Romancero* compiled by Durán.[6] His item
1362, listed under the heading of "Romances doctri-
nales," is "El que nascio sin ventura / solo va sin compañía" (No. 13), and item 1800, listed under "Romances
de varias clases, hechos de versos pareados . . ." is the
"Perqué de amores" (No. 10). For the reader's con-
venience I have appended to this study Núñez de Reinoso's poetry *in toto*. In the body of this text, in order
to make the poems cited easier to read and to clarify
meaning, I have made a few minor changes; while on
the whole remaining faithful to the original orthography
despite its inconsistencies, I have distinguished between
the use of "u" and "v," have supplied modern punctuation
and accent marks if their absence renders the passage
unintelligible, and have corrected such obvious errors
as *en barque*, when *embarqué* is the word called for. Two
impediments to complete comprehension of the poetry
can be attributed to the sixteenth-century publisher and
author. Because the book was printed in Italy, the poems
contain a number of typographical errors; indeed, the
Giolito press apologized "a los letores" for such printing
mishaps:

> Y siendo los que componian, estrangeros, y poco plati-
> cos en la lengua Castellana, no podra dexar de aver
> yerros de letras, que faltaran o sobraran, o estaran
> puestas unas por otras . . . (P. 135 of the original,
> see Appendix.)

In addition, Núñez de Reinoso was not always master

---

6. Madrid, 1851.

of his muse. He himself acknowledges his difficulties with
the hendecasyllable:

> solamente digo, que algunos versos que van escritos
> al estilo italiano, tienen y llevan la misma falta que
> vuestra merced les solia hallar, que era que sonaban
> algo en la sesta á las coplas de arte mayor ... (p. 432)

Núñez de Reinoso's novel was not printed in Spain
until the nineteenth century, when it was included in the
third volume of the BAE series: *Novelistas anteriores a
Cervantes.*[7] The rediscovery of his book was owing to
the antiquarian interest of the last century in collecting
and cataloguing works from Spain's literary past. However, since the reprinting of the novel, Reinoso's fame
as an author has not substantially increased and his romance remains an anthological item. He is not, perhaps,
even a major minor master; yet, his work deserves to
be read for what it reveals of the man and his times.

---

7. Ed. B. Carlos Aribau, Madrid, 1846, 431–68. Unless otherwise stated,
all prose quotations from the work of Núñez de Reinoso imply this
edition, and its orthography was followed. However, since the second
letter to Juan Micas, that which precedes the poetry, was not reprinted
in its entirety, I have always returned to the original Venetian edition
when referring to Reinoso's second introductory remarks.

ALONSO NÚÑEZ DE REINOSO:

The Lament of a Sixteenth-Century Exile

I

BIOGRAPHICAL ASSUMPTIONS

Alonso Núñez de Reinoso is one of the most enigmatic of those authors whose work Bataillon characterizes as the "littérature espagnole semi-clandestine" of the 1550s.[1] Contemporary references to him and his work are, within Spain, singularly lacking. No Spanish author or critic mentions his name until Nicolás Antonio in 1672.[2] Reinoso's own prose and poetry still remain our chief source for reconstructing the outline of his life. Such a life may be divided into three phases, each corresponding to the country in which this peripatetic author was then residing: Spain, his homeland and the country where he passed his formative years; Portugal, the land of his temporary exile, where he spent his mature years and developed his literary talents through contact with leading Portuguese writers; and Italy, the land of his permanent exile, where he lived out his old age, published his book, and enjoyed the protection of a wealthy Jewish family.

---

1. Marcel Bataillon, introduction to *La vie de Lazarillo de Tormès,* Paris, 1958, p. 67.
2. Nicolás Antonio, *Bibliotheca Hispana Nova,* I, Madrid, 1783, p. 39.

Spain

Sospiro menudamente
Lexos de Guadalajara.
(No. 2)
Following Nicolás Antonio's brief reference,

Alphonsus Núñez de Reinoso, Guadalaxarensis, edidit.

Historia de los amores de Clareo y Horisea [sic] *con
los trabajos de Isea.* Item *algunas Rimas.* Venetiis apud
Gabrielem Giolitum 1552. in 8³

belief has always persisted that Guadalajara was the
birthplace of Alonso Núñez de Reinoso. In consequence,
he is usually listed in books dealing with the history of
that province, books such as *Biografías de hijos ilustres
de la provincia de Guadalajara,*⁴ *Biblioteca de escritores
de la provincia de Guadalajara . . .,*⁵ and *Historia de
Guadalajara y sus Mendoza en los siglos XV y XVI.*⁶
Carolina Michaëlis de Vasconcelos is quite specific: she
declares that the town of Alcarria in the province of
Guadalajara was the site of his birth but, unfortunately,
she does not divulge the source of her information.⁷ The
original assumption, consecrated by time and repetition,
seems to have been based on nostalgic references Núñez
de Reinoso makes to that locality. By taking the line

---

3. *Ibid.*
4. Juan Diges Antón y Manuel Sagredo y Martín, *Biografías de hijos
ilustres de la provincia de Guadalajara,* Guadalajara, 1889, pp. 61ff.
5. Juan Catalina García, *Biblioteca de escritores de la provincia de
Guadalajara y bibliografía de la misma hasta el siglo XIX,* Madrid,
1899, pp. 370ff.
6. Francisco Layna Serrano, *Historia de Guadalajara y sus Mendoza
en los siglos XV y XVI,* IV, Madrid, 1942, p. 146.
7. Carolina Michaëlis de Vasoncelos, introduction to *Bernardim Ribeiro
e Cristovâo "Obras,"* I, Coimbra, 1923, p. 100.

"Lexos de Guadalajara" (No. 2), and superimposing it upon another, "Muy lexos de do nasçi" (No. 3), which appears in a gloss of the previous poem, one may conclude that he *was* born there. The poet's date of birth also poses a problem. One may induce from Reinoso's complaint that in 1552 he is "agora en la vejez" (No. 1), that he was born in the last decade of the fifteenth century. Equally, his statement,

> *Fue triste mi nasçimiento*
> . . . .
> *Han contra mi pregonado*
> *En la hora que nasçi*
>   (No. 14)

taken literally, could be an allusion to the Expulsion Order of 1492.

Lacking documentation for events in the life of Alonso Núñez de Reinoso, some critics have concentrated their attention on putative family connections. Juan Catalina García opines that he had a brother, "un Diego Núñez de Reinoso, natural de Guadalajara, estudiantón aventurero que anduvo corriendo universidades, no sé si por inquietud de ánimo ó por amor al saber." He further contends that Diego studied at Alcalá, Salamanca, and Coimbra "en cuya facultad de canones habia cursado 2 anos 6 meses y 20 dias, á contar desde Octubre de 1545."[8] Francisco Layna Serrano states that Diego was born in Guadalajara "hacia 1530,"[9] a date that would have him completing his university studies at the tender age of

---

8. Catalina García, p. 370. Only infrequently does he give sources for his information.
9. Layna Serrano, p. 146.

fifteen. Both Catalina García and Layna Serrano discover a third brother, one Martín de Reinoso who died in Madrid in 1567, leaving his estate to Diego, though the latter's whereabouts were unknown.[10] Catalina García concludes that "eran gentes de su familia un Diego de Reinoso y Dª. Petronila de Guzmán, vecinos de Guadalajara, que fundaron mayorazgo en 1550."[11] If this assumption is accurate, Alonso Núñez de Reinoso was a relative of the Señores de Autillo.

While the genealogical records of this family are confused and contradictory information is given in the available sources, be they reliable, semi-reliable, or pure fictions, it seems sure that one Diego de Reinoso of Guadalajara, the seventh Señor de Autillo, married his first cousin, Petronila de Reinoso, the widow of Francisco de Guzmán.[12] The name of Alonso Núñez de Reinoso

---

10. Catalina García, p. 370. Layna Serrano, p. 146.
11. Catalina García, p. 371.
12. Catalina García, p. 371, says that the document dealing with the founding of a "mayorazgo in 1550," in the form of "informacion de D. Petronila de Reinoso y Guzmán sobre dicho mayorazgo, impresa sin lugar ni año," can be found in the Biblioteca National (Madrid) under Varios 839. No such document can now be found under that listing. However, in the Archivo Histórico Nacional, there is a "Pleito" concerning the estate of "Diego de Reinoso y de las Salas y su mujer Petronila de Reinoso." In the intra-family lawsuit the relationships are difficult to determine. But in her will (1550), Petronila calls herself the "mujer de Francisco de Guzmán," and says that Diego was her first husband and Pedro, her son. Pedro apparently married Isabel de Guzmán, the issue of his mother's second husband and his first wife (also his cousin), Constanza de Sotomayor y Guzmán.
Alonso Núñez de Castro, in his *Historia eclesiastica y seglar de la muy noble y muy leal Ciudad de Guadalaxara*, 1653, pp. 342ff., gives a slightly different version. However, among the notable families of Guadalajara he does not list the Reinosos, the Señores de Autillo. In his discussion of the Guzmán family he notes that Petronila de Reinoso was the second wife of Francisco de Guzmán and that his daughter Isabel de Guzmán married a Pedro de Reynoso from San Martín de Málaga.
The Índice Salazar, D-35, deals in part, with the Señores de Autillo. According to the information given on Folio 99, Diego de Reinoso of Guadalajara married Petronila de Reinoso, his first cousin, the widow

does not appear in any of the various versions of the family tree. Such an omission would not in itself preclude the possible blood-relationship; for the climate of sixteenth-century Spain was such that anyone who ran afoul of the Inquisition could simply be written out of his family and become, in the terms of Américo Castro, a *persona sin ser*.

On the other hand, Alonso Núñez de Reinoso never does claim kinship to such an illustrious family as that of the Señores de Autillo. The caution that pervades his work is evinced in his very reluctance to reveal the names of those members of his family who remained in Spain. In the poem directed to "una señora su prima," he confesses, "Lloro porque nada sé / De mi padre ni hermanos," and asks for news of a brother, "Qué se hyzo de mi hermano, / Que si es bivo, muerto o sano" (No. 1). In yet another poem he speaks of his separation from two cousins, through death and distance:

> *De dos primas que tenia,*
> *La una ia me faltó,*
> *Y la otra me quedó.*
> *Donde vella no podia.* (No. 3)

Finally, he makes mention of a sister; hers is the only name of his immediate family that he reveals: "Y sospiro por mi hermana, / Doña Isabel de Reynoso"[13] (No. 2).

---

of Francisco de Guzmán y de Alballeque (?), and according to that on Folio 100, their son Pedro wed Isabel de Guzmán. The name of an Alonso Núñez de Reinoso does not appear.

13. Eduardo Toda y Güell, *Bibliografía espanyola d'Italia dels origens de la imprempta fins a l'any 1900*, III, Barcelona, 1929, item 3561, contends that this sister filed the will of Alonso Núñez de Reinoso in Madrid in 1567. Since Toda does not divulge the sources for this information nor does he give the name of the *escribano* who processed the document, it is impossible to check his statement. 1567 was the year that the will of Martín de Reinoso was filed; possibly Toda used Catalina García as a source and confused the two Reinosos. The tendency in writing on the life of Alonso Núñez de Reinoso has been for critics to repeat as fact assumptions of previous authors.

In order to please his family he studied law, though young Alonso had no sense of a legal vocation. Is not his anguish clear in the Horatian epistle addressed to Feliciano de Silva?[14]

> *Pero despues que por tener contento*
> *Mis caros padres a Iustiniano*
> *Sigo contino con asaz tormento.*
>
> . . . .
> *Padezco gran dolor y sufro males*
> *En leyes estudiar, . . .* (No. 15)

His statement, "Y que antes hazia tras Tormes yria," suggests Salamanca as the university attended. In two autobiographical poems (Nos. 13 and 14), Reinoso enumerates careers that he had contemplated pursuing but ultimately rejected, such as the life of the cloister—"Que en la santa Religion / Meterme yo no podia"—a life on the battlefield—"Buscar los campos de guerra / No sé si me convenia / Soy viejo para pelear / Armas"— or one of adventure in the New World—"Si en Indias me passava / No sé si a Dios serviria" (No. 13). To all such options did sixteenth-century *conversos* have recourse as a means of escaping the tense social situation in Spain or attaining a recognition that might otherwise be denied them. It is not clear if Núñez de Reinoso ever finished his legal studies,[15] but at all events, he

---

14. For a definition of the Horatian epistle. see Elias Rivers, "The Horatian Epistle and its Introduction into Spanish Literature," *Hispanic Review* XXII, 1954, pp. 174–94. Two of Reinoso's poems meet some of the requirements of this form; they are in *terza rima* (not always necessary but quite commonly used), there is a personal note at the beginning and end, they are somewhat colloquial in tone, and there is an attempt at moralization.

15. There is an all but illegible entry in the "Registros de pruebas de cursos" (1531) to suggest that he received his degree; a "bacca in legibus" was awarded to Alfonsi(?) Renexo (Romexo?), pp. 156–57.

ultimately rejected law as a vocation and returned to his first love, letters:

> *Pero letras de ganar*
> *Mi voluntad no queria.*
> *Soy amigo de las Musas.* (No. 13)

Turning to what may definitely be established about literary figures whom Núñez de Reinoso knew, we are on much firmer ground. He mentions two Spaniards whose historicity is verifiable. One is Juan Hurtado de Mendoza, Señor de Fresno de Torote, a relative of the famed Mendoza family of Guadalajara and author of *El buen plazer trobado en treze discātes* (1550).[16] Concluding his novel, Reinoso addresses a letter, dated March 1, 1552, to Juan Hurtado de Mendoza, in which he reveals that he had once written a play and contemplated dedicating it to the Duque del Infantado, the titular head of the Mendoza clan.[17] Such a declaration corroborates our suggested link between Núñez de Reinoso and Guadalajara. What prompted the letter to the Señor de Fresno de Torote could have been ambition, as the following words imply: "si esta mi obra en algun tiempo aportare á las riberas del rio Henares, . . . piadosamente será leida" (468a). Naturally, a man of Juan Hurtado de Mendoza's literary reputation and high social standing would have been useful in disseminating Reinoso's book in Spain. There may, however, be a further motivating factor: by reminding Hurtado de Mendoza of their own former relationship, common literary activity, and mutual friends, Núñez de Reinoso seems to ask the nobleman to commiserate with his former friend, neighbor and disciple,

---

16. This book is a model in caution. Evidently it was reviewed by numerous ecclesiastical authorities before publication.
17. Feliciano de Silva dedicated a book to the Duque del Infantado.

now languishing in exile. In a word, is it not possible that by ingratiating himself with the influential Mendozas, Núñez de Reinoso hoped to pave the way for his return to Spain? From the number of references in the poems to his longing for his native land, this would, indeed, seem to be his goal.

The other Spanish friend is, of course, the already-mentioned Feliciano de Silva, author of Books VII, IX, X, and XI in the Amadís series.[18] Born in about 1480, Silva had already launched his career when the as yet unpublished Reinoso, possibly still a student at Salamanca, began frequenting the literary circle at Ciudad Rodrigo. Their relationship seems to have been a close one; and, unlike Diego Hurtado de Mendoza[19] and Cervantes,[20]

---

18. *Lisuarte de Grecia,* Sevilla, 1514. *El noveno libro de Amadis de Gaula, que es la cronica del muy valiente y esforçado Principe y cauallero de la Ardiente Espada Amadis de Grecia, hijo de Lisuarte de Grecia, emperador de Constantinopla y de Trapisonda,* . . . , 1530? *La coronica de los muy valientes e esforçados e invencibles cavalleros don Florisel de Niquea y el fuerte Anaxartes, hijos del muy excelente Principe Amadis de Grecia;* . . ., Valladolid, 1532. *Parte tercera de la Crónica de D. Florisel de Niquea,* Medina del Campo, 1535. *Cuarta parte de D. Florisel,* Salamanca, 1551. In the latter, he interpolated pastoral verses, in both traditional and Italian meters, about which Cervantes wrote, "Y quisiera yo, ser que vuestra merced le hubiera enviado junto con *Amadís de Gaula,* al bueno de *Don Rogel de Grecia;* que yo sé que gustara la señora Luscinda mucho de Daraida y Garaya, y de las discreciones del pastor Darinel, y de aquellos admirables versos de sus bucólicas, cantadas y representadas por él con todo donaire, discreción y desenvoltura." *Quijote,* I, XXIV. (Francisco Rodríguez Marín, ed., *El ingenioso hidalgo don Quijote de la Mancha,* II, Madrid, 1927, 268-69.)
19. "Paréceos, amigo que sabria yo hacer, si quisiese un medio libro de *D. Florisel de Niquea,* y que sabria ir por aquel estilo de alforjas, que parece el juego de 'este es el gato que mató el rato,' etc., y que sabria yo decir 'la razon de la razon que tan sin razon por razon de ser vuestro tengo para alabar vuestro libro'? . . . Veis ahi a Feliciano de Silva, que en toda su vida salio más lejos que de Ciudad Rodrigo a Valladolid, criado siempre entre Nereydas y Daraydas, metido en la torre de Universo, a donde estuvo encantado, segun dice en su libro, diez y ocho años . . ." Diego Hurtado de Mendoza (?), *Carta del Bachiller de Arcadia, Sales Españoles o Agudezas del ingenio nacional,* recogidas por A. Paz y Melia. Primera serie, Madrid, 1890, p. 80.
20. ". . . ningunos le parecían tan bien como los que compuso el

Reinoso held a high opinion of his friend's ability. From Italy, Reinoso writes to Silva's daughter, María de Guzmán,[21] and expresses his nostalgia for the pleasurable moments he spent at the family hearth:

> *Que estoy en ciudad Rodrigo*
> *Muchas vezes finjo acá,*
> . . . .
> *Y digo contento hufano*
> *Y alegre podre llegar*
> *A casa de Feliçiano,*
> *A donde contino gano,*
> *Por tal ingenio tratar.* (No. 2)

There are numerous references to Silva in Reinoso's poetry and prose. Feliciano de Silva can probably be inferred from the names "Silvano," "Silvestre," "Floresindos," and "Felicindos." "Silvano" appears in Poem No. 11. Here, Reinoso's *Doppelgänger,* "Thomas

---

famoso Feliciano de Silva, porque la claridad de su prosa y aquellas entricadas razones suyas le parecían de perlas; y más cuando llegaba a leer aquellos requiebros y cartas de desafíos, donde en muchas partes hallaba escrito: 'La razón de la sinrazón que a mi razón se hace, de tal manera mi razón enflaqueze, que con razón me quejo de la vuestra fermosura.'" Miguel de Cervantes, *Don Quijote de la Mancha,* I, I. (Rodríguez Marín, ed., I, pp. 85–86.) This famous parody of Feliciano de Silva's style is based on a line from his *Segunda Comedia de Celestina,* not his *Amadís* series.

21. Of the three women, all bearing the name "María de Guzmán," whom Núñez de Reinoso might have known, Feliciano de Silva's daughter is the most logical choice as the addressée of the poet's letter. The "María de Guzmán," a possible descendant of Petronila de Reinoso, was probably not born until after Reinoso left Spain. While one of Silva's sisters was called "María de Guzmán," his daughters also often used the surname of Guzmán, thereby avoiding the socially-awkward maiden name of Silva's Jewish wife. In Reinoso's "Carta a la señora donna Maria de Guzmán" he also asks for news of an Isabel, the name of another of Silva's daughters (No. 2). In his epistle to Silva, Reinoso mentions "tu hija la hermosissima Maria" as well as an Isabel, the only two people to whom he alludes (No. 15).

Gomez," accuses him of "Fingiendo que en Lombardia /
Silvano pastor tenia / Amores con la tristeza," though
whether the poem is a reconstructed conversation or the
poet's indulging in self-criticism remains difficult to decide.
The mention of "Silvestre" occurs in yet another example
of poetic feigning; he is one of the shepherds present
at the burial of Darinel in the funereal elegy[22] (No. 6).
On this occasion, Núñez de Reinoso seems to be recalling not the circle of friends in Ciudad Rodrigo but
a second group in Portugal with which Feliciano de
Silva was also associated. The chivalric name, "Floresindos,"[23] could be identified with Feliciano de Silva. In
Reinoso's "Égloga de Baltheo y Argasto," one of the
shepherds who appears in a visionary sequence, an expression of intimate longing for former friends, is listed
as "Floresindos el mayor / Que no tiene ya descuento /
A su tristeza"[24] (No. 5) While in "Muerte de Lágrimas

22. The "Darinel," whose funeral "Silvestre" attended, also figures in
the only pastoral incident in Silva's otherwise chivalric tale of Amadís.
He and the significantly named "Florisel," a knight-turned-shepherd, love
the maiden Silvia. "Darinel" may be an imperfect anagram for Bernaldim; and in Bernardim Ribeiro's *Menina e moça*, "Bimnarder," an
anagram for Bernardim (*var.* Bernaldim), is a knight who has changed
his name and role and become a shepherd in order to court his lady. In
Núñez de Reinoso's novel there is an episode dealing with a knight
disguised as a shepherd who is the target of court gossip. It may be
that all three authors were treating an event in Ribeiro's life.
    Vasconcelos is of the opinion that Silva traveled to Portugal and was
in contact with Ribeiro's literary circle.
23. Teófilo Braga, *Renascença,* Lisboa, 1914, suggests the "Florisendos"
of Ribeiro's "Ecloga V" is derived from the name of the chivalric hero,
"Florisando," of Book IV of the *Amadís* series.
    In addition, note Núñez de Reinoso's debt to chivalric novels for the
christening of his title characters: *Floriseo* (1516), *Florindo* (1530),
Florambel de Lucea (1532), *Florisel de Niquea* (1532, by his friend
Feliciano de Silva), *Florando de Inglaterra* (1545), *Floramante de Co-
lonia* (1550), as well as *Clarián de Landanis* (1518, 1522, 1524), *Clari-
balte* (1519), and *Clarimundo* (1522). Even "Isea" is an apheretic form
of such names as "Belisea" or "Florisea."
24. Feliciano de Silva had a son of the same name with whom he
has been confused. "El mayor" would seem to distinguish father from
son.

y de Diana," the tearful shepherd suddenly interrupts
the catalogue of his woes to recall a hitherto unmentioned
"Floresindos": "Mas Floresindos pastor / No pena
como yo peno." (No. 4) Another "Florisendos", (a
minor variant) is similarly invoked in "Écloga V" written by a mutual friend, the Portuguese poet Bernardim
Ribeiro. There the shepherd "Agrestes" ("Argasto"),
who has been conversing with a fellow swain, "Ribeiro,"
laments his exile and cries out to an absent friend:

> *Em nada detreminando,*
> *De Florisendos me lembrando,*
> *Tambem a ele lhe falo.*
> *O' Florisendos pastor,*
> *Que se tu meu mal soubesses,*
> . . . .
> *Haverias dó de mi,*
> *Que em barbara terra vivo,*
> *Des que me apartei de ti,*
> *Florisendos, não me vi*
> *Ua hora sem ser cativo.*[25]

The "Felicindos"[26] of Reinoso's novel, like many a
fictional character created by Feliciano de Silva himself,
is a knight errant. His name, so evocative of Silva's,
has semantic significance, for "Felicindos," whose goal
is the "casa de descanso," where he hopes to terminate
his troubles, is a seeker after happiness.[27] In the introduction to the poems, where Núñez de Reinoso, apparently reacting to criticism, feels compelled to defend the

---

25. Marques Braga, *Éclogas de Bernardim Ribeiro,* Lisboa, 1923, p. 111.
All subsequent quotations from the poetry of Ribeiro imply this edition;
its orthography has been followed.
26. I use the spelling of the original, or Venetian edition of Reinoso's
work. The modern edition renders the name as "Felesindos."
27. Cf. the illusive heroine, "Felisinda," of Baltasar Gracián's seventeenth-century allegorical work, *El Criticón.*

serious purpose of his novel, he includes an interpretative legend to explain the significance of certain roles, that of "Felicindos" among them:

> . . . yo no la escreui para que seruiesse solamente de lo que suenan las palabras sino para auisar a bien biuir . . . Y ansi todas las mas cosas de aquella historia tienĕ secreto, . . . por Felicindos la fortaleza que los hombres de grande animo deuen tener, por poder llegar a aquella casa de descanso, adonde estaua la princesa Luciandra, porque aquella es la clara y uerdadera. (4-5)

"Felicindos, el caballero de las Esperas dudosas," is the hero of the chivalric adventures that constitute the second portion of Reinoso's novel, that sequence dismissed by most critics as too confused to be intelligible,[28] but which in reality is the most original as it owes no allegiance to the Byzantine tale that inspired the work. The travails of "Felicindos" are similar to those endured by a knight in the final episode of Silva's *Amadís de Grecia* and those recorded in the anonymous *romance*, "El sueño de Feliciano de Silva," dated 1544 and possibly published in Salamanca.[29] If we agree with Emilio Cotarelo, the allegorical events of the *Amadís* and the "Sueño" illustrate the obstacles that initially thwarted Feliciano de Silva in his desire to marry Gracia Fe, the daughter of a Jewish shoemaker.[30]

The name of the knight "Felicindos," the nature of

---

28. For such opinions, see Marcelino Menéndez Pelayo, *Orígenes de la novela*, II, Santander, 1943, 80, "su libro se convierte en uno más de caballerías, tan absurdo y desconcertado como cualquier otro . . . que ningún interés ofrece . . .," and Robert J. Palamo, "Una fuente española del *Persiles*," *Hispanic Review*, VI, 1938, pp. 57–68.

29. Henry Thomas, introduction to *Dos Romances Anónimos del Siglo XVI. El Sueño de Feliciano de Silva. La Muerte de Héctor*, Madrid, 1917.

30. Emilio Cotarelo, "Nuevas noticias biográficas de Feliciano de Silva," *Boletín de la Real Academia Española*, XIII, 1926, pp. 129ff.

his quest, and the allegorical treatment of the material coalesce to indicate that "Felicindos" is beyond reasonable doubt a portrait of Núñez de Reinoso's Spanish friend Feliciano de Silva, whose adventures the narrator (Isea-Reinoso) observed and recorded in a manner evocative of Silva's own literary style. In brief, that "Felicindos" and Feliciano de Silva are one and the same is a literarily compatible interpretation, consistent with Núñez de Reinoso's handling of his material—allegory for events occurring in Spain where he plays a subordinate role, allusion for adventures encountered in exile—and with his admiration for his friend's ability and his desire to pay him homage.[31]

Núñez de Reinoso's affection for Feliciano may also have been based on consanguinity. There is evidence to suggest that Feliciano de Silva and the Señores de Autillo (the Reinoso family) may have shared a common ancestor, one Aldonza de Guzmán.[32] The granddaughter

---

31. In his excellent study, "Alonso Núñez de Reinoso et les marranes portugais en Italie," *Revista da Faculdade de Letras*, III, No. 1, *Miscelânea de estudos em honra do Prof. Hernâni Cidade*, I – 21, Bataillon suggests Juan Micas for the role of Felicindos because of Micas's lengthy courtship of his cousin Reyna, the daughter of his aunt Beatriz de Luna. Such an interpretation is indeed possible but is heavily dependent on events, to the exclusion of style, and it also presupposes that the book is of one piece with only one cast of characters. I am led to my conclusions through the belief that the first part of the novel, a Byzantine segment where Isea is central to the action, is allusive and deals with Reinoso's wanderings and those whom he encountered in exile, and that the second part, primarily chivalric, where Isea is more of an observer, treats the adventures of a friend in allegorical fashion. Further, Felicindos and Isea part company on a mountainside near the "Rio del Olvido," an ancient name for the River Lima, which flows from Spain through Portugal, terminating in the city of Viana, the port from which Reinoso attempted to leave his Lusitanian refuge. Was it Reinoso's intention to indicate that Felicindos (Silva) had to work out his destiny in Spain while Isea (Reinoso) had to choose exile?

32. Índice Salazar, D–18, fol. 109. The parents of Feliciano de Silva are given as Tristán de Silva and Aldonza de Guzmán. Índice Salazar, D–33, fol. 153, reads "Diego de Reinoso casó con Isabel de Guzmán, hija de Aldonza de Guzmán y Toledo de Guadalajara." Is this the same woman? Núñez de Castro makes no mention of a *Diego* de Reinoso's marrying an Isabel de Guzmán.

of Silva, "el que compuso los Amadises," married Pedro de Reinoso, the eighth Señor de Autillo.[33] Perhaps the alliance of Silvas, Reinosos, and Guzmáns is one more instance of the predilection of the prominent *converso* families and others who composed the bureaucracy for marrying within their own group.[34] Furthermore, since Silva's family, like that of his son-in-law, Fadrique de Toledo, was of ancient *converso* origin, the opposition

33. Índice Salazar, D-18, fol. 109. His daughter Blanca de Silva married Fadrique de Toledo; their daughter Isabel de Silva y Toledo married Pedro de Reinoso, the eighth Señor de Autillo. Also, the already-mentioned "Pleito" in the Archivo Histórico Nacional (see note 12) says that Pedro de Reinoso y de la Quadra, eighth Señor de Autillo, was married to Isabel de Toledo, "bisnieta de los primeros duques de Alva."

34. The conflicting versions of the various genealogies preclude any definitive conclusions as to the *converso* origins of the Reinosos, while at the same time the omissions, obvious falsifications, and their predilection for intermarriage, especially with the Guzmán family argue for such a conclusion. Francisco de Guzmán had two wives, the first his cousin, Constanza de Sotomayor y Guzmán, the second, Petronila de Reinoso. Of the issue of the first marriage, Fernando de Guzmán married Ana de Reinoso, and Isabel de Guzmán married Pedro de Reinoso. Petronila de Reinoso, Francisco's widow, then married her first cousin Diego de Reinoso. Ultimately, Feliciano de Silva's granddaughter married into this very intermarried family of Reinosos and Guzmáns.

Not only was Silva's wife of very recent Jewish origin, but he was himself a Pacheco descendant. For information on the Pachecos, see Cardenal don Francisco Hurtado de Mendoza y Bobadilla, *Tizón de la Nobleza,* in which the sixteenth-century prelate reveals the *converso* ancestry of numerous illustrious families, including his own.

The *Enciclopedia heráldica y genealógica hispano-americana* by Alberto y Arturo García Carraffa does not offer any help. As to the name Reinoso, they say "este linaje desciende del de Cisneros, y recogen la tradición, . . de que un caballero Reinoso fué el primero que vió la Cruz aparecido en el cielo . . . el día de la batalla de las Navas de Tolosa" LXXVII, 1951, p. 454. For the name Silva they repeat the old legend that the family was descended from *Aeneas* and was related to Pope Pius II (Eneas Silvio) (LXXXIV, 1960, p. 184). It is interesting to note that while Silva's children avoided using his wife's surname, the Reinoso family added illustrious appellations so that one member is called Diego de Reinoso y de las *Salas,* the very safe surname of ancient and impeccable origin seemingly appearing from nowhere.

Another indication of New Christian origins is the choice of occupation; Américo Castro, *"La Celestina" como contienda literaria,* Madrid, 1965, p. 46, suggests that "regidor" was synonymous with "converso." Accordingly, we find that in the fifteenth century Silva's father was *regidor* of Ciudad Rodrigo, and in the sixteenth century Diego Reynoso, husband of Petronila, who was accused of "proposiciones escandalosas,"

to his marriage to Gracia Fe may have been based on family reluctance to sanction a union with a person of lower social status and more recent Jewish extraction. It was hardly politic to revive memories in *cristiano viejo* neighbors of one's *converso* origins, however remote, through a fresh infusion of Jewish blood. Silva seems not to have suffered during his lifetime from any accusations of religious unorthodoxy; however, his widow had to engage in a lengthy intra-family lawsuit in order to claim his estate,[35] and in 1596, one of his descendants, Fernando de Toledo y Silva, was barred from entrance to the order of Santiago because the "limpieza" of Silva's wife, Gracia de Fe, was declared doubtful by the inquisitorial board that investigated the matter.[36]

Alonso Núñez de Reinoso was not so fortunate as his friend Silva. While other members of Reinoso's family continued living in Spain, apparently indifferent to his plight, the shadow of doubt fell upon him and he was forced into voluntary self-exile.

Portugal

> *Los que biven en Castilla*
> *Tienen ya en Portugal*
> *Su sentido.* (No. 5)

Núñez de Reinoso does not indicate when and why he left Spain for Portugal. That he did so unwillingly is

---

was listed as "regidor en la ciudad de Guadalajara," AHN, *Inquisiciones,* leg. 222 (9). Because of the protection of the powerful Mendoza family, opposition to *conversos* came late to Guadalajara (see Francisco Márquez, *Investigaciones sobre Juan Álvarez Gato,* Madrid, 1960) ; in 1589 a document was filed in which Old Christians of that city protested the admittance of New Christians to public office, Índice Salazar, D-44, fol. 160.

35. Narciso Alonso Cortés, "Feliciano de Silva," *Boletín de la Real Academia,* XX, 1933, pp. 382-404.

36. Cotarelo.

clear from his many references to enforced exile. He undoubtedly joined the stream of Spanish refugees who crossed the frontier into Portugal before the establishment of the Inquisition in 1547, at which time the Lusitanian haven ceased to be. There were two logical routes open to him: from Salamanca, he could have followed the Tormes until it ran into the Duero, for access into the province of Entre Minho e Douro; or he could have trodden the well-traveled road that led from Salamanca through Ciudad Rodrigo, eventually terminating in the university city of Coimbra. He mentions both Portuguese localities in his poems. Perhaps, like Diego Núñez de Reinoso, he was connected with the university, although he is mute about his activities, if any, in Coimbra.

Since all evidence for his stay in Portugal must be drawn indirectly from what he intimates in his poems, we must accept the statement, "Acordé de hazer asiento / En lugar que los pastores / Basto llaman," (No. 5) as an indication that he spent some time in a place Carolina Michaëlis de Vasconcelos identifies as Cabeiceras de Basto, the country estate of António and Nunálveres Pereira, in the province of Entre Minho e Douro:

> Naquele antigo solar, sob o tecto hospitaleiro de Nunálveres e António Pereira (filhos de João Rodrigues, o Marramaque), tornado célebre pela Égloga *Basto* de Sá de Miranda e por uma *Carta* do mesmo, como pôrto principal a que haviam arribado, ou cabana abrigadora onde se haviam recolhido, fugindo das borrascas importunas da África, Índia e prenúncios da Inquisição, *pastores* nacionais e castelhanos.[37]

---

37. Vasconcelos, p. 99.

One of the cohosts, António Pereira, was accused of writing scandalous anticlerical tracts;[38] seemingly he attracted friends of heterodox thinking. Among those who found the atmosphere of the "Basto" congenial were Bernardim Ribeiro, Francisco de Sá de Miranda, and possibly Jorge de Montemayor. Poetic references further suggest that there was contact between the literary circle of the "Basto" in Portugal and that of Feliciano de Silva in Spain. Like Silva, Ribeiro (1482?-?), Sá de Miranda (1495?-1558), and Montemayor (1520?-1561?) were contemporaries of Núñez de Reinoso; and all contributed to the development of the pastoral. Doña Carolina maintains that during a stay in Italy, probably between 1522 and 1524, Ribeiro was the first Peninsular writer to wander "in Tempe or the dales of Arcady." She believes that he wrote his novel and the majority of his poems either in Italy or shortly after his return to the "Basto," and that he, in turn, influenced his younger friends.[39] Even though there is no evidence to indicate that Ribeiro himself essayed Italian verse forms, preferring instead the *décima*,[40] the logical conclusion of such a theory is

---

38. "O Indice Expurgatorio de 1624 chamou a atenção do publico para os seus escriptos sobre assumptos ecclesiasticos, contra os padres, e sobre a leitura da biblia, prohibindo, 'um seu tratado de mão sobre aquelle verso do Psalmo 81 . . .'" Vasconcelos, *Poesias de Francisco de Sá de Miranda,* Halle, 1885, p. 800. Menéndez Pelayo, *Historia de los heterodoxos españoles,* I, Madrid, 1965, p. 771, comments, "Cítase como partidario de ideas erasmianas a Antonio Pereira Marramaque, señor de Bastos."

39. Vasconcelos and others have employed various methods to try to establish the birthdates of Ribeiro and Sá de Miranda; indeed, Vasconcelos has changed her mind several times. Their exact age is not relevant to the problem at hand. Poetic evidence would seem to support her theory that Ribeiro was the elder.

40. Núñez de Reinoso and Sá de Miranda also employ the *décima.* In addition, Sá de Miranda essayed Italian verse form in imitation of Garcilaso, to whom he paid tribute in his eclogue "Nemoroso." All of Reinoso's bucolic poems are in traditional Peninsular meters; the only extant examples of his use of the hendecasyllable belong chronologically to a later period in his life.

that Peninsular pastoral antedates the conversation between Boscán and Navagiero and the poetic activity of Boscán and Garcilaso, and that the development of pastoral poetry and prose proceeded in unison.

While I shall later discuss the genesis of the pastoral, at this point it seems sufficient to state that we are evidently dealing with a literary academy such as flourished among Italian humanists of the sixteenth century. Here is a group of writers addressing each other by their poetic pseudonyms, reworking the same material, dealing with common topics. But more than that, the members of the "Basto," refugees from the activities of the Inquisition in Spain and from the intrigue of the court in Portugal, found in the pastoral a suitable vehicle for expressing their commonly felt religio-social problems.

Núñez de Reinoso probably joined the group during the decade from 1530 to 1540. He never refers to his Portuguese friends by name. But as he explains in the introduction to his poetry:

Estas obras de poesia las tengo por mas graues, de lo que las personas que no las entienden piensan: porque en ellas se an hallado señalados uarones, y hombres de gran erudicion. (3)

His avowed intention, then, is to celebrate the literary skill of the *cénacle*. Accordingly, in two poems, he conjures up an assembly of shepherds, many of whom bear the same names as those in the works of Ribeiro and Sá de Miranda: Silvestre, Silvano, Amador, Agrestes, Jano, Persio, Fauno, Floresindos, Nemoroso, and Andrés. Among the shepherdesses is "la linda Juana / La que las patas guardava / Por el Duero," (No. 5) who figures in Ribeiro's "Écloga II" as "Joana patas guardava / Pola ribeira do Tejo." (1) There are two theories current for identifying characters in Ribeiro's work: Delfim Guimarães discovers Ribeiro and Sá de Miranda beneath a multitude of pastoral disguises;[41] Vasconcelos would prefer to assign each name to a different person.[42] In Núñez de Reinoso's poetry, because of the repetitious nature of the complaints, it seems clear that Reinoso himself is usually the chief speaker. However, for the secondary figures who are present but inactive, whose function is to form a sort of background against which a dialogue may take place, or for those whose adventures are recounted as actions of the past, Núñez de Reinoso uses several names, in the form of other anagrams or attributes, for the same person: e.g., Lágrimas or Darinel (Bernaldiñ) may stand for the tearful Bernardim (Bernaldim) Ribeiro; Silvano and Silvestre (Silva), Felicindos (Feliciano), or Floresindos (Felicindos, FS), for Feliciano de Silva.

In addition to the duplication of names, there are innumerable instances of poetic reminiscence, of lines bor-

---

41. Delfim Guimarães, *Bernardim Ribeiro* (*O Poeta Crisfal*), Lisboa, 1908, *passim*.

42. Vasconcelos, *Obras*, pp. 101–2. Previously, in *Novos estudos sobre Sá de Miranda*, Lisboa, 1911, she seems to have been of another opinion. She suggests that Penamor (which she writes as Peñamor) may be Jorge de Montemayor. He is, of course, another example of a *converso* author who died in a foreign land, presumably in exile. Although younger than the others, his connection with the group can, perhaps, be established through the poem he wrote on the death of Silva ("Pues mi mayor amigo es ya perdido? / Perdí mi bien, perdí mi Feliciano," *Cancionero*, fols. 122–25), an exchange of poetic letters with Sá de Miranda in which Montemayor refers to "entre el Duero y Miño" (see Vasconcelos, *Poesias*, pp. 653ff) and an epistle to a friend in which he recalls a poetic gathering on the banks of the Mondego (see Menéndez Pelayo, *Orígenes*, II, p. 254, "Epístola a su amigo don Jorge de Meneses.") It is not beyond the limits of credibility that the traditionally bucolic names, Sireno and Silvano, of his *Diana* stand for Reinoso and Silva.

rowed from Ribeiro and Sá de Miranda. One curious example is a *villancico* sung by Argasto in the eclogue that bears his name; the song is a direct translation of one sung by Ribeiro's Agrestes in his "Écloga V." In his edition of Ribeiro's poetry, Braga is led to identify Agrestes as Sá de Miranda because the *estribillo* is almost identical with that in Sá de Miranda's "Vilancete II":

Sá de Miranda

Que mal avindos cuidados
Me tomárão antre si!
Nunca tais cuidados vi![43]

Ribeiro

—*Que mal avindos cuida-*
dos,
Me tem tomado antre si,
Nunca tais cuidados vi!—

VOLTA

Eu nunca vi tal cuidar,
Ou se o vi, não sei qual é,
E porem a minha fé
Ja mais se pode mudar;
E pois com grande penar
Me tem tomado antre si,
Nunca tais cuidados vi.[44]

Núñez de Reinoso

Desavenido cuidado,

Me a tomado entre si
Nunca tal cuidado vi.

Yo nunca vi tal cuidar
Ni lo entiendo ni lo sé,
Pero mi mal ni mi fe
No se pueden ya mudar,
Pero pues para penar,
Me a tomado entre si
Nunca tal cuidado vi.
(No. 5)

---

43. Vasconcelos, *Poesias,* p. 17. All subsequent quotations from the poetry of Sá de Miranda imply this edition; its orthography has been followed. In addition, its editor is always listed in this study by her married name, according to its modern spelling.

44. M. Braga, p. 100. A variation on this song appears at the end of the poem, pp. 125–26, suggesting that it not only functions as a poetic epithet but also as a *Leitmotiv.*

In the original (Ferrara) edition, this poem is listed as "A qual *dizem* ser do mesmo Autor." (italics mine)

A topic handled by all three is the love of a shepherd for a beautiful maiden he spies on the banks of a river. A friendly competition between members of the "Basto" could have led to the creation of the poems. Núñez de Reinoso's "Muerte de Lágrimas y de Diana" (No. 4) is a combination of Ribeiro's Écloga II" and Sá de Miranda's "Fabula de Mondego." The similarity of their opening is unmistakable: Ribeiro, "Dizem que havia um pastor / Antre Tejo e Odiana";[45] Sá de Miranda, "Entre el gran Tajo i Duero . . ."; Núñez de Reinoso, "Entre Tajo y Guadiana." In each case the girl flees when she notices that she is observed. In Ribeiro's poem, Joana leaves behind a shoe, which Jano fondles and covers with tears; in Reinoso's it is Diana's braid that Lágrimas bathes in tears, and so inconsolable is he that his weeping swells the waters that had claimed her life and he too drowns. In Sá de Miranda's version, Diego pines to death from unrequited love; in his honor, the river *Munda* is renamed *Mondego*. Núñez de Reinoso was also evidently at pains to provide a mythological and etymological explanation for the river's name; *Guadiana,* like Mondego, is a divisible word whose components are "Guadi" (River) and "Diana."[46]

Here, then, is sufficient textual evidence for Núñez de Reinoso's association with Ribeiro and Sá de Miranda and for his stay in Portugal. The inclusion in their poetry of common names, lines, and topics occurs before the publication of their works. The difficulty of assigning exact dates to the compositions complicates the matter; however, it would seem that the poems dealing with the

45. "Odiana—forma arcaica de Guadiana," M. Braga, p. 25.
46. Owing to the popularity of Ovid's *Metamorphoses* during the Renaissance, the creation of myths was a favorite poetic pastime. Here, of course, it is employed in the service of a fanciful etymology.

"Basto" *tertulia* were written at approximately the same
time. Doña Carolina suggests the decade of 1530-1540
for the penning of Sá de Miranda's eclogues.[47] Ribeiro's
"Écloga III" was published in folio in 1536;[48] this and
one other poem are his only compositions to appear
before the Ferrara edition of his work in 1554. Verse
form and subject matter suggest that at least two of
Núñez de Reinoso's poems, Nos. 4 and 5, also date
from the 1530s.

An episode in Reinoso's novel may recreate his friend-
ship with these Portuguese writers; but—"Et in Arcadia
ego!"—their idyllic existence is abruptly interrupted by
death, presumably that of Ribeiro.[49] Interpretation of
the episode is dependent on accepting Bataillon's thesis
that sex in Reinoso's novel is often reversed: *i.e.,* the
narrator, Isea, is Núñez de Reinoso; and her sometime
patron, "el gran Señor,"[50] is really a woman. Accordingly,
two sisters whom Isea meets in exile could be identified
as Ribeiro and Sá de Miranda. Her description of them
is affectionate: "las cuales tenian fama de muy avisadas
y sábias . . . nos queríamos y amábamos como si fuéramos
muy cercanos deudos. . . ." Isea comments that the plea-
sure afforded by their company "disminuia mi soledad."

---

47. Vasconcelos, *Poesias,* p. 774.
Rodrigues Lapa, in the introduction to *Sá de Miranda, "Poesias,"*
Lisboa, 1942, p. xv, mentions that the poet essayed about a dozen versions
of the "Basto" eclogue.
48. *Trouas de dous pastores. Feytas por Bernaldim Ribeyro . . . 1536.*
49. The exact date of Ribeiro's death is not known. Most critics give
credence to the rumors of his banishment from court, his subsequent
melancholy and eventually madness, and his death prior to the publication of his novel. Vasconcelos, *Obras,* supplies the most logical reconstruction of his life. The polemic over his identity continues, ranging from
the "fraudulent" document of 1642 to Rego's theory that he was León
Hebreo.
50. Bataillon, "Alonso Núñez de Reinoso . . .," suggests Gracia Nasi
(Beatriz de Luna) for "el gran Señor," pp. 13-17.

At times all three retire to a pastoral setting where "recebíamos gran contento, estando leyendo, ó cantando, o tañendo. . . ." (453b) One of the friends dies suddenly. After an extravagant display of grief during which she pays tribute to her dead companion's eternal literary fame, "aquella gloria . . . que con tus claras obras acá ganaste," the heroine says, "Muerta esta hermosa ninfa, yo acordé de partirme, porque mi deseo era irme en Alejandría. . . ." (454a)

If Núñez de Reinoso's ultimate destination was not the Levant, as symbolized by the novelistic reference to Alexandria, it was at least Italy, the land to which many *marranos* migrated.

Italy

> *Acordé de me passar*
> *A los Alpes de Alemaña*
> *A bivir.*   (No. 5)

With the probable demise of his friend and the mounting offensive of the Inquisition, Núñez de Reinoso left Portugal. After many years of opposition on the part of prominent *conversos,* of edicts and counter edicts, and struggle between the crown and papal authority, the Inquisition authorized in 1536 became officially activated in 1547. The number of Spanish and Portuguese *marranos* who fled the country, despite occasional travel restrictions, increased in this period, particularly after the first *auto-de-fe* held in Lisbon in 1540.[51]

---

51. For information on the Inquisition, see Alexandre Herculano, *História da origem e estabelecimento da Inquisição en Portugal,* Lisboa, 1867, and Lucio D'Azevedo, *Historia dos Christãos novos portugueses,* Lisboa, 1921.

Núñez de Reinoso outlines what was probably a first (and abortive) attempt to escape:

> *Acordé de me passar*
> *A los Alpes de Alemaña*
> *A bivir,*
> *Y como los que desaman*
> *El remedio a sus dolores*
> *Yo me fue.* [sic][52]
> *En una çiudad que llaman*
> *Viana los moradores*
> *Embarqué.*   (No. 5)

But a storm at sea drove the ship back to land. The passengers disembarked at Lisbon,

> *Y por Coymbra passamos*
> *Do cresçio mi soledad*
> *Por la ver.*
> *Y volvime en fin . . .*
> *Como de la mar sali*
> *Por el Duero*
> *A vivir en este Basto.*
>   (No. 5)

But reach Italy he did, probably before 1550. Documentation for his stay in that country is both more substantial and more abundant; the identity of his acquaintances can be established. The Juan Micas[53] to whom

---

52. Present-day "Ladino" pronunciation, apart from regional Peninsular dialects, may help explain the syntactically incorrect phrase "Yo me fue" which must rime with "Embarqué." Sephardic Jews pronounce first person singular preterite endings of "ar" verbs as "í"; *i.e.,* the lines in question could be read aloud as "Yo me fui" and "Embarquí." (See Rafael Lapesa, *Historia de la lengua española,* Madrid, 1959, p. 337, for examples of the substitution of "í" for final "e.")

53. There is no substance to the statement initially made by B. Carlos Aribau in his introduction to *Novelas anteriores a Cervantes* (*BAE* III, p. xxix) and repeated by the usually careful Julio Caro Baroja in *Los*

Reinoso dedicated his book, was not, as Menéndez Pelayo
supposed, a "caballero italiano,"[54] but a member of a
well-known and wealthy Marrano family who fled Portugal, took up residence in Antwerp, moved to Italy, living
first at Venice, later at Ferrara, in which city most of
them openly reembraced Judaism. The clan eventually
emigrated to Turkey. There Juan Micas, or João Miquez
as he was called in Portugal, assumed the Jewish name
of Joseph Nasi. He rose to a position of power in the
court of the sultan, who named him Duke of Naxos, and
engaged in espionage against Spain for the Duke of
Orange. His aunt was the equally famous Beatriz de
Luna who married Francisco Mendes of the international
banking family; it was she, as Gracia Nasi, who led the
mass migration of Peninsular Jews to Turkey.[55] In the
Viaje de Turquía, Laguna describes the entrance of doña
Gracia and her retinue into Constantinople in 1553:

> ... entre los quales fue vn dia vna señora portoguesa
> que se llamaba doña Beatriz Mendez, muy rica, y
> entró en Constantinopla con quarenta caballos y quatro
> carros triumphales llenos de damas y criadas españolas.
> No menor casa llevaba que vn duque d'España, y
> podialo hazer, que es muy rica, y se hazia hazer la
> salba; destaxó con el Gran Turco desde Veneçia, que

judíos en la España moderna y contemporánea, I, Madrid, 1962, p. 223,
to the effect that Feliciano de Silva dedicated his *Segunda comedia de
Celestina* (1536) to Juan Micas. Micas was at that time about sixteen;
his family was in the process of moving from Portugal to Flanders.
Silva dedicated the various editions of this book to 1. Francisco Zúñiga
Guzmán y de Sotomayor (Medina del Campo, 1534) and 2. Lope de
Soria (Venice, 1536).
    54. Menéndez Pelayo, *Orígenes,* II, p. 82.
    55. For information on Juan Micas and Beatriz de Luna, see Cecil
Roth, *The House of Nasi: Doña Gracia,* Philadelphia, 1948, and his *The
House of Nasi: The Duke of Naxos,* Philadelphia, 1948; Jacob Reznik,
Le Duc de Naxos, Paris, 1936; Juan Bautista Avalle-Arce, "Espionaje
y última aventura de José Nasi 1569-1574," *Sefarad,* XIII, 1953, pp.
157-286. Núñez de Reinoso is not mentioned in any of these works.

no quería que le diese otra cosa en sus tierras sino que
todos sus criados no traxesen tocados como los otros
judios, sino gorras y vestidos a la veneçiana. El se lo
otorgo, y más si más quisiera, por tener tal tribu-
taria. . . . Quando menos me caté vierais a la señora
doña Beatriz mudar el nombre y llamarse doña Graçia
de Luna *et tota Hierosolima cum illa.*"[56]

Laguna then records a conversation with Juan Micas
on the subject of his conversion to Judaism:

Desde a vn año vino vn sobrino suyo en Constantinopla,
que hera año de 1554, que en corte traia gran fausto
ansi del Emperador como del Rei de Françia, y me-
resçialo todo porque hera gentil hombre y diestro en
armas y bien leido y amigo de amigos; y hai pocos
hombres de quenta en España, Italia y Flandes que
no le conosçiesen, al qual el Emperador habia hecho
caballero, y llamabase don Juan Micas; y porque
aquella señora no tenia más de vna hija; a la qual daba
tresçientos mill ducados en dote, engañole el diablo y
circumçidose y desposose con ella; llamase agora Iozef
Nasi. Los gentiles hombres suyos vno se ponía don
Samuel, otro don Abraham y otro Salomon. Los primeros días que el Juan Micas estubo alli christiano, yo
le iba cada dia a predicar que no hiziese tal cosa . . .
y hallabale tan firme, que çierto yo volvia consolado . . .
Quando menos me caté supe que ya hera hecho miembro
del diablo. Preguntado que por qué habia hecho aquello,
respondio que no por más de no estar subjeto a las
Inquisiçiones d'España . . .[57]

That Núñez de Reinoso knew both aunt and nephew
can hardly be doubted. Although he dedicates his work

---

56. Andrés Laguna, *Viaje de Turquía,* (attributed to Cristóbal de
Villalón) ed. Manuel Serrano y Sanz, *Autobiografías y memorias*
(N.B.A.E., II), p. 131a.
57. *Ibid.,* pp. 131a–b.

to Juan Micas, in his poems he acknowledges his undying
gratitude to a patroness:

> *Es verdad que sirvo: a quien*
> *Es justo que el mundo alabe*
> . . . .
> *Pero yo jamas dexar,*
> *De querer, ni de amar*
> *Muy grato siendo contino.*
> . . . .
> *Y tengo por bien dexado*
> *A mi padre y natural.*
> . . . .
> *A quien soy tan obligado*
> *Sin ingrato nunqua ser.* (No. 1)

His attitude toward her is distant, one of respect.
He always mentions her in terms of what Curtius calls
the "inexpressibility topos":[58]

> *El bien que en ella se esmalta,*
> *No lo digo ni lo toco.*
> . . . .
> *Porque en cosa que es tan alta*
> *Dezir mucho es dezir poco.*
> (No. 1)

Similar is Isea's lengthy eulogy of the "Gran Señor" who
has rescued her from prison; in part she comments that
"sus bondades y grandezas son tantas, que ninguna riqueza
de palabras bastaria para podellas loar," adding "que
no son menester palabras para loar á quien por sus obras
de todos y entre tan conocido es" (433a), and finally de-
claring:

---

58. Ernst Robert Curtius, *European Literature and the Latin Middle
Ages,* New York, 1953.

Y ansí su fama es y será, después de largos tiempos de
vida, inmortal, y la mayor que jamás ha sido; y esto,
entre tanto que los espíritus vitales en mí no faltaren,
podré yo decir y pregonar. (453b)

Reinoso was apparently employed in the household as
a tutor, as suggested by the following remarks of Isea:

Porque andando así como digo peregrina, perdida, acosada y estranjera, . . . sin tener de mí mas noticia ni
mas deuda ni obligacion que aquella que á su gran
valor tiene, me recogió en su casa y servicio, para que
sirviese á unas sus hijas. (453b)

Presumably doña Gracia's aid was disinterested; Reinoso
was just one more Peninsular refugee she helped:
". . . peregrina gente, de ella siempre resçibio" (No. 1).
In his *Consolaçam ás tribulaçoens de Israel,* Samuel
Usque, who had also benefited from her generosity, re-
counts the assistance she rendered to thousands:

Esta aos que jaa sahiam, e em frandes, e noutras partes
chegauam vencidos da pobreza, desconsolados do mar,
e em periguo de nã passar adiante, cõ dinheiro e muitos
outros remedios e cõfortos a suas minguoas com mão
liberalissima socorreo. Esta na aspereza dos fragosos
Alpes de Alemanha e outras terras lhes deu fauor . . .[59]
(III, lii-r-lii-v)

Since the events recorded in Reinoso's novel apparently
hold to no chronological consistency, it is impossible to
determine whether he discharged his tutorial duties in

---

59. Samuel Usque, *Consolaçam ás tribulaçoens de Israel,* edition of
Joaquim Mendes dos Remedios, Coimbra, 1906–1908. All subsequent
quotations imply this edition.

Portugal or Italy. The novelistic description of his position in the Nasi household (in the guise of Isea) occurs
before the previously mentioned episode recalling the
happy association with Ribeiro and Sá de Miranda (the
"two sisters"). The location of the episode and the reversal of genders occurring in the novel plead strongly
in favor of Núñez de Reinoso's acquaintance with doña
Gracia and his employment in Portugal, where he would
have been tutor to Juan Micas and his brother Bernardo.
It is an incontrovertible fact that they did not attend the
University of Louvain before 1542 and 1540 respec-
tively.[60] If, however, the locale is Italy, Reinoso would
have been tutor to Gracia Nasi's daughter Reyna and
niece, also called Gracia.

Where and when the family employed Núñez de
Reinoso's services broaches the question of the date
of his departure from Portugal. He may have left as
early as 1536, as they did.[61] However, it is likely that
he first met them in Portugal, rejoined them in Flanders
and accompanied them to Italy, following the route
that Usque outlined. While there is no record of Núñez
de Reinoso's having stayed in Flanders, his residence
there can be inferred from the fact that Ribeiro's
romance, "Ao longo de hua ribeira / que vay polo pee da
serra," was first published by the Martín Nucio press in

---

60. Bataillon, "Alonso Núñez de Reinoso . . .", p. 9, gives as his
source, Arch. Gén. du Royaume, à Bruxelles; Univ. de Louvain, No. 24,
Liber quartus intitulatorum, fol. 160 1°, "Dominus Johannes Micas
lusitanus intitulatus in specie nobilis—Louvain 1, Sept. 1542." He wonders
if the "Bernardinus Michas lusitanus" (7 April 1540, fol. 131 v°) is
Juan Micas' brother. Although Cecil Roth, *Doña Gracia,* p. 66, confesses
that he cannot uncover the Christian name of the brother, the records
of a secret trial in Venice, seen by this writer, clearly establish that
Bernardo Micas was indeed his name.

61. This is the date that Roth suggests. Presumably he chose 1536 because it was the year of the establishment of the Inquisition as well as
that of the death of Francisco Mendes, the husband of Beatriz de Luna.

Antwerp in 1545. "Polas ribeiras de ums rio," the initial words of the version of the eclogue "Basto" that Sá de Miranda dedicated to Nunálverez Pereira, suggest that that poet was alluding to Ribeiro's *romance* and evoking the companionship of the three bards. Since Sá de Miranda's poem was written between 1530 and 1540, the implication is that Ribeiro's *romance* was composed long before its publication date of 1545.[62] Was it Núñez de Reinoso who delivered his friend's poem to the Martín Nucio press when he was passing through Antwerp on his way to Italy?

In Italy, his closest literary associate was Ortensio Lando, an Italian author whose ironic sense of humor and unorthodox religious beliefs scandalized many;[63] Núñez de Reinoso seems to have secured the patronage of the Nasi family (for his friend Lando.) The *Dialogo di M. Ortensio Lando nel qual si ragiona della consolatione e utilità, che si riporta leggendo la Sacra Scrittura* . . . is dedicated to Beatrice de Luna (Gracia

---

62. For more detail on the poem, see Vasconcelos, *Nótulas relativas á "Menina e Moça" na edicão de Colónia (1559)*, Coimbra, 1924, pp. 27–28. In *Poesias*, p. 775, she denies that there is any connection between Sá de Miranda's eclogue and Ribeiro's *romance*. Eugenio Asensio, "El *romance* de Bernardim Ribeiro 'Ao longo da ribeira,' " *Revista de Filología Española*, XL, 1957, pp. 1–19, voices his opposition to Teófilo Braga's autobiographical interpretation of the poem. Asensio also believes that the ballad was written shortly before Ribeiro's death. Guimarães, pp. 125ff., does not even believe this poem is by Ribeiro.

63. Jacob Burckhardt, *The Civilization of the Renaissance in Italy*, II, New York, 1958, pp. 336–37, comments that Lando ("Landi") " . . . published an anonymous *Commentario*, . . . which contains among many follies not a few valuable hints on the unhappy ruined condition of Italy in the middle of the century." The *Biographie Universelle ancienne et moderne*, XXIII, Paris, p. 146, succinctly sums up Lando's character with the remark that he and his friend Aretino were "deux hommes faits l'un pour l'autre et bien dignes d'habiter ensembles un hôpital de fous." As to his religious beliefs, a friend, Ginnagiolo Odone, wrote, "C'est un grand ennemi de la religion . . . Il n'osait pas montrer ses sentiments en Italie . . ." *Ouevres de Gilbert Cousin*, I, 313.

Nasi).[64] In addition, his *Due Panegirici nuovamente composti de quali l'uno é in lode della S. Marchesana della Padulla et l'altro in comendatione della S. donna Lucrezia Gonzaga da Gazuolo,* published in the same year and by the same press as Reinoso's volume, bears two dedications: one "Al magnanimo et generoso s. il. s. Gioan Michas," and the other to his brother Bernardo. On page 56 of this work there is a poem "Del S. Alphonso Nunnez, de Reynoso [sic] al S. Hortensio Lando."[65]

Lando is the only contemporary critic to comment upon Núñez de Reinoso's work during his lifetime. In his *Sette Libri de Cathaloghi a'varie cose appartenenti, non solo antiche ma anche moderne . . .,* he lists "Alphonso Numez de Reynoso [sic], poeta de giocondissimo stile," among such illustrious Spaniards as "Il Boscano Garcilasso della Vega [sic], D. Diego di Mendozza, D. Girolamo di Vrea [sic], Giovanni di Mena."[66] The inclusion

---

64. *Dialogo di M. Ortensio Lando nel quale si ragiona della consolatione e utilità, che si riporta leggendo la Sacra Scrittura, e si tratta eziandio dell'ordine da tenersi nel leggerla, mostrandosi esser le Sacre Lettere di vera eloquenza e di varia Dottrina alle Pagane superiori,* Venezia, Segno del Posso, 1552. The copy I examined (Biblioteca Marciana) was missing the first few pages so I am unable to verify the name of the printer and the contents of Lando's dedication. There is a letter by Girolamo Ruscelli "Alla molto illustre et honoratissima S. la S. D. Beatrice de Luna," pp. 60–71.

65. Gabriel Giolito de Ferrari et fratelli, Venice, 1552.

66. *Sette Libri de Cathaloghi a'varie cose apparteneti, non solo antiche, ma anche moderne: opera utile molto alla historia et da cui prender si po materia di Favellare d'ogni proposito che ci occorra,* Gabriel Giolito de Ferrari e Fratelli, Vinegia, 1552 (Libro VI, p. 476)

Il Boscano Garcilasso della Vega
D. Giorgio Manrich
D. Diego de Mendozza
El Marchese di Santiglia
D. Girolamo di Vrea
Giovanni di Mena
D. Hernando di Cugna
Garcí Sanches di Badasoz
Alphonso Numez di Reynoso, poeta di giocondissimo stile.

of Reinoso's name can be attributed less to his renown than to a sixteenth-century example of book promotion, for Lando's book was published February 26, 1552, by Gabriel Giolito de Ferrari, just four days before Núñez de Reinoso's work left the same press.[67] Furthermore, Lando's mention of his friend suggests that he was repaying a debt of gratitude to Reinoso for introducing him to the Nasi family and securing him their patronage.[68]

Doña Gracia's interest in publishing is well known. She was evidently the patroness of the first Jewish-Spanish press in Italy, that of Abraham Usque in Ferrara.[69] Its enduring achievements were: the celebrated "Ferrara Bible" (1553), the Jewish version of which was dedicated to her and signed with the Jewish names of the printers Abraham Usque (Duarte Pinel) and Yom Tob Atias (Jerónimo de Vargas), while the Christian version, dedicated to Ercole II, the Duke of Ferrara, bore their *converso* names: Samuel Usque's *Consolaçam ás tribulaçoens de Israel* (1553), containing

---

It is interesting to note that Lando has made a common error in assuming that Boscán and Garcilaso were one person. Urrea, whose life is shrouded in mystery, was the author of the chivalric novel, *Clarisel de las Flores* (1550?), whose title may have inspired Reinoso in the selection of names for his principal characters.

67. Because the calendar in use at that time in Venice began the new year on March 1, it is impossible to determine whether Lando's and Reinoso's books were published the same year or one year apart. There is little reason for believing that Reinoso dated his letters according to the Venetian custom; presumably for him, January 24 and March 1 belonged to the same calendar year. An examination of the records of the Giolito press does not clear up the confusion because, although Reinoso's book was published with the official imprimatur, his name does not appear among the lists of authors submitted by the press to the authorities in order to secure permission to print.

68. Lando, in his *Sette Libri di Cathaloghi,* p. 26, mentions that among the richest moderns are the *Mendesi.* Is this not the Italian for Mendes and a good indication that he sought the patronage of this international banking family?

69. For information on the activity of the Usque Press, see Cecil Roth, *The History of the Jews in Italy,* Philadelphia, 1946.

two lengthy eulogies of her and her good works—one in the dedication, the other within the text—and Ribeiro's *Menina e moça* (1554), the only Portuguese novel published outside the Peninsula during the sixteenth century.

To judge by the volumes dedicated to them, the Nasi family authorized the publication of a certain number of books by privately owned firms in Venice. The bulk of these books were printed before the founding of the Usque press, though at times it appears that the choice of firm was dictated by subject matter and author. The works published by Abraham Usque met a less rosy fate than those issued by the independent presses: Ribeiro's novel appeared on the Portuguese Index of 1581 and Samuel Usque's *Consolaçam*, printed without the official "Imprimatur," was placed on the Spanish (Madrid) Index of 1690. Conceivably, Gabriel Giolito de Ferrari was one of the beneficiaries of the Nasi family's interest in publishing. This press was noteworthy for its publication of Spanish works and translations, especially so for the reprinting, under the editorship of Alfonso de Ulloa, of *La Celestina* and other masterpieces.[70] An Italian critic points out that "Queste stampe spagnole furono quasi tutte del 1552 e del 1553." However, his proffered explanation for the cessation of such activity, "che le spagnoleri incontrassero poco favore presso gli italiano, e che gli spagnoli ch'erano fra noi non fossero molto usati di comprar libri,"[71] seems unlikely. It is more probable that money destined to

---

70. See Benedetto Croce, *La Spagna nella vita italiana durante la Rinascenza,* Bari, 1917; also, Salvatore Bongi, *Annali di Gabriel Giolito de Ferrari,* Roma, 1890.

71. Giuseppe Clerico, *Giornale delle Biblioteche fondato e diretto da Eugenio Bianchi,* Genova, 1869, p. xlviii.

subsidize such books was no longer supplied to Gabriel Giolito de Ferrari after the Nasis left Italy in 1553.

Another Italian critic puzzled over the connection of a man of so dubious a reputation as Lando, with the highly-esteemed Giolito press.[72] It should be pointed out that the house itself encountered difficulties with the Inquisition and that some of its books were confiscated.[73] Additionally, when one examines the non-Italians connected with the firm, such as the Nasi family and Ulloa,[74] all of whom were indicted or imprisoned by the Venetian authorities, it begins to look as if it were no ordinary press that published Núñez de Reinoso's work in 1552.

Was Núñez de Reinoso unaware of the religious beliefs of his patrons? Hardly. Bataillon suggests that Reinoso dedicated the book to Juan Micas rather than to his aunt because, while she was at that time living openly in Ferrara as a Jewess, Micas was still considered a Christian.[75] The passage previously quoted from Laguna's *Viaje de Turquía* would seem to support such a conclusion. However, records indicate otherwise. The entire family had too many brushes with authority for the public to ignore their Jewish persuasions. Diogo

72. Bongi.

73. Filippo Salveraglio, *Catalogo d'una raccolta di opere stampate dai Gioliti di Ferrari in Venezia,* Milano, 1890, pp. 105ff.

74. A. M. Gallina, "Un intermedio fra la cultura italiana e spagnola nel sec. XVI: Alfonso de Ulloa," *Quaderni Ibero-Americani,* XVII, 1955, pp. 4–12. Ulloa was condemned to life imprisonment on January 19, 1567, for crimes against the state. The supposition was that he was not executed because he had the protection of a noble Venetian accomplice. He died in jail from a fever, June 16, 1570. He was the editor of *De los Sonetos canciones, mandriales y sextinas de gran POETA y orador Francisco Petrarca,* traduzidos de toscano por Salomon Usque, Hebreo, Casa de Nicolao Bevilaqua, Venezia, 1567. Salomon Usque was a friend of the Nasi, possibly their business agent.

75. Bataillon, "Alonso Núñez de Reinoso," p. 6.

Mendes, the head of the banking firm and Beatriz de Luna's brother-in-law, was first accused of Judaizing in Antwerp in 1532. He survived this and subsequent denunciations, thanks to the intervention of Carlos V and other heads of state to whom he had lent money. Although Carlos V knighted Juan Micas in 1546, when the family was still domiciled in Antwerp, Micas was himself later detained in Milan on a similar charge. Beatriz (Gracia) was arraigned and imprisoned in Venice in 1549; it was rumored that her release was obtained through the intervention of the Grand Turk himself who, at the instance of his physician Mosén Amón, the son of emigré Spanish Jews, sent a special ambassador to Venice to carry out the negotiations.[76] Among the Inquisitional records of the State of Venice can be found a document listed under "Ebrei anonomi," in which on Wednesday, January 11, 1550, "Juã Miches" was implicated in an accusation of practicing Judaism. This charge was evidently not followed up.[77] It may be noted that 1550 was the year in which Micas petitioned the governing body of Venice, the Council of Ten, for the purchase of an island as a refuge for Peninsular *mar-*

---

76. See either of Roth's books on the Nasi family for details of the various charges.

77. Archivio di Stato, Venezia, *Santo Uffizio*, "Ebrei anonomi." There are no other documents, such as those of corroborating witnesses, to substantiate the accusation, nor evidence of a trial. Presumably prestige and money led to the accusation's being ignored and filed under "anonymous" even though the document clearly states the name "Juã Miches." The introductory paragraph, written in Latin, contains the all but obliterated name of the accuser, possibly an "Alphonsus spanuolo"; is this Alonso (Alfonso) Núñez de Reinoso? The testimony itself begins with words very reminiscent of Ribeiro's novel: ". . . me pigliorno da mia madre che io potovo aver da tre in quatro anni [et] me menorno in Fiandra . . ." ("me leuará de casa de minha may para muyto lonje . . ." p. 3). For further discussion of the document, see C. H. Rose, "New Information on the Life of Joseph Nasi, Duke of Naxos: The Venetian Phase," *The Jewish Quarterly Review*, LX, 1970.

ranos.[78] At the time of the publication of Reinoso's work, dedicated, as we have said, to Juan Micas, Micas himself was engaged in a spectacular affair that culminated in the Council of Ten's meeting in extraordinary session of March, 1553, and voting to apprehend the entire Nasi-Mendes family, including their servants, and to offer a generous reward for their capture, dead or alive. The records of this trial, held *in absentia* and the correspondence, listed under "Secreta," the section reserved for the most heinous crimes, indicate that Juan Micas, not his aunt, was held to be the chief culprit.[79]

Despite the fact that it must have been common knowledge that the entire family was Portuguese and Jewish, we come upon strange statements such as Girolamo Ruscelli made in a laudatory letter, dated April 27, 1552, to Beatriz de Luna, where he stated that he was happy to have lived "in quella città gloriosa [Venice], nelle qualli sono & nati, & vivuti il miracoloso Signor Ortensio Lando, & la Signora Donna Beatrice di Luna."[80] But how could Ruscelli, a friend of Lando and the Usques, have been unaware of Beatriz de Luna's

---

78. Reznik, p. 85.
79. Archivio di Stato, Venezia, Consiglio de Dieci, Criminales "Essendo il caso de Zuan Miches di quella importanza che é nota, á cadauno di questo conseglio; Nel quale si ricerca maggior pena di quello che per l'ordinario si pó dare, Stante la parte de XI, Luglio, 1549." Other names mentioned are: "Bernardo Miches fratello di Zuan Miches portoghese," "Rodrigo Nunes, servitor di D. Breanda di Luna" (supposedly Beatriz's sister), "Alexandro Calado, Ferãndo Rodriges portoghesi servitori de Zuan Miches," "Diego Mendes portoghese," "Agustin Henrichez portoghese" (Enríquez, otherwise known as Abraham Benveniste, was a relative and an employee; perhaps an informer, he was one of the few apprehended and released). One accusation reads "Zuanne Miches, et compagni raptori di Beatrice Mendes: li quali fugendo con la detta Beatrice rapita. . . ." Beatrice de Luna's maiden name was Benveniste, her married name Mendes. For more information about the trial, its causes and consequences, see Rose, "New Information. . . ."
80. Ruscelli's letter appears in Lando's *Dialogo . . .,* p. 71.

national origins?[81] Again, among the *Lettere* of Lucrezia
Gonzaga is an epistle, dated May 12th, to "S. Giovanni
Michas, a Vinegia," in praise of Charles V,[82] written
as if the Spanish monarch were at that time a friend of
Juan Micas—an unlikely assumption, given the flight
of Beatriz de Luna from Spanish territory after her
refusal to let her daughter marry a Gentile chosen by
the royal family,[83] not to mention the long-drawn-out
negotiations between Micas and Charles V over the
confiscation of the family fortune.[84]

The *Lettere,* which supplies further connections
between Reinoso, Lando, and the Nasis, was evidently
Lando's idea of a literary joke (he, rather than Lucrezia
Gonzaga, is usually considered to have authored the
volume).[85] Can one consider as serious the bizarre letter

81. In his *Delle lettere di Principi, le quali o si scrivono da principi,
o a principi, o ragionan di principi,* Venetia, 1562 (1564-77), Ruscelli
makes reference to "Odardo Gomez," who can be identified as doña
Gracia's Italian agent and possibly as the writer "Salomon Usque."
Gómez also contributed a sonnet to Ruscelli's *Del Tempio alla divina
Signora Donna Giovanna d'Aragona, fabricato da tutti i più gentili
spiriti, & in tutte le lingue principali del mondo,* Venetia, 1555. Roth,
"Salusque Lusitano," *Jewish Quarterly Review,* N.S., XXXIV, 1934,
tries to clear up the confusion surrounding the many Usques.

82. *Lettere di Lucrezia Gonzaga da Gazuolo: con gran diligentia
raccolte à gloria del sesso feminile nuovamente in luce posto.* Scotto,
Venezia, 1552, pp. 264-65.

83. See Roth, *Doña Gracia,* pp. 43-45, for this incident.

84. See Reznik, pp. 52-72, for this correspondence.

85. It is usually listed under Lando's name. Burckhardt, p. 336, says
of Lando's predilection for pseudonyms: "Ortensio Landi . . . is so
fond of playing hide-and-seek with his own name, and fast-and-loose
with historical facts, that even when he seems to be most in earnest he
must be accepted with caution and only after close examination." It
should be noted that his idea of humor included the writing of mock
funeral sermons on the death of a dog, a rooster, etc.

However, Lucrezia Gonzaga cannot be dismissed as the possible author.
Educated by Bandello, she was capable of writing the *Lettere.* Also the
record of the Gonzaga family is one of extreme liberality toward all
religious groups. The court at Mantua favored Jewish writers and
musicians (Roth, *Personalities and Events in Jewish History,* Philadelphia, 1953, p. 284) ; in Naples Lucrezia's cousin Giulia supported the unorthodox religious group that formed around another Spanish literary exile

addressed to "Solimano imperadore di Constantinopoli,
& di Trapesonda . . .," in which Lucrezia purportedly
asks the Sultan to rescue her husband from the prison
of the Duke of Ferrara (where, indeed, he was held
captive), and suggests sending Rustan Basciah on such
a mission?[86] That such a request could be made by a
noble Christian lady, at a time when the sultan's fleet
was menacing the Mediterranean, is to say the least
improbable. The letter has the quality of an "inside"
joke, while the request is suspiciously redolent of the
events surrounding doña Gracia's release from jail in
Venice. Presumably Lando and his circle of friends had
full knowledge, as did Núñez de Reinoso, of the identity
and activities of the Nasi family. Either they shared
the family's religious views, or remained indifferent
because they benefited from the association.

Also among the *Lettere* can be found a "thank-you
note" to Núñez de Reinoso for his contribution to the
Due panegirici. Dated June 15th, the epistle reads in part:

> . . . ma hauendomi uoi nella uostra canzone castigliana
> tanto honoratamente lodata come fatto hauete; non
> vego io come far possa per renderui altrettante lodi;
> saluo se alla sembianza dell'Echo, io non ui rimandassi
> le uostre medesime uoci: Ben poteuate S. Reynoso
> risparmiare queste tante lodi, che mi date; anzi
> impiegare le doueuate in donna che ne fusse piu degna
> di me.[87]

from a *converso* family, Juan de Valdés (see Christopher Hare, [Pseud.,
Marion Andrews] *A Princess of the Italian Reformation Giulia Gonzaga
1513–1566: Her Family and her Friends,* New York, 1912, for information
on the entire Gonzaga family; and Juan de Valdés, *Alfabeto Cristiano,*
edición de Benedetto Croce, Bari, 1938, for information on Giulia and
Juan de Valdés.)

86. In Turkey, Rustan Basciah, the vizier, was Juan Mica's most
useful ally in the court of the sultan. See Roth, *The Duke of Naxos.*

87. *Lettere,* p. 77.

Following this letter, there are no further references to Núñez de Reinoso. He either accompanied Juan Micas to Turkey or remained in Italy, settling in Venice or Ferrara.

The dukedom of Ferrara was a haven for Peninsular *marranos*; Ercole II[88] and his wife, the Protestant Renée of France, welcomed religious refugees of all sorts. In 1549, upon her release from the Venetian prison, doña Gracia moved to Ferrara with her family, as did other *conversos* who received letters of protection guaranteeing immunity from religious persecution in that community.[89] The influx increased following a decree in 1550 by the Venetian Senate expelling *marranos* from the Republic. There are indications that Núñez de Reinoso had spent some time in Ferrara prior to the publication of his novel; its Chapters XI and XII describe life at the court of the fictional Duque de Atenas on the Ínsula de la Vida, a cipher for the dukedom of the Estes. Reinoso's heroine comments upon the social gatherings, the witty and elevated conversation, and the tolerant attitudes of the ladies and gentlemen of the court who speak

> . . . con mucha cordura y discrecion, . . . ni tractando de los linajes, ni de las tierras ó naturales, la cosa mas baja y menos usada entre personas avisadas y celosas de tener buen nombre; porque los hombres de precio y valor sus obras han de tener por padres, y sus virtudes por natural y tierra . . . (442b)

The remark is both a criticism of Spain, where *linajes* were all-important, and a tribute to the enlightenment of the Duke and Duchess of Ferrara. Presumably it was

---

88. In Usque's *Consolaçam*, Ercole II is the only Gentile eulogized.
89. Andrea Balletti, *Gli Ebrei e gli Estensi*, Reggio, 1930, pp. 77-78.

Núñez de Reinoso, attached to the Nasi household in
Ferrara, who delivered the manuscript of *Menina e moça*
to the Abraham Usque press which, it will be remembered,
was sponsored by Gracia Nasi.[90] A passage from
Reinoso's novel may be interpreted as a vow to see
Ribeiro's work published: Isea (*i.e.,* Reinoso), com-
muning with the spirit of her dead friend, says, "Está[s]
en aquella gloria y descanso que con tus claras obras acá
ganaste" (454a).

With the printing of his own work in 1552 and that
of Ribeiro in 1554, each in some way sponsored by the
Nasi family who left Italy in 1553,[91] the final chapter in
the life of Núñez de Reinoso comes to a close. The
events of his old age, like those of his youth, have
perished in oblivion; even the date of his death, like
that of his birth, remains a mystery.[92] Indeed, after the
year 1552, nothing further is heard of the man known as
Alonso Núñez de Reinoso.

---

90. Vasconcelos, *Obras,* I, p. 105, and Bataillon, "Alonso Núñez de
Reinoso," suggest this possibility.
91. The date of their departure is usually given as 1552 but the
Venetian documents clearly state that they were in Italy in 1553.
92. The date of 1567, given by Toda, is unprovable (see n. 13).

2

THE CONVERSO PREDICAMENT
AND LITERARY TRADITION

¿Tú piensas que no te entiendo?
¡Dom 'a Dios que vas huyendo
de la Santa Enquesición!

Torres Naharro,
Comedia Jacinta, III, 146-48[1]

We have seen how Núñez de Reinoso was closely associated in Italy with a group of people who had fled the workings of the Holy Office of the Inquisition, but in order to ascertain how he himself felt about the situation and how he expressed the *converso*'s predicament, we must examine his poetry.

The Method

Interpretation of Núñez de Reinoso's poetry depends on understanding a series of literary transpositions he employed. The poet could count upon his reader's familiarity with certain literary traditions and awareness of social circumstances for the transmitting of his recondite message. Pastoral poetry had, since time of Virgil,

---

1. Joseph Gillet, ed., *Collected Plays,* Pennsylvania, 1964.

been used for presenting contemporary personages in the guise of shepherds who made reference to topical events. Imbued with a reverence for, and a desire to imitate and assimilate the classical past, Renaissance humanists revived this tradition. We have already seen, in the discussion of the "Basto" academy, how sixteenth-century Spanish and Portuguese writers attempted to reproduce the atmosphere of a literary society of antiquity. Accordingly, in their poetry and prose contemporary figures were fashioned into shepherds bearing such traditionally bucolic names as Silvano, Coridón, and Melibeo, as well as those of their own invention. In order to remind the reader of the masquerade, such authors underscored the transformation by pointing out role changes: e.g., in *Menina e moça*, Ribeiro's narrator remarks, "Deveis de saber . . . que este pastor e um cavaleiro" and "O pastor da frauta que nam era pastor."[2] Furthermore, Ribeiro's "pastor-cavaleiro" deems it necessary to rechristen himself: forsaking his former mistress "Cruelsia" for amorous allegiance to "Aonia," "Narbindel" assumes the name "Bimnarder." By extension, it was possible for the reading public to conclude that behind the fictional character of knight-turned-shepherd there existed a real person, in this case, the author Bernaldim (Bernardim) Ribeiro.

The social circumstance underlying such fictional transformations, that made role-playing understandable and acceptable to the reader was that of religious conversion. Literary tradition and social reality converged. Not only did some of Núñez de Reinoso's friends use poetic pseudonyms, but others employed aliases in their daily

2. *Obras,* II, Pt. I. All further references to Ribeiro's novel imply the edition of Anselmo Braamcamp Freire, which is based on the original or Ferrara version of 1554.

life. It was often customary, as Cecil Roth points out, for *cripto-Judeos* to have both a Christian or baptismal name by which they were known in society and a Jewish name by which they were called within the family and to which the reverted after reaching a land of relative safety where they could openly reenter the faith of their ancestors.[3] Among Núñez de Reinoso's associates were Juan Micas-Joseph Nasi, Beatriz de Luna-Gracia Nasi, Duarte Pinel-Abraham Usque. In the case of a translator of some Petrarchan verses, there are three known names: Duarte Gómez reverted to Salomón Usque and wrote under the name of Salusque Lusitano.[4] On the other hand, no Christian name has been put forward for Samuel Usque, and the true identity of Ribeiro, if indeed this is a pseudonymn as Bataillon believes,[5] may never be known.

---

3. *The House of Nasi: Doña Gracia,* p. 5.

4. See note 80, Chapter I, for reference to Roth's discussion of "Salusque Lusitano."

5. Bataillon, "Alonso Núñez de Reinoso," p. 3, says that this is just a feeling on his part, based on the fact that the name was frequently found in *romances*. Américo Castro, *De la edad conflictiva,* Madrid, 1961, p. 211, calls Ribeiro a *converso* but does not elaborate upon the subject. I believe that the following excerpt from Ribeiro's Écloga II contains autobiographical material indicative of his *converso* status:

> Quando as fomes grandes foram,
> Que Alentejo foi perdido,
> Da aldea que chaman Torrão
> Foi este pastor fogido.
> . . . .
> Que Alentejo era enxuito
> De agoa, e mui seco de prado.
> . . . .
> E Jano, pera salvar
> O gado que lhe ficou,
> Foi esta terra buscar. (26–27)

The foregoing might explain the residency of Ribeiro, a native of Torrão, in the "Basto" refuge in 1528, because *conversos* in Alentejo were blamed for droughts and other natural disasters in the late 1520s (much as they were later held responsible for the Lisbon earthquake).

Coinciding with the literary practice of poetic pseudonyms and religio-social necessity of aliases, was another
factor that may figure in the creation and deciphering of
names: the popularity of the *Cabala* among humanists,[6]
and particularly among both Jewish and Christian
mystics.[7] It should be remembered that the last book
of the *Cabala*, the *Libro de Esplendores*, was written in
Spain. A Biblical work, frequently cited during the sixteenth and seventeenth centuries, was the "Lament of
Jeremiah" (I shall later discuss its relevance to Reinoso's
novel); its composition was based on the cabalistic prin-
ciple of employing acrostic verses.[8] Vasconcelos attributes
the predilection of Ribeiro and others for inventing names
based on anagrams and other types of verbal clues to
the influence of the *Cabala* on this group.[9] The informed
reader could be counted upon to make the necessary
linguistic transformation or rearrangement of letters in
order to uncover the identity of the fictional character.
This was but one more method of alerting the audience
to the fact that the method bespoke a fiction that masked
a reality.

Thus, it can be assumed that Núñez de Reinoso con-
sciously led his readers through a series of transformations to put them in a properly receptive frame of mind
for his topic—change or conversion—and that he used

---

6. Among them, Pico della Mirandola.
7. Doña Benvenida Abravanel, daughter-in-law of the rabbinical
authority Isaac Abravanel, and sister-in-law of the neo-platonist Judah
Abravanel (León Hebreo) was known to have had an interest in the
Cabala as well as in the mystical Messianism of David Reubeni.
8. The prologue of the *Celestina* contains the famous acrostic verses.
Is the influence here that of the *Cabala,* or of troubador tradition where
such devices, as well as riming games, were popular, and which came
down to Rojas through the works of earlier poets such as Manrique?
9. Vasconcelos, *Obras,* I, pp. 230f., where, incidentally, she points out
Columbus's interest in the *Cabala*; he was known to have recorded dates
according to the Hebraic calendar.

a literary tradition, pastoral poetry, for its potential as a vehicle for the dramatization of his problem. In his discussion of the homiletic and responsa literature of Spanish Jews, Benzion Netanyahu asserts that

> . . . when the discussion turned on conversion in general, . . . the audience sensed quite clearly whether the author has these matters in mind, or whether he used them merely as a ruse to express his opinion on the Marrano problem.[10]

Was not Núñez de Reinoso sincere in urging his readers to look for the hidden meaning in his work when, in the second introduction, he employed familiar literary formulae to proclaim, "debaxo de su inuencion ay grandes secretos," and "ninguna palabra escreui que primero no pensasse lo que debaxo queria entēder"? (4-5)

To the strain of pastoral poetry as it had come down from classical times and was revived in the Renaissance through the works of such writers as Boccaccio and Sannazzaro, must be added a Peninsular variety, rustic poetry, such as the *Coplas de Mingo Revulgo*, where conditions in contemporary Spain were discussed. Juan del Encina brought both elements together when he recast Virgilian eclogues in *sayagués*. Other early masters of the drama, such as Torres Naharro and Gil Vicente, made use of rustic poetry for setting forth their ideas and attitudes on the personal, religious, and social problems that the sixteenth-century *converso* faced.[11] Thus,

---

10. Benzion Netanyahu, *The Marranos of Spain From the Late XIVth to the Early XVth Century According to Contemporary Hebrew Sources,* New York, 1966, pp. 79-80.

11. Encina, Torres Naharro, Sánchez de Badajoz, Fernández, Vicente, and other early dramatists were *conversos*. For amplification of this statement and its implications, see Castro, *De la edad conflictiva, passim.* Stephen Gilman, "Retratos de conversos en la *Comedia Jacinta* de Torres

pastoral poetry, ancient and modern, foreign and native, had often been employed for the transmission of topical matters in transmuted form. In more recent times, in the hands of *converso* authors, it had been employed to express the *converso* predicament.

While Núñez de Reinoso used the tradition of pastoral poetry for presenting contemporary figures and events, there was available to him a medieval literary tradition that could be employed for conveying double meaning. This was the poetry of courtly love as it came down to him through the fifteenth-century writers of the *cancionero*. In the first place, the forces that contributed to its development made such poetry capable of adaptation for expressing a religio-social topic. The poetry of courtly love was a fusion of two poetic streams whose nature had already been subject to religious transformation: the mock-serious devotion to the God of Love, derived from Ovid, and the cult of the Virgin as expressed in *marianas*. The poetic offspring of such a union could voice blasphemous or pious thoughts. The courtly love songs of the troubadors were early associated with the Manichaean heresy.[12] In Spain, secular material that

Naharro," *Nueva Revista de Filología Hispánica*, XVII, 1966, pp. 20-39, discusses this *comedia* in relationship to the exiled *converso* situation. For more information on Juan del Encina, see J. R. Andrews, *Juan del Encina, Prometheus in Search of Prestige*, Berkeley, 1959, wherein Andrews discusses Encina as a self-advertiser but does not relate this characteristic to a projection of the *converso* personality as Castro would have done. It is further interesting to note that, while Andrews discusses the role-playing in the two eclogues, "Reqüesta de amores," in terms of social mobility possible through poetic ability (being able to write in both high and low styles—courtly love or rustic pastoral), it is possible to interpret Gil's conversion in a religious sense, an assumption made possible by Encina's desire to attain religious acceptability as well as social recognition.

12. For further discussion of courtly love, see C. S. Lewis, *The Allegory of Love: A Study in Medieval Tradition*, New York, 1959, and Denis de Rougemont, *L'amour et l'occident*, Paris, 1962; for this tradition in Spain, specifically, see Joseph E. Gillet and Otis Green,

had its origins in amorous poetry to the Virgin was restored to its original purpose when "contrahecho a lo divino"; lines from popular songs were often employed in artistic secular compositions and then reworked, sometimes by the same poet, as in the case of Álvarez Gato, "a lo divino."[13] Given the history of its development and use, it is not surprising that such poetry could be invoked to convey the love-hate conflict of the Spanish *converso*.

The characteristics of the poetry of courtly love, partially reflecting life in the medieval manor, could be made applicable to a contemporary social conflict: the superiority of women (i.e., religion or homeland), obedience to her every whim and service without thought of reward, the spiritual anguish and mental confusion caused by the loss of the lover's soul to his lady, the physical transformation or deterioration endured by the rejected but steadfast lover, the exile or banishment of the man from the presence of the great lady, and finally the transmutation of amorous suffering into joy.

Such poetry had borrowed much of its terminology from religious sources. It is precisely this flexibility and duplicity of language that made it serviceable to Núñez de Reinoso. The words "fe," "firmeza," "pena," "gloria," "mudanza," and so on, were capable of being interpreted in either a secular, literary fashion or a religio-social context.[14] Critics have noted the natural reticence, the note of caution, that pervades the work of Ribeiro and

---

Propalladia and other Works, IV, *Torres Naharro and the Drama of the Renaissance*, 1961.

13. Bruce Wardropper, "Hacia una historia de la lírica a lo divino," *Clavileño*, V, 1954, pp. 1–11.

14. The interchangeability of religious and amorous sentiments can further be illustrated through Garci Sánchez de Badajoz's conversion of verses from Job to those of erotic despair (*Cancionero general*, No. 273) and Villegas's similar treatment of Psalm 137 ("Super flumina Babilonis") in his *Ausencia y soledad de amor*.

Sá de Miranda.[15] Núñez de Reinoso is, perhaps, even more guarded, for it seems that he unrealistically entertained the hope of returning to Spain.[16] He refrains from saying anything too openly dangerous, yet the import of his words must have been intelligible to the informed reader. The development of a cryptic language to express religious thoughts has been noted by Netanyahu: "Between the writer and his audience there developed . . . a special system of communication, or a kind of secret code."[17] Núñez de Reinoso, then, adopted the poetry of courtly love, for the possibilities its tradition of transformation of theme, situation, and language presented, as a means of expressing his own personal anguish resulting from the religio-social tensions of the times. His readers had been conditioned to accept such material. Much as the courtier recorded his despair and examined his tragic emotion, Reinoso reveals himself as the rejected lover for whom there can be no "remedio" because he cannot forget the land that exiled him.

---

15. Some examples from the poetry of Sá de Miranda:

> No siguió Ribeiro mas.
> Antes como era cuidoso
> . . . .
> Estuvo un rato pensoso.
>
> ("Alejo," *Poesias,* p. 123)
>
> Porque este mundo é tal
> Que é milhor ca nos desertos
> Sofrer e calar o mal
> Que descobrir os secretos
> D'este nosso Portugal.
>
> ("Montano," *Poesias,* p. 406)

16. ". . . si esta mi obra en algun tiempo aportare á las riberas del rio Henares . . . (468a) The Portuguese version of Reinoso's novel (exemplar, Harvard College Library) omits reference to this river, which flows through Guadalajara.

17. Netanyahu, p. 79.

Portrait and Self-Portrait

Given the methods employed and their appropriateness for expressing the situation, let us now turn to the poetry itself, where Núñez de Reinoso manifests many of those attitudes Américo Castro considers typical of a *converso*. Reinoso exhibits the mental confusion of a man who has left one country and cannot find peace in another, who has left one religion and cannot embrace another. In a frankly autobiographical poem, he writes to a friend, "Ya no soy / Quien ser solia."[18] (No. 2) Typical of his state of mind is the following:

> *Firmeza no sé tener,*
> *Ora bivo, ora me mato,*
> *Ora no quiero plazer,*
> *Ora no sé qué me hazer.*
> *Pues no ato ni desato:*
> *En nada tengo sentido*
> *En nada puedo acertar. (No. 1)*

He records his indecision: "No me sé determinar / No me determino en cosa" (No. 14), and describes himself as a man divided: "Soy me enemigo mortal / A mí mismo mal hazia / Conmigo traigo batalla" (No. 13). Such commonplaces, which ordinarily refer to the change a great passion has wrought, permeate the poetry of his companions Ribeiro and Sá de Miranda as well: Ribeiro, "De mi eu me desavim / E pois eu me sam imigo," "Ja não sam quem ser soia," "Contra mi mesmo pelejo," "Que a mi mesmo mal digo";[19] Sá de Miranda, "Comigo

18. Cf. "Non sum qualis eram bonae / Sub regno Cinarae." Horace, *Odes,* IV, 1, 3. Unlike his model, Reinoso's transformation results from the rigors of exile.
19. M. Braga, "Écloga IV," 78–79, 153, 312, 325.

me desavim," "Io no soi el que era entaño."[20] Yet the
subject in the works of all three poets is social, not
amatory, suffering.

Núñez de Reinoso acknowledges that his "desaso-
siego," a condition Castro considers typical of *conversos,*
is innate: "Pero mi dessasossiego / En la leche lo mame"
(No. 5). His view of life is negative, and expressing
himself in the Heraclitean and Petrarchan terms that are
reminiscent of *La Celestina,* he says, "Que es el hijo
contra el padre / Y el hermano contra hermano /
. . . . Pues el mundo todo es guerra"[21] (No. 5). In addition, he is referring to conditions in Spain where families
and friends divided over religious matters. Efodi, in *The
Shame of the Gentiles,* a work written, "as a means of
defense against the 'rebels' (converts) who connive
against the faith," employs a similar phrase to express the
dissension among Spaniards of Jewish ancestry: "the
entire people is at strife."[22] In one of Sá de Miranda's eclogues, an embittered exile exclaims,

> *O pai contra o filho vai,*
> *O irmão contra o irmao,*
> *O filho vai contra o pai,*
> *Um mao contra outro mao! (396)*

---

20. Vasconcelos, *Poesias,* "Cantiga VII," p. 15.
21. "Todas las cosas ser criadas á manera de contienda ó batalla, dize
aquel gran sabio Eráclito en este modo: 'Omnia secundum litem fiunt.' "
Rojas expounds upon this statement, making frequent references to
Petrarch. (ed. of Julio Cejador y Frauca, I, Madrid, 1963, pp. 15-16)
Cf. Sá de Miranda, "Sempre dos seus olhos augua / A Heraclito corria
/ Polo que ouvia e que via, / De que tudo tinha magoa," "Carta IV.
A seu irmão Mem de Sâ." *Poesias,* p. 230; in addition consider
the words of a seventeenth-century *converso* author, Antonio Enríquez
Gómez: "Llora como Eraclito en esta del Mundo. Quexase de aver
naçido. . . . Democrito del hombre se a reido. Eraclito le llora." *La
Culpa del primer peregrino,* Roán, 1644.
22. Netanyahu, p. 88.

The similarity of the utterances is not coincidence, for Sá de Miranda was evidently recording a remembered conversation he had had with Núñez de Reinoso, and in the figure of the shepherd Gil, he was creating a portrait of his friend. The locale for both poems is the "Basto"; the conversation that served as the source of inspiration probably took place before 1536. The participants in Sá de Miranda's eclogue are Gil (Reinoso), a willful man, and Bieito (Sá de Miranda), an upright man. Possibly Ribeiro was dead at the time Sá de Miranda wrote this series of poems, for he is mentioned as an absent friend who, at some time in the past, had tried to advise the unhappy Gil. Bieito recalls his own silent attendance at such a meeting:

> *Trouxeste me ora á lembrança*
> *Aquele amigo fuão (Um amigo do Torrão)*[23]
> *Que, ó tempo d'essa mudança*
> *Tua, foi te assi á mão*
> *Como quem os dados lança.*

---

23. Vasconcelos, *Poesias,* gives three different versions of this eclogue, plus variants; they are listed as No. 103, "Egloga II: Basto," No. 116, "Egloga VI: Basto," and No. 164, "Redacçao nova da Égloga II." The passage cited is from No. 103, does not appear in its entirety in No. 116, and in No. 164 reads as follows:

> Tornaste me ora á lembrança
> Um amigo do Torrão
> Que ao tempo d'essa mudança
> Tambem 'si te foi á mão.
> Ora eu i no tal ensejo,
> Escutei (lembra me tudo):
> Falou te como sesudo,
> Parece me ora que o vejo. (553)

Delfim Guimarães proposes that Gil is Ribeiro and Bieito is Sá de Miranda. He is hard-pressed to explain just who is "aquele amigo fuão," otherwise identified as "um amigo de Torrão," Torrão supposedly being the birthplace of Ribeiro; he ultimately suggests that this friend is possibly Pero de Carvalho. However, in No. 116 the friend is clearly identified as Ribeiro, "O meu bom Ribeiro amigo."

> *E lembra me ora bem tudo*
> *(Que era eu i no tal ensejo)*
> *Inda que então me fiz mudo*
> *Falou te como sesudo;*
> *Parece me ora que o vejo. (169)*

In another version it is Gil who comments, "O meu bom Ribeiro amigo, / Que em milhor parte ora sê, / Conheceu bem o perigo" (391). In the "Epitalemio Pastoril," both Gil and Ribeiro are spoken of as absent; other shepherds recount one of their song contests. The "Epitalemio" written shortly after 1535[24] to honor the marriage of Sá de Miranda's niece to her granduncle aids us in dating the period when the three poets lived together.

In Núñez de Reinoso's "Ecloga de los dos pastores Baltheo y Argasto" (No. 5), it is more difficult to determine the identity of the interlocutors because the arguments voiced by Miranda's Gil are uttered by both of Reinoso's principals. Argasto, who could be modeled after Sá de Miranda because it is he who arrives singing the snatch of song from Sá de Miranda's "Vilancete II," is actually from Spain. In answer to the self-posed question, "Quien te truxo a Portugal / En Soria siendo nasçido / Y criado?"[25] he admits that he has been banished from his homeland, "Y la sentençia dezia: / 'Argasto por desleal / Se condena!'" It is therefore more

---

24. For information about Sá de Miranda's family, consult the genealogical table, an insert that concludes Vasconcelos's *Poesias*.
25. Ribeiro's "Écloga V" gives the speech to Ribeiro who asks "Quem te trouxe por aqui, / Agrestes, triste pastor?" (103) Wardropper, p. 5, lists the following as an example of verses that were *hecho a lo divino* and *contrahecho*:

Juan Álvarez Gato	*Juan del Encina*
Quien te trajo, caballero	Quien te traxo, criador
Por esta montaña oscura.	Por esta montaña escura.

logical to assume that Sá de Miranda was expressing
Reinoso's discontent in the *vilancete*, rather than his own
Weltschmerz. And although M. Braga has already sug-
gested Sá de Miranda for Agrestes in Ribeiro's "Écloga
V"[26] it is quite possible that that poem actually refers to
the discussion between Ribeiro and Reinoso that Sá de
Miranda mentions in the passage quoted from his eclogue
"Basto." For Reinoso's Argasto is at one time accidently
listed as "Argeste," and more importantly, Ribeiro's
Agrestes' complaints about life in a foreign land are
directed both to his fellow shepherd Ribeiro and to his
absent friend Florisendos (Silva).

It is not unreasonable to hypothesize that the poems
by all three deal with an identical subject: Reinoso's exile.
Sá de Miranda's "Basto" is particularly useful as a
means of substantiating the nature of Reinoso's complaints. For example, there is the complaint directed
against authority:

Núñez de Reinoso	Sá de Miranda
Los señores y los amos	*Que eis que achei ca tais amos*
Que son Iulios de la tierra Principales	*Que se têm por deus da terra.*
Comen trigo y dan avena, Beben y nos sudamos Sin caudal.	*. . . . . Vivem dos nossos suores, O como não digo eu;*
. . . . Comen de nuestros sudores, El cómo, no digo yo.	*. . . . . Comem trigo e nos d'avea, Eles bebem . . . (389)*

Not only do the idle lords and *hidalgos* live off the work
of others—undoubtedly the industrious *converso* artisans

---
26. P. 100.

and administrators—but a worse evil has invaded the
land: Núñez de Reinoso, ". . . Quieren nos quitar / El
entender que nos dio / Solo Dios"; Sá de Miranda, "O
entendimento que é nosso / Não no-lo querem deixar."
(389) Such a statement seems to refer to religious sup-
pression: those in power wish to govern the manner in
which their subordinates, Jews and *conversos,* think—
i.e., they wish to deprive them of their religion.[27]

Sá de Miranda's eclogue also performs the service of
supplying additional information that clarifies some of
Núñez de Reinoso's more guarded statements. Gil con-
firms that he adopted the role of shepherd because of
previous troubles he had endured:

> *Tu sabes como escolhi*
> *Esta vida de pastor.*
> *Polo mal que fora vi,*
> *Cuidei que esta era a milhor. (388)*

His sarcastic outburst against his father,

> *São doente, meu pai não,*
> *Digo outro tal da virtude!*
> *Pola ventura sou são,*
> *Porque meu pai tem saude?*
> *Não, que compre outra mezinha! (398)*

---

27. "Entendimiento," *Diccionario de autoridades*: Valverde, *Vida de
Christo,* lib. 3, cap. 13. "Y este entendimiento de la Divina ley, en ella
quedó espressado con claridad." In addition, this is precisely the manner
in which the *converso* exile, Antonio Enríquez Gómez, uses the word:
"hoy se vean ricos y mañana pobres, por un delito del flaco entendimiento
del padre . . .," *Política angélica,* Rouen, 1647. However, Rodrigues Lapa,
in a footnote to Sá de Miranda's passage writes, "entendimento = a
libertade de pensamento," and Carlota Almeida de Carvalho, *Glossário
das Poesias de Sá de Miranda,* Lisboa, 1953, p. 164, defines the word
as "inteligência, razâo." Still another interpretation is possible: "entendimiento" is one of the faculties of the soul; possibly the meaning of
the passage is that those in authority wished to strip Jews and *conversos*
of their birthright, their innate intellectual superiority, either by de-
preciating intellectual activity or by depriving them of positions as
administrators, tutors, etc.

helps to explain a long "wish" found in Reinoso's eclogue,
which otherwise might defy interpretation.

> *Mis padres viendome assi*
> . . . .
> *Mueran todos mis plazeres*
> *Muera todo mi descanso*
> *Y holgar*
> *Ellos gozen sus averes,*
> . . . .
> *Ellos vistan terçiopelo*
> *Coman su leche y su trigo*
> *A plazer.*

Sá de Miranda's Gil then adds poverty to parental in-
difference,

> *Não tenho de meu em pão*
> . . . .
> *Que negra consolação*
> *Que foi meu bisdono rico!*
> *Bons donos certo honra são,*
> *(Que eu tambem bons donos tive)*
> *Mas quem como eles não vive,*
> *Os que honrão os deshonrão. (399)*[28]

28. A strange literary coincidence suggests a possible explanation of
Núñez de Reinoso's disassociation from his family. One Andrés Ortiz
is listed as the author of a sixteenth-century chivalric *romance* (Durán,
No. 287), whose hero, "Floriseo," is challenged by his own father,
"Perineo," (Pedro de Reinoso, Señor de Autillo?). The unusual name
"Perineo" is coupled with that of "Andrés" in Reinoso's pastoral eclogue
(No. 5). Argasto brings news from home that Baltheo's lady has
married another: "Y a Andrés dixo de 'si,' / Pero el 'no' que a ti
quedó / La condena." Then the exiled Baltheo remembers that he already knows this: "Perineo ser desposada / Y bivir en dulce gloria
/ Me contó." "Andrés" is the only poet (shepherd) for whom there is
no pseudonym, and "Perineo" is only mentioned this one time in Reinoso's
poem.
Now if there be any connection between the two poems other than
the supposition that the chivalric tale *Floriseo* (1516) served as the
basis of Ortiz's *romance* (Thomas, *Spanish and Portuguese Romances
of Chivalry*, Cambridge, 1920, p. 138) and supplied Reinoso with a name
for one of his characters, the foregoing yields the possible interpretation

Such complaints seem excessive for describing conditions in Portugal, where, for example, confiscation of property by the Inquisition was more or less prohibited until the year 1547, certainly a date later than the composition of the poems. Nor does it seem that the plethora of family lawsuits, which plagued Spain after the establishment of the Inquisition, was as yet a common occurrence in Portugal.[29] However, it is the coupling of loss of money with that of honor which would seem to mark Gil, a stranger to the *sierra,* as Spanish. The implication is that because he encountered difficulties with the authorities, members of his family saved themselves by disowning and disinheriting him. And Núñez de Reinoso, speaking in his own name, acknowledges leaving Spain, the land "Ado passé mi niñez / Y lo mejor de mis años / Sin ganar honra" (No. 1), without obtaining honor, that most precious of Spanish possessions. In Reinoso's eclogue, one shepherd contrasts conditions in Spain, "la tierra / Que tu sabes," which he disdains to name, with those in Portugal, "esta sierra" where he now resides, once more emphasizing the economic retaliation, in the form of confiscation of property, that could be brought against Spanish *conversos:*

> *Ningun juego de perder*
> *Seguro que en esta sierra*
> *Iamas halles*
> *Como lo suelen hazer*
> *Los pastores de la tierra*
> *Que tu sabes*
> *Pues se fingen verdaderos*

---

that Spain (the lady) preferred Old Christians to New Christians ("Andrés" to "Baltheo"). Furthermore, even if *conversos* had worthy grandparents ("bons donos" as Sá de Miranda's "Gil" says), fathers were willing to disown sons who brought dishonor upon the family.

29. At least, Herculano and D'Azevedo do not deal with such matters.

Hasta que de todo acaben
Los averes.

Reinoso's constant references to his losses, principally
of wealth and "gloria," are reminiscent of the innumerable losses suffered by the characters in his novel where
the cause, indirectly stated in a long digression, is given
as *envidia*.[30] "Envidia" is termed "destruccion de las
honras, . . . poniendo [las familias] en pleitos, discordias,
trabajos, desventuras, poco ó ningun reposo ni sosiego."
Once again honor is connected with money as that very
Spanish activity—the family lawsuit—is brought in. A
direct result of envy is "aquella falsa y perversa acusacion,
que aunque después el pobre acusado se quiera defender
ó desculpar no le aprovecha" (448a). In the eclogue,
Reinoso, still contrasting conditions between the two countries, speaks out against the *malsín.*

> *Aquí no biven ladrones*
> *Ni cossarios desleales*
> *Sino claros corazones*
> *Con pensamientos boçales*
> *De maldad.*
> *No moran aqui traydores*
> *Desseosos de los males*
> *De tu tierra,*
> *Ni saben, aqui de olores*[31]
> *Si no son los naturales*
> *De la sierra (No. 5)*

In an epistle to a friend, Núñez de Reinoso is more specific about the damage a *malsín* can do. He strays from his

---

30. Ribeiro's "Agrestes" also says that envy was the cause of his
troubles and exile: "O ciume é que me mata." (112)

31. "Parecerse o tener señas y visos de una cosa, que por lo regular
es mala. *Este hombre me* HUELE *a hereje*," *Dic. de la len. esp.*

announced theme to interject a tirade against the world, which bears some resemblance to a portion of Pleberio's lament:[32] "A otros buelves cosarios y ladrones / En pena de lo cual pierden su vida / Por las públicas calles con pregones." The euphemisms that Reinoso employs, "ladrón," "cosario," and so on, are similar in tone to the expressions used in responsa literature for *converso*: "criminal" and "rebel."[33]

Núñez de Reinoso emerges as a bitter, inconsolable man, disowned or ignored by parents, bereft of friends and estate, whose pessimistic outlook, ". . . el mundo todo es guerra" (No. 5), expands to include all of life:

---

32. Núñez de Reinoso's invective against the world begins:

> Porque dime traydor mundo engañoso,
> En que para todo lo que tu vendes
> Que es dulze plazer breve y amargoso.
> Porque o mundo falso nos offendes*es*
> O mundo manjar de duros gusanos
> Y di porque no sueltes los que prendes.
> Tus queridos regalos siempre vanos
> Tus galas todas tus cortes penosas
> Que bien les dan a los tristes humanos,
> Tus altas damas galanas hermosas
> Se convierten tambien en dura tierra
> Por muy mas lindas o por mas graçiosas.
> O mundo vano que contina guerra
> Das siempre a los que siguen tu real
> O bivan en poblado, o en agra sierra. (No. 16)

Cf. ¡O vida de congoxas llena, de miserias acompañada! ¡O mundo, mundo! Muchos mucho de tí dixeron, muchos en tus qualidades metieron la mano, a diuersas cosas por oydas te compararon; yo por triste esperiencia lo contaré, como a quien las ventas e compras de tu engañosa feria no prósperamente sucedieron, como aquel mucho ha fasta agora callado tus falsas propiedades, por no encender con odio tu yra, porque no me secasses sin tiempo esta flor que este dia echaste de tu poder. *La Celestina* (II, 203).

While the provocation for Pleberio's lament is understandable, Núñez de Reinoso's outburst appears in an epistle addressed to Lope de Guzmán, where the subject seems to be the writing of poetry. Reinoso encourages his friend and praises his ability.

33. Netanyahu, p. 79, discusses such terms.

Núñez de Reinoso   Sá de Miranda

Mas quien pudiesse saber
En que va este secreto
Tan dubdoso
Que no ay cosa en esta vida.   *Ves tu cousa nesta vida*
Porque diga solo esto   *Por que deva de ser ledo?*
Me contenta   *Eu a tenho comprendida*
Yo la tengo comprehendida   *Inda mal, que foi tam cedo.*
¡Ay de mi, que vi tan presto   *Que em fim a verdade era*
Su tormenta!   *Ir polo fio de gente.*
Que yr al hilo como siento   *Não vai mal quem vai con-*
Trabajo cierto me diera   *tente.*   *(388)*
Menos fuerte,
No va mal quien va con-
tento.

Despite the almost cynical attitude projected, Reinoso could not follow the crowd ("yr al hilo") in order to live in peace. It was necessary for this willful man, "voluntario," as Sá de Miranda dubs him, to leave Portugal when conditions worsened in that country.

Vasconcelos has suggested that Sá de Miranda's eclogue "Basto," of which there are fourteen versions, was written to depict an internal struggle between two sides of the poet's nature.[34] There is precedence for such an interpretation in the medieval tradition of debates between the body and soul and in the dialogues created by early humanists, such as Petrarch, in which the internal conflict is externalized through the use of allegorical figures. However, because of the duplication of material in the poems by Sá de Miranda and Núñez de Reinoso, it seems more likely that the poems recreate an actual

---

34. Vasconcelos, *Poesias,* pp. 773–74.

debate between the two men.[35] Gil's tirade on the evil nature of man, representative of an attitude Castro would consider typical of *converso* mentality,[36] marks him as the unhappy exile, Reinoso; the more moderate view advanced by Bieito, the upright man ("ás direitas") who tries to counsel Gil, as Sá de Miranda.

Núñez de Reinoso's account of life on the road and in Italy seems to bear out the terms of a recurring prophecy that runs through the eclogues of Ribeiro and Sá de Miranda.[37]

35. While this study can only attempt to deal with a few of the innumerable examples of similar lines in the works of Núñez de Reinoso, Ribeiro, and Sá de Miranda, the extent of their poetical borrowing is made clear by the appearance of hitherto unmentioned personages such as the "Luzia" in Reinoso's eclogue.

Núñez de Reinoso	*Sá de Miranda*
O con luego me comendar	Se não visse inda Luzia
A mis padres sin tardanza	Não podera repousar.
Y a Luzia. (No. 5)	("Basto," 399)

36. Castro, *La realidad histórica de España,* pp. 533ff.

Gil is a name that had previously been associated with pastoral or rustic poetry; in the *Coplas de Mingo Revulgo,* he is the city dweller or *converso* and in Encina's *Reqüesta de amores* he is the *escudero* who becomes a shepherd (as I have previously indicated in note 10, such a *conversion* invites a religious interpretation).

37. In Ribeiro's "Écloga II," Pierio utters the prophecy to Jano:

> Em terra que inda não viste,
> Polo que nela has de ver,
> Vejo-te o coração triste
> Pera em dias que viver
> Has de morrer de ũa dor,
> ....
> A terra estranha irás. (44)

In the various versions of Sá de Miranda's "Basto," it is Ribeiro ("Um amigo do Torrão") who warns Gil (Reinoso?) (Gil na sua mocidade / Muita de terra correra," 385) and comments upon his own peripatetic existence:

> Andarás muitos lugares,
> Verás muito, e porem
> O que não esprementares,
> Não cudes que o sabes bem. (389)

Núñez de Reinoso	Ribeiro
Ando assi de sierra en sierra	*Andarei de vale em vale,*
	E de lugar em lugar. (57)
. . . .	
De una tierra en otra tierra	
Como si fuesse gitano	
Peregrino.	

Reinoso adds that he cannot return to Spain, ". . . ya no espero / Salir de tierras agenas," but must spend his life "Biviendo por los mesones, / Durmiendo por los passares / Sin plazer." His later remarks about Italy sound typical of a stranger in a foreign land, yet such Senecan expressions of dissatisfaction can be found in Ribeiro's "Écloga V" voiced by the exiled Agrestes:

Núñez de Reinoso	Ribeiro
Que no soy acostumbrado	*A's agoas não costumado,*
Á los çielos de esta tierra	*Nem me posso acostumar*
Ni a sus aguas usado.	*Não posso delas gostar;*
(No. 1)	*Assi malaventurado,*
Las aguas, que acá avia	*A sede me quer matar:*
. . . .	*O manjar é desgostoso*
Aunque en oro las bevia,	*Alheo do meu comer.*
No me matan la sed mia,	*(108)*
Mas quedo muerto de sed.	
El manjar es desabrido.	
(No. 2)	

Ribeiro's complaint, "Cuidados são meu manjar, / Beber as lagrimas são" (109) is echoed in Núñez de Reinoso's reply to "Thomas Gomez" "Mi comer sean enojos, / Y tristezas me bever." (No. 12)[38]

---

38. "Cura dolorque animi, lacrimaeque alimenta fuerent." Ovid, *Metamorphoses*, X, 75.

In Italy, Reinoso found himself the object of that
hostility which awaited Peninsular exiles, most of whom
the Italians considered to be *marranos* :[39]

> *Los hombres de aquesta tierra*
> *Son mas falsos que Medea. (No. 2)*
>
> *Pues que sin lo meresçer*
> *Aqui todos me combaten,*
> *A puñaladas me maten. (No. 3)*

He admits experiencing the loneliness that was predicted
in both his own eclogue and those of Ribeiro's:

Núñez de Reinoso	Ribeiro
Andarás muchos lugares	*Andarei de vale em vale,*
Sin saber tu solo a quien	*E de lugar em lugar,*
Tu mal cuentes	*Não acharei quem me fale,*
Porque lo que no passares,	*Nem com quem possa falar*
No pienses sabello bien	*Nem quem diga que me*
Por las gentes. (No. 5)	*cale.* *(57)*
Y no tengo solo acá	*Não tenho nemhum amigo*
Ni amigo, ni amiga	*Que me queira consolar.*
Ni persona que me diga	*(109)*
¡O hombre, cómo te va!	
(No. 2)	

He misses his friends: "Grito, peno, lloro, clamo, / Y
por mis amigos llamo: / Pero ninguno responde" (No.
2). He passes sleepless nights and troubled days; he
can find neither "reposo" nor "descanso."

In the eclogue, Reinoso foresaw the hopelessness of his
situation and the uselessness of change: "Que aunque
mudes lugar / No mudara tu dolor / Ni tu pena." This
Horatian aphorism, which also appears as a warning in
Ribeiro's "Écloga III,"

---

39. Francisco Márquez Villanueva, *Investigaciones sobre Juan Álvarez
Gato*, p. 50.

Não aproveita andar
De ũs vales em outros vales,
Que aproveita tal mudar,
Pois que mudando o lugar
Não s'hão de mudar os males. (72)

was frequently cited by sixteenth- and seventeenth-century writers, including Quevedo, who used it in the ending of the *Buscón*[40] and in a gloss of one of the lines of his rendition of *Las lágrimas de Jeremías*.[41] Employers of the aphorism as well as translators of and commentators upon this book from the Bible can be divided into two groups: those who upheld the orthodox Christian view that the destruction and exile that befell Israel was the justifiable punishment meted out to the wicked; and those, perhaps, *conversos,* to whom it signified the inevitable sad outcome of life in a hostile world.[42] To many a *converso* the despair experienced by Núñez de Reinoso, and others like him, had been fully presaged;

---

40. ". . . pues nunca mejora su estado quien muda solamente de lugar, y no de vida y costumbres." *La vida del Buscón llamado don Pablos,* edición crítica por Fernando Lázaro Carreter, Salamanca, 1965, p. 280. Dale B. J. Randall, "The Classical Ending of Quevedo's *Buscón,*" *Hispanic Review,* XXXII, 1964, pp. 101-8, puts forth the theory that the aphorism is Senecan: "animum debes mutare, non caelum." He does not, however, totally dismiss Horace as the potential source: "Though Quevedo knew Horace's epistles," p. 106.

41. "Aphorismos morales sacados del primer alphabeto de Ieremías." "Gimel. Necio es quien siendo malo y vicioso peregrina, por uer si muda con los lugares las costumbres. El que así lo haze está, si peregrina, en otra parte, pero no es otro. . . . Al que castiga Dios en Ierusalem por malo, también le castigará donde fuere, si lo fuere: y assí es bien mudar de vida y no de sitio." *Lágrimas de Hieremias castellanas,* p. 36.

42. In the introduction to the 1953 edition of the above-mentioned work by Quevedo, E. M. Wilson and J. M. Blecua note, "Casi todas las traducciones españolas de los trenos entre los años 1550-1600 son heterodoxas." (xi). Later, the Jesuit, Francisco de Borja treated the "Lamentations" as an ascetic prayer or sermon directed toward her (Israel, and by extension, those of Jewish ancestry) as a sinner. For the various versions and attitudes, see the introduction to Quevedo's work. The subject will be further elaborated upon in Chapter 4 below. Discussion of Quevedo's statements as indicative of an orthodox anti-semitic attitude can be found in C. H. Rose, "Pablos' *damnosa heritas,*" *Romanische Forschungen, LXXXII,* 1970.

his sentence had been handed out thousands of years
before:

> Y esparcirte ha Jehová por todos los pueblos desde el
> un cabo de la tierra hasta el otro cabo de la tierra;
> . . . Y ni aun en las mismas gentes reposarás ni la
> planta de tu pié tendrá reposo: que allí te dará Jehová
> temeroso y caimiento de ojos, y tristeza de alma. Y
> tendrás tu vida colgada delante, y estarás temoroso
> de noche y de día, y no confiarás de tu vida. Deuter-
> onomy 28:64-66.[43]

Such was the punishment for those who had turned away
from God and the religion of their ancestors.

It would seem that Núñez de Reinoso found himself
cast in the role of the Wandering Jew. The actual intensity of his religious beliefs, however, is quite another
matter. Perhaps he can be included in that group whose
"Jewishness" was created by the Inquisition. As Netanyahu points out,

> . . . the minority that still adhered to Judaism in the
> three decades preceding the establishment of the Inqui-
> sition was . . . constantly diminishing in size and in-
> fluence; that it would have, in all likelihood, soon
> faded into nothingness, had not the process of assimila-
> tion been violently interfered with by the repellent and
> bewildering actions of the Inquisition; and that thus
> it was due to the Inquisition itself that the dying Mar-
> ranism in Spain was given a new lease on life.[44]

The Conflict Restated

In their eclogues, Núñez de Reinoso, Ribeiro and Sá

---

43. *Santa Biblia.*
44. P. 3.

de Miranda present a situation in which one shepherd sets forth his complaints and then is advised and consoled by a more experienced shepherd (at times, each in turn consoles the other). Such a tradition came down to these poets not only through Virgil, but also through Biblical sources, where, for example, Job uttered his lament in the presence of Eliphaz, Bildad, Zophar, and Elihu. A similar format was utilized, within a well-developed pastoral setting, by Samuel Usque in his *Consolaçam ás tribulaçoens de Israel*, where Ycabo, an anagram for Yacob, outlines the history of his grievances and is consoled by Numeo (Nehum) "The Comforter," and Zicareo (Zacarias) "The Remembrancer." While the interlocutors of the poems written in the "Basto" supposedly present their "casos de amor," the amount of topical material included and their infrequent references to the ladies in question indicate that the authors' attention is directed elsewhere—on survival in a hostile world. And Sá de Miranda's eclogue "Basto" dispenses with all pretense that it is anything other than social protest. In Núñez de Reinoso's and Ribeiro's eclogues, the "querella," carefully couched in the terminology of courtly love, has a religio-social interpretation: upon reexamination, the pastoral debates begin to sound very much like the polemic that was carried on both by inquisitors and rabbinical authorities as each group struggled to establish a standard to determine just what behavior constituted that of a true Christian or a true Jew.

Two shepherds meet. Noting the change for the worse in his old friend, one comments upon the other's unkempt appearance. As described by Núñez de Reinoso, the change wrought by suffering is of a more unwholesome nature than that normally attributed to lovesickness; it reminds one of Job.

Núñez de Reinoso

¡O Baltheo, ay de ti!
Qué es aquesto,
Cómo te veo mudado,
. . . .
Cómo podras tu cuidado
En cubrillo?
La barba cumplida tienes,
Y el gesto todo arrugado
Y amarillo.

Ribeiro

Que bem pasmado estou
De te ver mudo, e mudado,
Ó Amador, quem cuidou,
Que fosses tão descuidado.
(63)

As the dialogue gets underway, it is usually conceded that, although the unhappy shepherd has changed in appearance, he has not changed his faith. Such firmness is both applauded and given as the cause of his present unfortunate state:

Núñez de Reinoso

(Baltheo to Argasto)
Y pues que llagado vienes
Sin poder tu firme fe
Ya mudar.

Ribeiro

Agrestes, firme pastor,
. . . .
Ja se sabe a tua fé,
E a causa que te condena,
Tudo bem craro se vê.
(104-5)

The shepherd bewails his loss of wealth and worldly goods (bienes), time, and fame (gloria). Several remedies are offered to alleviate his suffering or cure his sickness. The standard remedy is prescribed in

Reinoso's eclogue, where the group at the "Basto" is seen as chorusing that "En las cosas sin remedio / El olvido es mejor medio." Acceptance of the situation is counseled in a Ribeiro poem: "As cousas que não tem cura, / Amador, não cures delas" (63). Two unusual suggestions are put forth. First, in Ribeiro's "Écloga I," Jano comments,

> *Que a vertude esforçada,*
> *No grande medo e temor,*
> *Se estima e é estimada,*
> *Não te espante esta mudança*
> *Que o tempo traz consigo. (21)*

Such an utterance brings to mind the problem of forced conversion. While Christian theologians pondered whether or not those who had converted in order to conform to nationally stated policy were sincere, the debate in responsa literature was devoted to determining whether or not a seeming conversion, based on the element of fear, was justifiable or whether it placed the secretly practicing convert outside the Covenant of Abraham. The second suggestion, even more startling since it comes from Sá de Miranda's Bieito, the "upright" man, is to "ir al fio da gente," and "Não has tu sô de enmendar / O mundo; e o meu conselho / seria dissimular" (393). Dissimulation had become a way of life to many a sixteenth-century *converso*.

Evidently conditions made it impossible for Núñez de Reinoso to accept such solutions: that time would solve his problems; that forgetting his old allegiances, either religious or national, would help; that he could live as a Christian and secretly practice Judaism because his conversion (or that of his ancestors) had been made under duress; that he could dissimulate. Or perhaps he followed a more orthodox line of thinking. In rabbinical circles, Maimonides had been invoked to uphold the tenet that for the true believer (the expression true lover is employed) exile was an obligation, and that the convert who was secretly practising the Jewish religion was

> justifiably subject to heavy censure . . . when he refuses to leave the land of persecution and settle in a country where he can worship in freedom. He (Maimonides) considers such transfer so important for the believer that in his opinion nothing should stand in its way, not even love for wife and children—let alone considerations of a pecuniary nature.[45]

Núñez de Reinoso acknowledged wanting to leave Portugal:

> *Acordé de me passar*
> *A los Alpes de Alemaña*
> *A bivir,*
> *Y como* los que desaman
> *El remedio a sus dolores*
> *Yo me fue.* [sic] *(No. 5, emphasis mine)*

The foregoing presupposes that Núñez de Reinoso was a practicing, religious Jew and that in accordance with the strictest interpretation of the law he accepted exile rather than risk jeopardizing his faith. There are other reasons that could be advanced for substantiating such a view. In his frequent references to his loss of "gloria," he does not use this word in its Christian context: i.e., the glory that awaits the true believer when he is united with his maker after death. Rather, for him

---

45. Netanyahu, p. 15; his summary of a passage from Maimonides's *Iggeret ha Shemad.*

"gloria" seems to be a state that is obtainable during one's lifetime; it embraces fame, well-being, happiness, honor. This emphasis on the here-and-now suggests the Judaic attitude of focusing on life as it must be lived on this earth. Another reason for supposing that he might have been a *cripto-Judeo* concerns a remark made by "Thomas Gomez,"[46] who warns Núñez de Reinoso that his present behavior may lose him the good will of the patroness who has welcomed him into her family, "No como hombre desterrado / Mas hermano aqui nasçido" (No. 11). Writing on the correct attitude to be held toward those *conversos* who wished to reenter the faith, the Chief Rabbi of Granada had stated that ". . . the Marranos must be received not as strangers, but as brethren."[47]

Note, however, that Gómez merely describes the reception afforded Reinoso by the Mendes-Nasi family; he makes no attempt to ascertain the intensity of Reinoso's beliefs. Indeed, it was because he sensed an internal conflict in the man that he felt impelled to lecture him. Furthermore, Reinoso's distress about the elusiveness of terrestrial "gloria" may simply reflect the *converso*'s concern with material or intellectual rather than religious pursuits.

Rather than a man of firm faith, Núñez de Reinoso appears to be a man of divided loyalties. As previously

---

46. On previous occasions, I have questioned whether Gómez wrote this poem or whether he represents Reinoso's conscience. Two Tomás Gómezes can be found whose lives may have crossed that of Núñez de Reinoso: the name occurs in a list of Spanish refugees in Antwerp in 1560 (J. A. Goris, *Les colonies marchandes méridionales à Anvers,* Louvain, 1925), and again in an inquisitional denunciation in Venice in 1583 (Roth, "Les Marranes à Venise," *Revue des études juives,* LXXXIX-XLI, 1930–31, p. 215).

47. Netanyahu, p. 64; summation of the contents of part of a statement by Rabbi Saadia ben Maimon ibn Danan, Chief Rabbi of Granada.

indicated, he could have been one of those about whom the famous rabbinical thinker and father of León Hebreo, Isaac Abravanel, wrote:

> Thus, as the irony of history would have it, they who so systematically abandoned all practices of Jewish religion, are now maligned that they perform Judaism in secret. They who made every effort to assimilate, so that their relationship with Israel be forgotten, are constantly regarded as Jews and so designated to their great vexation and dismay.[48]

A scene from the novel may help to reveal Núñez de Reinoso's state of mind; interpretation of the episode is again somewhat dependent on accepting Bataillon's theory on the reversal of gender that occurs in the work. After an allegorical journey to hell where she observes the burning bodies of the damned, the heroine Isea (Reinoso) decides to "meterme monja, por acabar mi vida sirviendo a Dios, porque tenia gran temor de las cosas que habia visto en los infiernos, que en otra cosa no pensaba" (466b). Witnessing an *auto-de-fe* (the vision of the erotic hell) would have convinced many a *converso* of the desirability of entering a religious order. The narrator applies at a convent, which like many a religious

---

48. Netanyahu, p. 154. Netanyahu also points out that Isaac Arama, in his *Aqedat Yizhaq*, connects the fate of the *conversos* with the Biblical prophecy (Deuteronomy 28:64), when he writes about "thousands and myriads of Jews in this Diaspora who changed their religion as a result of the persecutions," fulfill the prophecy, *"For although they assimilated among those nations entirely,* they will find no peace among them; for they, the nations will always revile and beshame them, plot against them, and *accuse them falsely in matters* of faith." Incidentally, M. A. Cohen, the English translator of Usque's *Consolaçam,* believes that Abravanel influenced Usque's work; for details on this theory, see *Consolation for the Tribulations of Israel,* Philadelphia, 1965, pp. 15–16, 274–87.

establishment of its time, was seemingly populated by *conversos* who sought refuge there from the conflict but who carried with them many of their previous attitudes. The ensuing scene is similar to one that takes place in *El Crotalón* and in the fragment apparently dislodged from Chapter XV of the first continuation of the *Lazarillo*,[49] works also presumed to be by *converso* authors. The conditions for entering the convent are given as "traer mil ducados de dote, y ser de don y de buen linaje." While the nuns erupt into arguments and begin beating each other with their shoes,[50] Isea leaves because "no tenia dineros para entrar allí, ni menos se podia saber quién era" (467a). Fear, not faith, is the reason given for wishing to enter the religious order and thereby profess Catholicism; lack of money, family credentials, and proof of *limpieza* barred the way. Such a commentary does not reflect an attitude of strong religious conviction.

Núñez de Reinoso's national or cultural ties were evidently stronger than any religious feeling he may have possessed. In his poems, Reinoso's role is that of the rejected lover. For this tormented man there was no "remedio" because he could not forget the land that had exiled him. His undying love for Spain seems to be the principal cause for his unhappiness in Italy, where he found refuge with the most prominent Jewish family of his time. Thematic to his work is *ausencia y soledad de*

---

49. For a discussion of the missing chapter, see Robert H. Williams, "Notes on the Anonymous Continuation of 'Lazarillo de Tormes,'" *The Romanic Review*, XVI, 1925, pp. 223–35. Raymond Foulché-Delbosc reproduces the fragment in his article, "Remarques sur 'Lazarille de Tormes,'" *Revue Hispanique*, VII–VIII, 1900–01, pp. 81–97.

50. Sebastián de Covarrubias, *Tesoro de la lengua castellana o española*, 1611, comments upon the practice: "Chapinaço, el golpe que da la muger con el chapín, que toman cólera suelen descalçársele y vengar con él sus injurias."

España.[51] As he expresses it,

> *Soledad de España siento*
> . . . .
> *Aqui en esta ciudad*
> *Adonde peno en ausençia*
> *Y muero con soledad. (No. 2)*

And so he must be viewed as neither Jew nor Christian but as an exiled Spanish *converso* who had faith in nothing, least of all himself:

> *Ora no sé qué me hazer,*
> *Pues no ato ni desato:*
> *En nada tengo sentido*
> *En nada puedo acertar. (No. 1)*

---

51. For a definition of "soledad" and examples of this emotional yearning, see Karl Vossler, *La soledad en la poesía española,* Madrid, 1941. *Ausencia y soledad de amor* is the title of the *novela* contained in Villegas's *Inventario,* Medina del Campo, 1565. It was probably written earlier, as the *Inventario* was approved for publication in 1551. The text of this pastoral novelette, with an introduction by Francisco López Estrada, can be seen in "Estudio de 'Ausencia y soledad de amor,'" *Boletín de la Real Academia Española,* XXIX, 1949, pp. 99–133. I believe this to be another example of a *converso*'s lament for the loss of his lady, Spain.

3

ADVERSE FORTUNE AND
THE WANDERER

. . . para aquellos hombres la vida no podía ser sino
huída o ataque. Huir del país materialmente, a donde
no fuesen conocidos como conversos, refugiarse en
una orden religiosa, o en la apartada irrealidad de
alguna imaginación bella y melancólica.

Such is Américo Castro's description of what life
held in store for a *converso* in the sixteenth century
in Spain.[1] Leaving aside the alternative of aggres-
sion (practised by such *chocarreros* as Francisco de Villa-
lobos or Francisco de Zúñiga), let us observe how Alonso
Núñez de Reinoso, who chose flight, expressed the *converso* situation through the novelistic life of Isea, the
protagonist of *La historia de los amores de Clareo y
Florisea y de los trabajos de la sin ventura Isea*. Her life
is one of endless motion as she flees from country to
country and suffers countless reversals at the hands of
adverse fortune. After being turned away from a convent
where she seeks refuge in a religious order, she retires
to a pastoral island; there, giving way to perpetual

---

1. Américo Castro, *España en su historia (Cristianos, moros y judíos)*,
Buenos Aires, 1948, p. 577.

melancholy, she spends her days in the composition of the novel that relates the unfortunate events that have befallen her.

Before examining how Alonso Núñez de Reinoso, wanderer, solitary exile, alienated *converso,* recorded the disquietude of his peripatetic existence and fashioned a fiction that is a surrogate life, it would seem necessary to say a few words about the structure of the novel and to determine what use he made of his source materials. The binary structure of the work is manifest in the title: the first part, dealing with the loves of Clareo and Florisea, is a partial adaptation, via an Italian translation, of Achilles Tatius's *Clitophon and Leucippe*;[2] the second, dealing with the travails of Isea, is primarily an original chivalric tale. The entire novel is set within a pastoral frame; in addition, there are a number of interpolated tales. A brief synopsis of the complex plot follows.

Isea, in self-imposed exile on the Ínsula Pastoril, implores prospective readers to hear the sad story of her life. However, she begins her tale by recounting the adventures of Clareo and Florisea, two young people of good family, who have run away from home, vowing to live together as brother and sister for a year before marrying. We first encounter them as they sail for Alexandria (it is here that Reinoso begins to make use

---

2. There is little agreement as to the dates of Achilles Tatius and his more famous contemporary Heliodorus. Their rank of "bishop" may have been conferred centuries later by monks whose religious scruples prompted them to confer honorary episcopal titles upon authors of secular works that they were transcribing. See the introduction to Moses Hadas's translation, *An Ethiopian Romance: Heliodorus,* 1957, for a discussion of these matters.

of Tatius's novel.)[3] However, the beauty of Florisea (Tatius's Leucippe) attracts the attention of the brigand Menelao, who kidnaps her. Clareo (Clitophon) gives chase by ship, only to witness what he believes to be Florisea's decapitated body being thrown into the sea. Sorrowing in Alexandria, Clareo is seen by a young widow Isea (Melitte), whose husband Tesiandro has been lost at sea. The sight of Clareo is enough to arouse her passions and to cause her to forget her unhappiness. Clareo finally accepts her offer of marriage on the condition that it remain unconsummated. They leave for Isea's native land of Éfeso and suffer a number of misadventures along the way, including a shipwreck that casts them upon the shores of the Ínsula de la Vida, where they enjoy a brief respite from their troubles (an incident of Reinoso's invention.)[4] To complicate matters, Tesiandro reappears, the accounts of his death being somewhat exaggerated. Clareo is imprisoned for adultery. There he persuades himself that he is responsible for Florisea's death, and in an ungentlemanly fashion implicates Isea. He is brought to trial, freely confesses his supposed guilt, and receives a death sentence. Isea awaits a separate trial

---

3. Reinoso made use of an Italian work, *Amorosi Ragionamenti. Dialogo nel quale si racconta un compassionevole amore di due amanti, tradotto per Ludovico Dolce, dal fragmento d'uno antico Scrittor Greco . . .*, Venice, 1546, itself a translation of a Latin translation of Tatius's work, *Narrationis amatoriae fragmentum e graeco in latinum conversum, Annibale Cruceio interprete*, 1544. Both translations are fragmentary, dealing only with the last two books of Tatius's novel; therefore, Núñez de Reinoso had to invent a means for getting his story underway. The opinion of Stanislav Zimic, "Alonso Núñez de Reinoso, traductor de *Leucipe y Clitofonte*," *Symposium*, XXI, 1967, pp. 166–75, to the effect that Reinoso was acquainted with and made use of the complete version of Tatius's tale in an Italian translation by Francesco Angiolo Coccio, 1550, is irrelevant to this study.

4. Bataillon, "Alonso Núñez de Reinoso . . .", suggests that this episode refers to Reinoso's stay in Ferrara. (See Chapter 1 above for further references to Ferrara.)

because she has denied complicity in the plot. In the meantime, Florisea is alive, if not well. She was first held in servitude in the very same city of Ephesus. After an exchange of letters with Clareo, who was overjoyed to learn she was alive, she managed to escape from her lascivious master—into the arms of Tesiandro, who was also captivated by her beauty. It was the second report of her death, a rumor circulated by Tesiandro, that caused Clareo to make his false confession. Managing to elude Tesiandro, Florisea arrives in the nick of time at the place of execution, reveals her presence to the judges, and obtains Clareo's release. The reunited young lovers leave for home, where they obtain parental permission to marry.

At this point Reinoso's dependence on Tatius's novel ceases. For reasons the author does not make abundantly clear, Isea leaves her homeland to take up a life of wandering. Presumably she feels disgraced. Her first venture ends in a shipwreck. Upon disembarking from another vessel, Isea is detained by local authorities who accuse her of traveling with brigands.[5] A stranger in town, the "Gran Señor," obtains her release from prison and employs her in his household as tutor to his daugh-

---

5. An obvious autobiographical reference. Presumably Reinoso was at some time imprisoned, probably in Portugal, and found guilty because his travelling companions were known Judaizers. Since there were, from time to time, travel restrictions—only Spanish refugees of substantial means were allowed to settle in Portugal—possibly the fact that Isea had lost her money in the shipwreck should be interpreted as meaning that Reinoso, deprived of his wealth, was cast into jail when he attempted to enter that country. The locale might also be Holland as "El gran señor" (Doña Gracia) is termed a foreigner ("era estranjero y venido de lejos de aquellas partes," 453a). However, although she is usually considered as Portuguese, some contemporaries suggest that she was Spanish. For the arrest of Peninsular refugees in the Low Countries, see Goris. (There is no Alonso Núñez de Reinoso listed among those detained.)

ters.[6] Next she becomes friendly with two sisters who
live nearby,[7] but when one of them unexpectedly dies,
she, inexplicably, feels that she must move on. On the
road she encounters the knight errant Felicindos; his
mission is to find his love, Luciandra, who has been removed to the "casa del Descanso."[8] Isea accompanies
him as he participates in several adventures that are
transcribed in allegorical terms. Finally they arrive at
the house of the "gran sabio Rusimundo," who takes
them on a trip to the underworld (modeled after that in
the *Aeneid*), where they see the condemned burning in
hell.[9] Rusimundo counsels Isea and Felicindos that they
must go their separate ways. Isea travels to Spain, where
she is turned away from a nunnery she wishes to enter.
She then retires to a pastoral island to write her memoirs.

As can be observed from the plot summary, Reinoso's
novel is a compendium of the Byzantine, chivalric, and
pastoral, but it is in no sense, as Menéndez Pelayo as-
serted, "la más antigua imitación de las novelas griegas
publicada en Europa."[10] Taking their lead from him,

---

6. ". . . me recogió en casa y servicio, para que sirvese á unas sus
hijas que tenia" (453b), an autobiographical allusion to Reinoso's employment in the Nasi household.

7. For interpretation of this episode, see Chapter 1, where I suggest
that the two sisters who "tenian fama de muy avisadas y sábias"
represent Sá de Miranda and Ribeiro.

8. While Núñez de Reinoso explains the symbolism of these adventures
—"por Felicindos la fortaleza que los hombres de grande animo deuen
tener, por poder llegar a aquella casa de descanso, adonde estaua la
princesa Luciandra" (p. 5)—Felicindo's quest seemingly refers to
Feliciano de Silva's courtship of Gracia Fe.

9. ". . . me partí de allí con intencion de irme á alguna ciudad y
meterme monja, por acabar mi vida sirviendo á Dios, porque tenia tan
gran temor de las cosas que habia visto en los infiernos, que en otra cosa no
pensaba" (466b). Whether the incident represents the witnessing of an
auto-de-fe or is merely descriptive of the hot social climate of Spain
cannot be definitively determined; however, Isea's reaction to the situation coincides with Reinoso's oft-expressed desire to forsake the world.

10. *Orígenes*, II, p. 83.

contemporary critics have perpetuated the mistaken notion that *Clareo y Florisea* pertains to the vogue for the Byzantine novel throughout Europe during the sixteenth and seventeenth centuries and that it influenced the course of Spanish literature. For example, Robert Palamo endeavors, none too successfully, to prove that Reinoso's novel was a source of Cervantes's *Persiles*;[11] and Stanislav Zimic pays homage to Reinoso for "su indudable influencia en el desarrollo de la novela española posterior."[12] But as Avalle-Arce protests, "Esto no es más que una verdad a medias. . . ."[13] All such assertions concentrate on that portion of the work which is, more or less, a faithful transcription of Tatius's tale and ignore Reinoso's original contribution as well as his ordering of the material.

Further, it can be demonstrated that in an age when literary catalogues were fashionable, Reinoso's name does not appear on any of the long lists of authors cited by such writers as Cervantes or Gracián. And while Tatius's name is often linked with that of the more famous Heliodorus when the Byzantine novel is discussed, Núñez de Reinoso's imitation of Tatius's work is ignored.[14] Indeed, Ágreda y Vargas, author of the only extant version of

---

11. "Una fuente española del *Persiles*," *Hispanic Review*, VI, 1938, pp. 57–68. Menéndez Pelayo, *Orígenes*, II, p. 79, had written, "Y es cierto que Cervantes había leído con mucha atención de los *Amores de Clareo* [*sic*].

12. Zimic, p. 166.

13. Avalle-Arce, *La novela pastoril española*, Madrid, 1959, p. 31.

14. While Heliodorus's *Aethiopica* was immensely popular in the sixteenth century and was translated into a number of languages, in Spain interest in Tatius's work is not manifest until the seventeenth century, when preceptists and authors become concerned with the epic in prose. Perhaps the first to associate these two hellenistic authors is Alonso López Pinciano, *Philosophia antigua poetica*, ed. de Alfred Carballo Picazo, III, Madrid, 1953, p. 165, where he claims that the works of both Heliodorus and Tatius "son tan épica como la Ilíada y la Eneyda."

Tatius's romance, which he entitled *Los más fieles amantes* (1617),[15] does not mention Reinoso's novel. Seemingly he was totally unaware of its existence. It is exceedingly doubtful that *Clareo y Florisea,* unpublished in Spain until the nineteenth century, was read in the Peninsular in Reinoso's lifetime or the century thereafter.[16]

As suggested, misconceptions about Reinoso's work seem to have arisen because his novel was indeed partially based on that of Tatius, and critics *a posteriori* have concluded that his aim was a literary one—that of fashioning a Byzantine tale, of participating in the renaissance of that popular type of prose fiction. In any case, while Núñez de Reinoso freely acknowledges as the source of inspiration for his novel a work called *Ragionamenti amorosi,* "habiendo en casa de un librero visto entre algunos libros uno que *Razonamiento de amor* se llama, me tomó deseo, viendo tan buen nombre, de leer algo en él" (431), he also signals his departure from his model when he proclaims that he is "imitando y no romanzando" (431). In other words, he found the work of sufficient literary prestige to permit him to use it as a basis for his own creative efforts and a vehicle for the projection of his thoughts. He is strangely reluctant to

15. Ágreda y Vargas's work is a paraphrase rather than a translation. Menéndez Pelayo, *Orígenes,* II, pp. 73, 84, mentions that both Quevedo and Pellicer de Ossau Salas y Tovar claim to have essayed Spanish versions of Tatius's romance, but if so, both works have been lost.

16. Reinoso's book seems not to have undergone a second printing in Italy; there was a French translation, *La plaisante histoire des amours de Florisée et de Clareo, et aussi de la peu fortunée Isea,* trad. du castillan en françois par Jacq. Vincent, Paris, 1554, and an anonymous Portuguese version, without date of publication. While the French version is quite faithful to Reinoso's original, the Portuguese edition, clearly written after 1552, is a condensation in which most of the dialogue is merely summarized, thus emphasizing the adventures. (It is not, as both Menéndez Pelayo [*Orígenes,* II, p. 83] and Michaëlis de Vasconcelos [*Obras,* I, 104] conjectured, either a source for or an earlier version of Reinoso's novel.)

reveal the identity of the author of the *Ragionamenti*, a man who could not have been a stranger to him because the Italian work was a translation of the last two books of Tatius's novel by one Lodovico Dolce, an editor for the firm of Gabriel Giolito, which published Reinoso's work, and the contributor of one of the two laudatory sonnets that preface Reinoso's volume.[17] Indeed, Reinoso is proud of the fact that a man of Dolce's reputation has so honored him and he compliments the Italian in the following extravagant terms: ". . . es uno de los mas escelentes autores que agora en toda Italia se sabe, y por quien las musas florecen y toda la poesía tiene vida y gala" (432). In Chapter 1 I suggested that the Nasi family, Reinoso's patrons, supplied money to the Giolito de Ferrari press, Dolce's employers. Therefore, Reinoso's initial statement to the contrary, it is apparent that the selection of the *Ragionamenti* as source material was by design, not by accident.

Reinoso is not so guarded about the purpose of his novel as he is about identifying the author of the *Ragionamenti*. While he demonstrates the humanist's usual interest in moral philosophy,

> . . . yo . . . escreui . . . para auisar á bien biuir, como lo hizieron graues autores, que inuentando Fiçiones, mostraron a los hombres auisos para bien regirse, haziendo sus cuentos apazibles, por induzir a los letores a leer su abscondida moralidad . . . (4)[18]

---

17. Poi che del Beti e del gran Tago infiora
　　Con pure voci e note alte e faconde
　　Reinoso le superbe altere sponde,
　　Che di ricchi trofei Cesare onora;
　　. . . . .
　　E, se ben vinse le provincie e i regni
　　Alzando lei nel ciel Pallade e Marte,
　　La bella Italia mia non se ne sdegni. (432)
18. The anonymous sonnet that also prefaces the work emphasizes the

his real reason for writing the work would seem to be revealed in two statements he makes concerning his relationship with Juan Micas. In the epistolary dedication to Micas, dated January 24, 1552, Reinoso states,

> Luego que tomé la pluma en la mano, fué con propósito de componer aquesta obra, debajo del nombre y favor de vuestra merced; porque de otra manera no tuviera yo presuncion de publicalla ni de sacalla á luz; . . . y dado caso que el servicio sea pequeño, vuestra merced no por tanto deje de recebillo, porque no menos loor es recebir pequeños servicios, que hacer grandes mercedes, cuanto mas que yo este no lo tengo por pequeño; porque yo no doy obra, sino ánimo y voluntad . . .
>
> (431)

thus acknowledging that Micas is his patron, without whose aid and influence it would be impossible to publish the book, and that he, Reinoso, wrote it because he feels indebted to Micas. In a letter to Juan Hurtado de Mendoza, dated March of the same year, Reinoso reiterates that repaying Micas motivated the writing of the work:

> Y por tanto me pareció de poner aquí la causa que me movió á mudar propósito, haciendo imprimir este libro. La cual no fué otra mas que querer servir en algo á este caballero, á quien esta obra va dirigida, en

---

idea of moral philosophy, as well as Renaissance literary precepts based on Horatian principles:

> Quien junto querrá ver encadenado
> Lo útil con lo dulce en compañía,
> La virtud, discrecion y cortesía,
> Y el modo de vivir limpio y cendrado:
> Quien sotil invencion, quien el traslado
> De toda la moral filosofía,
> . . . .
> Pues ha dejado á sí, con su escritura,
> Y á vos fama inmortal el de Reinoso. (432)

lugar de otros servicios de los que pueden en esta tierra
mas que yo le suelen hacer; porque yo le tengo tanta
obligacion, que no solamente doy por bien empleado
todo el tiempo que en esto he gastado, pero soy cierto
que jamás me pesará de lo que hice en su servicio, sino
de lo que no puedo hacer. (432)

It should be noted that Núñez de Reinoso at no time
mentions Tatius or his novel. He knew the Italian version to be a partial translation of an earlier work:[19] "vi
que aquel libro habia sido escrito primero en lengua
griega, y después en latina, y últimamente en toscana;
y pasando adelante hallé que comenzaba en el quinto
libro"; and acknowledges his desire to appropriate the
plot: "no uso mas que de la invencion" (430). His aim
was not solely literary. A poor man whose only talents
lay in the field of letters,[20] he set out to discharge a debt
of gratitude by composing a novel and some poems on
a subject that would be of interest to his benefactor,
Juan Micas. His work was, in other words, primarily
directed toward a group of "enterados," Micas and his
acquaintances, who had fled the Peninsula. Reinoso wrote
for a "minoría selecta" of Spanish and Portuguese *ma-*

19. Authors of chivalric works often claimed to have translated the
material from a Greek—or other—ancient manuscript.
20. As mentioned in Chapter 1, Reinoso acknowledged his debt to
a patroness, presumably doña Gracia, in his poems where he indicates
that he cannot perform for her services that others can but instead will
praise her, seemingly through his writing:

> No me deven de culpar
> En cosas grandes no dar
> Pues que lo que tengo doy.
>
> Los otros serviçios dan
> De trabajos que passado
> En servilla siempre han,
> . . . .
> Pero yo tan solamente,
> Mi voluntad con desseo.
> (No. 1)

rranos residing in Italy, whose experiences, paralleling his own, permitted them to pierce the secret meaning of his novel, its "escondida moralidad."[21] The subject of his discourse seems to have been nothing less than the Second Diaspora as it affected their lives. For what apparently attracted Núñez de Reinoso to Dolce's *Ragionamenti Amorosi* was the opportunity he saw for developing the theme of fortune as it related to suffering and to endless travel.

The changes that Núñez de Reinoso makes in his source material, what he chooses to emphasize, add, or omit, indicate that he wished to depict the agonies of exile. As mentioned, in order to give external unity to the disparate parts of the work, Reinoso enclosed the entire tale within a pastoral frame. For internal unity, he employed as narrator Isea, who figures in both plots, rather than Clareo (Clitophon) as in Tatius's original. To carry out this change, Reinoso had to transform the rather calculating, sensuous "other woman" of Tatius's novel into his long-suffering protagonist. The linking of sequential events through the figure of Isea permits Reinoso to extend the theme of fortune throughout the work. Because of the change of focus imposed by Reinoso, it is Isea's story and it is she who suffers at the hands of adverse fortune: in the first part, she is unsuccessful in love; in the second, unfortunate in all aspects of life. Fortune is presented as an abstract force that has complete sovereignty over Isea's life and that has singled her out for an unhappy lot in this world.

---

21. Enrique Moreno Báez, *Lección y sentido del "Guzmán de Alfarache,"* Madrid, 1948, p. 21, dismisses Reinoso's claim as just one more example of a current literary formula signifying nothing when he speaks of ". . . libros tan de puro entretenimiento como *La historia de los amores de Clareo y Florisea* . . . de Alonso Núñez de Reinoso, en la que lo moral no aparece por ninguna parte."

Fortune

Before turning to a study of the novel itself, it is necessary to examine the theme of fortune that Núñez de Reinoso found present in Tatius's work and adapted to his own use. "Fortuna" has been called the one goddess of classical times who survived into the Christian era.[22] Her role has been subject to various interpretations: for Dante, she was one of God's ministers;[23] for Machiavelli, an irrational force responsible for the haphazard events in man's life, but one that could be used by a "virtuoso".[24] In Spain, Manrique reflected an attitude common to the

---

22. Howard Patch, *The Goddess Fortuna*, Cambridge, 1927, p. 3.
23. Dante delineates his *ancilla dei* theory in the following manner:

> Colui lo cui saper tutto trascende
> Feci li cieli, e diè lor chi conduce,
> Sì c'ogni parte ad ogni parte splende,
> Distribüendo igualmente la luce.
> Similemente a li splendor mondani
> Ordinò general ministra e duce,
> Che permutasse a tempo li ben vani
> Di gente in gente e d'uno in altro sangue,
> Oltre la difension de senni umani:
> *Divina Commedia,* I, VII, ll. 73-81.

24. Machiavelli believed that fortune could be opposed by the stoic quality of *virtù* or manliness:

> Et assomiglio quella a uno di questi fiumi rovinosi, che, quando s'adirano, allagano e'piani, ruinamo li arberi e li edifizi. . . . E, benché sieno così fatti, non resta però che li uomini, quando sono tempi quieti, non vi potessino fare . . . provedimenti e con ripari et argini, in modo che, crescendo poi, o andrebbono per uno canale, o l'impeto loro non sarebbe né sí licenzioso né sí dannoso. Similmente interviene della fortuna: la quale dimonstra la sua potenzia dove non è ordinata *virtú* a resisterle . . . (124-155)

> Concludo, adunque, che, variando la fortuna, e stando li uomini ne'loro modi ostinati, sono felici mentre concordano insieme, e come discordano, infelici . . . la fortune è donna et è necessaria, volendola tenere sotto, batterla et urtarla. (129) *El Principe,* introduzione e note di Federico Chabod, Torino, 1927. Cf. the neo-stoic attitude in *El Abencerraje*: ". . . Abindarráez, quiero que veas que puede más mi *virtud* que tu ruin Fortuna." (ed. Claudio Guillén, New York, 1966, p. 120; italics mine.)

fifteenth century: that fortune, together with time and death, was one of the three forces that inevitably limited human existence.[25] While Otis Green holds to the opinion that by the sixteenth century the concept of fortune had been reduced to a meaningless formula,[26] evidence he himself supplies would seem to indicate otherwise. For example, he mentions that the Inquisition in Portugal either expressly forbade references to fortune or instructed that they be interpreted in a Christian context.[27] It may be only coincidence that seemingly innocuous remarks—references to fortune and fate—are deleted from an early reprinting of Ribeiro's *Menina e Moça*.[28] But in any case, such censorship seems to have derived from official disapproval of what could be termed a heretical point of view on the part of dissident thinkers who maintained that divine providence did not extend to the sublunary world[29] where fortune or blind chance regulated men's lives and their survival was based on their ability to overcome adverse circumstances. In other words, fortune was a cipher for environmental factors or social pressures in this essentially anthropocentric view.

As a class, none felt more subject to the whims of the fickle goddess than did Spain's *conversos*, who display a disproportionate interest in the theme of fortune. They are early associated with translations of the standard

25. For Manrique's attitude toward fortune and that of the fifteenth-century *cancionero* writers, see the excellent study by Pedro Salinas, *Jorge Manrique o tradición y originalidad*, Buenos Aires, 1948.

26. Otis H. Green, *Spain and the Western Tradition*, II, 1964, pp. 279–337. He maintains, for example that in the *Diana*, Montemayor uses the concept of "fortune" only to advance the plot. (309)

27. *Ibid.*, p. 282.

28. Vasconcelos, *Nótulas relativas*, pp. 18–26.

29. Charles Fraker, "The Importance of Pleberio's Soliloquy," *Romanische Forschungen*, LXXVIII, 1966, pp. 515–29, asserts that such a view of the world, expressed by many *conversos*, derived from Maimonides.

works on this subject: Alonso de Cartagena of the famous
Santa María family translated Boccaccio's *De casibus*,
and Francisco de Madrid, Petrarch's *De remediis*. Stephen Gilman, who has illustrated the importance of the
theme to Fernando de Rojas,[30] has recently advanced the
theory that "fortune" was for a few writers almost a
euphemism for the Inquisition.[31] Indeed, Luis Vives used
the word in precisely that fashion; writing to a friend, he
lamented: "La Fortuna continua siendo igual y fiel a sí
misma, contra mi padre, contra todos los míos y aun contra mí mismo."[32] It is not unusual, then, that an exiled New
Christian author such as Núñez de Reinoso would seize
upon a work that emphasized the workings of fortune
in order to set forth his own experiences.

Reinoso's Novel

As indicated, the theme of fortune was part of Núñez
de Reinoso's literary heritage. For models, he chose to
imitate those authors whose works treat this subject.
Among those he acknowledged are Ovid and Seneca;[33]
among those not acknowledged, though their influence
is evident, are Virgil, Petrarch, and Boccaccio. It is not
by accident that entire lines from the *Aeneid* find their
way into *Clareo y Florisea*, for Núñez de Reinoso seems
to have seen an analogy between the unhappy Dido and
the unfortunate women in his book who welcome the
handsome stranger, the shipwrecked Clareo or the

30. Gilman, *The Art of "La Celestina,"* Madison, 1956; "Fortune and
Space in 'La Celestina'," *Romanische Forschungen,* LXVI, 1955, pp. 342–
61; "The Fall of Fortune from Allegory to Fiction," *Filologia Romanza,*
IV, 1957, pp. 337–54.
31. Gilman, "The 'Conversos' and the Fall of Fortune," *Collected
Studies in honor of Américo Castro's Eightieth Year,* Oxford, 1965.
32. Letter of January 25, 1525, to Francisco Cranevelt, quoted from
Castro, *La realidad histórica de España,* Mexico, 1954, p. 551.
33. "Cuanto á en esta mi obra en prosa haber imitado á Ovidio en los
libros de *Tristibus,* á Séneca en las tragedias . . . no tengo pena." (432)

wandering Feliçindos, only to be spurned. Indeed, he models his heroine, Isea, after Dido, transformed by then-current opinion into a "víctima de la mudable Fortuna."[34] An example of Reinoso's debt to Virgil can be seen in the words employed by the abandoned Estrellinda as she curses the departing Felisindos:[35]

34. For the Spanish interpretation of Dido as a long-suffering heroine abandoned by Aeneas and pursued by adverse fortune, see María Rosa Lida, "Dido y su defensa en la literatura española," *Revista de Filología*, IV, 1942, 209-52, 313-82.

35.

Reinoso	Virgil
ESTRELLINDA	DIDO

Reinoso (Estrellinda):

¡Oh duro y sin fe ninguna, Felesindos! Y, ¿es posible que te baste el ánimo á partirte de mí, que tanto te quiero, y á peregrinar por ajenas tierras, podiendo hallar comigo ciudades y castillos . . ? Y ¿es posible que sabiendo tú cierto, que después de tu partida yo no podré vivir, que no te detenga esto y que quieras antes navegar por los mares bravos, y caminar por los estranjeros reinos, que sosegar y casarte conmigo? . . . ¿Y que estas lágrimas mias no te detengan, y la fe y palabra qu me diste . . ? . . . . Pues pídote, por el amor que te tengo, y por cualquier servicio que de mí hayas recebido, . . . que no te partas; . . . que mi muerte no podrá tardar . . .

Virgil (Dido):

Dissimulare etiam sperasti, perfide, tantum
posse nefas tacitusque mea decedere terra?
Nec te noster amor, nec te data dextera quondam,
nec moritura tenet crudeli funere Dido?
Quin etiam hiberno moliris sidere classem,
et mediis prosperas aquilonibus ire per altum,
crudelis? . . .

. . . .

. . . Per ego has lacrimas dextramque tuam te
(quando aliud mihi iam miserae nihil ipsa reliqui),

. . . .

oro, si quis adhuc precibus locus— exue mentem.

Reinoso (Felesindos):

FELESINDOS
Las grandes mercedes y beneficios que de vos, señora Estrellinda, yo he recebido, jamás negaré; porque en cuanto el alma mia acompañare mi cuerpo, siempre de vos y dellas tendré memoria . . . por los dioses inmortales, que yo no puedo, porque los hados ordenaron traerme así desasosegado hasta llevarme . . .   (461b–462a)

Virgil (Aeneas):

AENEAS
. . . Ego te, quae plurima fando enumerare vales, numquam, regina, negabo
promeritam; nec me meminisse pigebit Elissae,
dum memor ipse mei, dum spiritus hoc regit artus.

. . . .

Me si fata meis paterentur ducere vitam
auspiciis et sponte mea componere curas,
(IV, 305-11, 314-15, 319, 333-36, 340-41.)

Reinoso	*Virgil*
ESTRELLINDA	DIDO
Yo creo verdaderamente, que hombre tan sin piedad no puede ser nacido sino de algunos tigres de Hircania, ó criado entre algunos duros saxos . . . Ora pues, cruel, sigue tu camino, que yo espero que los piadosos dioses me den venganza de tí, y yo te prometo que muchas veces me nombres. (462a)	*Nec tibi diva parens, gene-ris nec Dardanus auctor, perfide; sed duris genuit te cautibus horrens Caucasus, Hyrcanaeque admorunt ubera tigres.* . . . . *I, sequere Italiam ventis . . . Spero equidem mediis, si quid pia numina possunt, supplicia hausurum scopulis, et nomine Dido saepe vocaturum.* *(IV, 365-67, 381-84)*

Also, because the destruction of Troy as a theme of civic misfortune captured the imagination of the Renaissance, it is not to be wondered at that that epic, which dealt with unhappiness, wanderings, shipwrecks, and the effort to found a new homeland, should have come to mind. Lastly, the theme of fate (*fatum*) is basic to the *Aeneid;* it will be seen in Reinoso's work that the workings of fate and fortune cross, so that both the *Aeneid* and *Clareo y Florisea* deal with people who are not in control of their own destiny.[36]

Further, when Reinoso's characters refer to "fortuna," it is usually in the sense of "adverse fortune," although the tradition admits of both "próspera" and "adversa." As Claudio Guillén points out, in his edition of the *Lazarillo*, "adversidades" and "fortunas" are syn-

---

36. Núñez de Reinoso, in connection with the theme of fortune, employs expressions usually associated with that of fate: "hados," "parcas," etc.

onyms.[37] In *Clareo y Florisea*, however, there is no attempt to combat or change one's fortune; Isea simply flees before what she apparently considers her inexorable fate.

Núñez de Reinoso initiates his tale of suffering by delineating a personal disaster in the field of love. That fortune's sphere of influence extended to that of love is not original with Reinoso. Howard Patch points out that the personalities of Fortuna and Eros were similar enough to permit the goddess to assume the activities of the God of Love and notes that from the time of the loves of Abelard and Heloise, "Fortuna is found meddling more or less in love-affairs."[38] That Fortune's control over love was not confined to the literature of countries other than Spain can be seen in references to two Spanish works contemporary with that of Núñez de Reinoso. In Avendaño's *Comedia Florisea* (1551), a play having little correspondence with Reinoso's novel beyond coincidence of title, the Goddess Fortuna is invoked to settle the love affair of the hero, Floriseo, and the financial matters of the Caballero Muerte. Here Fortuna functions both in her most common sphere, that of distributing worldly wealth (*bienes*), and in the territory of love. The play ends with the *refrán*: "contra fortuna y amor / ¿quién será resistidor?"[39] In the *Diana* (1559), Montemayor points out that fortune operates like love: "Amor y la fortuna / autores de trabajos y sinrazones."[40] There was, then, ample literary precedence

---

37. P. 136 (note 13).
38. Patch., p. 32.
39. See the edition of Bonilla y San Martín in *RHi,* XXVII 1912, pp. 398–422. It is quite possible that the Caballero Muerte is a "converso." *Comedia Florisea* may be the first Spanish play in three acts.
40. Jorge de Montemayor, *Los siete libros de la Diana,* ed. y pról. de López Estrada, Madrid, 1946, p. 167.

as well as contemporary usage for linking fortune with
love.

The following examples, all original with Reinoso,
reveal his method of handling the theme of fortune:
lines with which a character reacts to misfortune in
love (in part one) are equally applicable to other
problematic situations (in part two). Such treatment of
the material eventually allows Reinoso to subordinate the
love story and to emphasize suffering.

The subject of the first quotation is rejection; Isea,
having received information that Clareo has spurned
her offer of marriage, directly identifies the activities of
Fortune with those of Cupid and berates both deities:

> ¡Oh cruel fortuna, y cómo quieres ganar honra con
> una sin ventura y flaca mujer, vencida de la voluntad,
> sin poder obedecer á ninguna cosa sino al amor que
> con flecha dorada mis tiernas entrañas ha traspa-
> sado. . . . ¡Oh cuitada de tí, Isea triste y estranjera,
> y cómo podrás sufrir tantos dolores. . . . ¡Oh amor,
> y cuántos daños has sido causa, haciendo siervos los
> que son libres, tornando locos á los que son sabios!
> (437b)

The second deals with separation from a loved-one:
Clareo, having discovered that Florisea did not die upon
the sea, now believes that he has lost her once more:

> ¡Con cuánta razon me puedo quejar de tí, ó fortuna,
> y de mi suerte, y de mis tristes hados, viendo cuán
> presto mi bien acabó y aquella mi gloria se pasó! ¡Oh
> triste y sin ventura! Y ¿para qué me mostró fortuna
> tan pequeño placer con tornar la vida á Florisea, pues
> que tan presto se la habia de tornar á pedir . . . (450a)

The third treats the death of a loved-one: Clareo em-

braces what he assumes to be Florisea's headless body
and cries:

> ¡Oh desdichada y sin ventura Florisea, y qué muerte
> tan dura los hados te quisieron dar, cortando y ras-
> gando la hoja de tu vida en tan tierna edad, no
> guardando las parcas la órden que á tus tiernos años
> era debida! (436a)[41]

Later, as Isea leaves Alexandria to begin her endless
travels, she directs some remarks to the readers ("gene-
rosas señoras"); the paragraph from which the quotation is taken marks the transition from the first part of
the book to the second. The subject is her exile:

> . . . yo, á quien fortuna, no harta de mis trabajos ni
> de mi contraria suerte, aflige, y de un trabajo en otro
> mayor lleva, alongándome de mi tierra, y trayéndome
> por las ajenas queriendo que siempre crezca mi mal, y
> que jamás sepa de ningun bien, sino para presto
> perdello . . . (452a)

Isea speaks of death, employing the same classical

---

41. Clareo's long and grotesque variation on the *ubi sunt* formula,
a literary device often employed in conjunction with the theme of fortune,
concludes with the only reference to fortune present in the original
passage:

Reinoso	*Tatius* (Via Dolce)
Pero pues que la envidiosa for-	Ma por che la invidiosa fortuna
tuna me quitó poder besar tu	mi toglie hora di poter basciar
hermoso rostro, á lo menos no me	la tua faccia; io non questo san-
quitará que yo abrace este san-	guinoso tronco a cui il bel collo
griento cuerpo . . . (436b)	congiungeva. (8)

The line in Tatius causes a modern critic (Donald Blythe Durham,
"Parody in Achilles Tatius," *Classical Philology*, XXXIII, 1938, p. 18)
to accuse him of "rhetoric gone mad," but Núñez de Reinoso far outdoes
him in displaying poor taste: cradling what he thinks is Florisea's
headless body, Clareo employs the *ubi sunt* formula to exclaim, "Y qué
es de aquella hermosa cabeza. . . . Adonde son agora aquellos y
hermosos ojos?"

formula as did Clareo: ". . . parecióme . . . irme por ese mundo hasta ver en qué lugar la muerte querria acabar mi vida, y las duras parcas cortar los hilos de la triste tela." (452a) Later after having been shipwrecked, bereft of companions and worldly possessions and cast into prison, she once more cries out to Fortune:

> ¡Oh fortuna, y grande debe de ser la injuria que de mí recebiste, pues no cansada de me haber puesto en los trabajos pasados, agora me has traido á tal estado . . . (452b)

Important to the extension of the theme of fortune from the first to the second part of the novel is the identification of the role of Fortune with that of Venus, made possible because both goddesses were associated with the sea. The interconnection of amorous misadventures and general suffering and the relation of such affairs to a sea hostile to man's interests are evinced through two speeches of Isea, the first of which Núñez de Reinoso found in Tatius's work. Isea, very much in love with Clareo, tries to persuade him to break his vow that they will live as brother and sister rather than as man and wife:

> . . . pero que yo sabia que cierto que todo lugar era conviniente á los amantes; porque siendo el amor dios, en toda parte defendia á todos aquellos que su señorío obedecian; y que la diosa Venus, madre del amor, era hija del mar, y que forzadamente habia de favorecer los que á su hijo eran sujetos, y que la diosa de las bodas seria muy contenta que aquí se celebrasen, y que la fortuna las enderezaria á próspero fin . . . (441a)

Later, in her prison lament (the initial words have already been quoted), Isea recognizes that her interpretation that the sea was a favorable place for consummating the marriage was entirely erroneous. Having addressed Fortune and blamed her for the new disaster, Isea continues:

> ¡Oh mar, mar, y cuán mas cortés has sido siempre con todos de lo que fuiste comigo, cuando por tí navegaba! Y di ¡mar, mar! y ¿qué te costaba . . . no traerme á esta dura y triste prision, en la cual las bodas que pensaba hacer con Clareo se verifican bien; porque la hermosa y linda cámara es aqueste escuro lugar, y la blanda y rica cama es la dura y áspera tierra . . .
>
> (452b)

Fortune is often depicted as directing the winds that stir up the seas, causing man's light craft to founder. Indeed, Corominas suggests, "En cuanto a la explicación semántica, . . . [Fortuna] es eufemismo, destinado al principio a evitar lo alarmante de voces como *procella, tormenta, tempesta.* . . ."[42] Accordingly, Núñez de Reinoso made use of the Byzantine novel's predilection for depicting storms and shipwrecks in order to advance the theme of fortune. His characters display an awareness of the symbolism of the "sea-figure" and comment upon its relevance. For example, in explaining Clareo's presence to her husband, Isea says, ". . . quiso su ventura que navegando por la mar, la fortuna le fué contraria; perdida toda la hacienda que tenia" (447b). Her reference here, more explicit than Tatius's line upon which it is based, is to Clareo's loss of wealth, an act commonly attributed to Fortune. When Clareo and Isea arrive at the Ínsula de la Vida and are asked the reason for their coming, they answer, ". . . la tormenta nos habia echado en aquella tierra" (442a). As the storm abates, Isea understands that ". . . como la fortuna me fuese tan

---

42. *Diccionario crítico etimológico de la lengua castellana,* II, Madrid, 1954, p. 558b.

contraria, quisieron mis hados que no muriese allí, porque viniese á padecer y sufrir" (441b). Much later, after suffering fresh maritime disasters, Isea decides to continue her journey by land: "acordé de hacer mi camino por tierra, por andar tan cansada de la fastidiosa mar" (454a).

Isea is not the only one who expounds upon the connection between fortune and the sea. In his lament (part of which has already been quoted) before what he thinks is Florisea's headless body, Clareo, after berating fortune and the fates for her untimely death, adds, "Yo te saqué, querida señora mia, de casa de tu padre, . . . yo te truje por los mares bravos, no siendo usada en tales fortunas ni trabajos" (436a). But Florisea is not really dead; it has all been a ghastly trick and a case of mistaken identity. Upon her reappearance, she too associates fortune and the sea; in a letter to the seemingly unfaithful Clareo, she bewails her enslavement:

> . . . no merecia esto el haber navegado (por tu causa) la brava mar, sufriendo los grandes peligros della; . . . siendo por tu solo respecto robada de cosarios y perdida por la mar, en galardon de las cuales cosas y grandes *fortunas, trabajos* y *adversidades,* . . . soy [contenta] tambien en llorar mi gran fortuna.
> (444b; italics mine)

Núñez de Reinoso, then, appropriated the Byzantine novel's locale, the sea, and used it to supply underlying metaphor to his work. The fictional misadventures serve as a gloss of the popular "lugar común." He emphasizes the symbolic role of the sea as a means of uniting theme and action through endless repetitive disasters and through comments he allows his characters to make.

The sea figure occurs with frequency, in a symbolic

sense, in Usque's *Consolaçam*. For example, in Ycabo's last lament, he speaks of the storms that have perpetually beset the people of Israel, pursued as they were by adverse fortune:

> . . . e ynda tee o presente dia nhũa destas tormētas cessa de offenderme, antes *como nao de diuersos e tempestosos ventos em alto mar* muy combatida, que pera nhũa das quatro partes do mundo pode com seguridade voltar a proa, tal me acho eu atribulado ysrael no meo de minhas *fortunas* ynda agora.
>
> (III, xxxviiii-v-xl-r; italics mine)

Like Isea, Israel (Ycabo) seeks a refuge from the storms of life:

> Os ariscados mareantes que por meo da *soberba e perigosa tormenta* tiuerom suas vidas postas em hum dado; vesitaos depois a *boa ventura e tempo prospero,* e com suas riquezas e pessoas saluas alegres arribam a seguro e desejado porto; e contra mi contado a *trabalhosa fortuna* jamais cessa, nem de minhas esperãças vejo o porto.
>
> (III, xl-v-xli-r; italics mine)

Further, Ycabo clearly connects the "sea of fortune" with his own tribulations:

> Mas Ay mizquinho de mĩ q̃ deuaneo achome no meo das fortunas do mar alagado e ameaço os que estam no sossego da terra contemplandome . . . (I, xlix-r)[43]

Samuel Usque had no need to mask his message. He was a Jewish author whose work was published by a Jewish printing press under the auspices of, perhaps, the outstanding Jewess of his century; his avowed intent was to reaffirm the faith of those *marranos* who had sup-

---

43. English translator Martin A. Cohen misses the point here, when he writes, "I am drowning amidst the *hazards* of the sea." *Consolation for the Tribulations of Israel,* Philadelphia, 1965, p. 102 (italics mine.)

posed that the route to survival lay in conforming to Christianity and to reclaim them for Judaism.[44] His use of the sea figure is ornamental; he is clearly speaking of the troubles that assailed the people of Israel during the First and Second Diasporas.

One of the safe ports that Usque lists is the Duchy of Ferrara, and he praises Ercole II in the following manner:

> O setimo caminho que a grande cosolaçam te guia, he o *porto seguro e sosseguado* que pera se acolherem teus cansados membros e desterrados filhos das *tormentas de mar e terra* a enfinita misericordia do ceeo te aparelhou, no felice animo daquelle alto principe do sangue ytaliano o mais sublime e generoso, . . . Quem se lembra depois que tuas *desuenturas e pelegrinaçoes* tiuerom principio, estranho algum de tua ley assi fauorecer tua baixeza, recolher com tanto amor teu esparzimento.   (III, liii-r; italics mine)

Ferrara, termed the "Ínsula de la Vida" by Reinoso,[45] serves as a refuge for the shipwrecked Isea and Clareo; and Ercole II, or the "duque de Atenas," and his wife are the object of Isea's gratitude:

> . . . la gran deuda en que yo era á [los duques de Atenas], por las obras que en la ínsula de la Vida dellos habia recebido; porque, fuera de la gran deuda en que soy á aquel gran señor de Egipto, porque esta es la mayor que yo tengo ni pienso tener, soy en gran obligacion á todos los de la ínsula de la Vida. (460a)

Núñez de Reinoso and Usque, then, intended that the

---

44. "Pello que eu comouido, & vendo esta nossa naçāo seguida & afugentada agora dos reinos de Portugal vltimamente hūs por pobreza, outros por temor, & os mais delles pella pouca costancia q̃ jaa de abinicio ē nossos animos repousa, vacilar & mais do deuer someterse aos trabalhos & deixarse vencer delles (I, prólogo).

45. Bataillon, "Alonso Núñez de Reinoso."

symbolism of the sea figure be applied to an identical
historical situation, one dealing with wandering punctu-
ated by continuous misfortunes (storms and shipwrecks).
And it should not be overlooked that the Jewish editors
chose as the illustration for the title page of the "Ferrara"
Bible and the colophon of the Usque press,[46] which also
published the *Consolaçam*, a drawing of a ship attempting
to ride out a storm—an indication that they, too, identified
this symbol, the "sea of fortune," with the tribulations of
exiled Sephardim.

Núñez de Reinoso, on the other hand, claimed to be
writing fiction; seemingly he could not afford to be open
and direct, as could Samuel Usque. Therefore, Reinoso
couched his version of historical reality in allusive terms.
One description of a storm that threatens Isea is a
reworking of a passage from Ovid's *Tristia*:[47]

Núñez de Reinoso	Ovid
. . . *y las bravas ondas parecia que unas veces nos subian al cielo, y otras nos bajaban á los abismos; y ansí el patron de la nao no sabia qué hacerse . . .* (441b)	*Quanti montes volvuntur aquarum! Jam jam tacturos sidera summa putes. Quantae diducto subsidunt aequore valles! Jam jam tacturas Tartara nigra putes. (II, 19-22) Rector in incerto est: nec, quid fugiatve petatve . . . (II, 31)*

---

46. A reproduction of the colophon may be seen in Toda.
47. The use of Ovid's description of a storm at sea is just one more
example of the predilection of Renaissance writers for employing well-
known phrases from the works of classical authors as commonplaces. In
this instance, however, it seems that Núñez de Reinoso, who acknowledges reading *Tristia*, considered his situation to be analogous to that
of Ovid.

Yet a similar passage appears in Núñez de Reinoso's eclogue, where one of the interlocutors describes the storm that thwarted his attempted escape from Portugal:

Y las ondas que venian
Que las velas nos llevavan
. . . .
A las estrellas subian
Y subiedas abaxavan
A la tierra.

. . . .
El marinero no sabe
Que azer.   *(No. 5)*

Storms, in Núñez de Reinoso's work, are open both to literal and figurative interpretation, because, like Ovid's, from whom he borrowed a number of lines, the subject of his discourse is his own exile. For while Samuel Usque, through the voice of Ycabo (Israel), recounted a group experience, Núñez de Reinoso, through the voice of Isea, related the suffering of one individual.

The Fall of Fortune

In Núñez de Reinoso's novel, as in all literary treatment of the theme, the fall of fortune implies a loss of some sort—of wealth, position, a loved-one, friends, life, liberty, or homeland. Accordingly, Clareo loses his beloved to the sea (though he is subsequently reunited with her), later is jailed, and then is threatened with death; Florisea almost loses her life and does lose her freedom upon becoming a slave; a young girl dies suddenly; Isea thinks she has lost her first husband to the sea, does lose her second (Clareo), loses her companions and money in a shipwreck, suffers imprisonment, and is condemned to a life of ceaseless wandering and exile.[48] In each case fortune is blamed for the loss. However, in Reinoso's book, there is no attempt to affix sin in order to explain the fall of fortune in accordance with Christian beliefs.[49] Neither Adam and Eve, original sin, or any of the subsequent causal arguments have any bearing on the outcome of the novelistic events. Isea, the victim, is blameless; the cause of her fall does not emanate from her own acts; there is no hint that she may have been responsible for her own misfortune. While infidelity was often a reason for fortune to deal out punishment, Núñez de Reinoso deleted Melitte's (Isea's) seduction of Clitophon (Clareo) from his rendering of Tatius's work; and, it must be observed, infidelity caused the original Melitte no harm as she passed the test of her chastity by employing a mental reservation.

If the fault does not lie within Isea, one must look elsewhere for the cause of her suffering. There is a strong hint in the novel that the cause is *envidia*. Traditionally,

---

48. Cf. Petrarch's treatment of the theme, in Part Two of *De Remediis*. It is curious to note that various misfortunes are the chapter headings that correspond to incidents in Reinoso's book:

> De la servitud
> Dela perdida del dinero
> Dela muger robada por fuerza
> De la infamia
> Dela muerte del amigo
> Dela ausencia de los amigos
> Del naufragio o peligro del mar
> De la carcel
> Del destierro
> De la imbidia
> De la muerte ante de tp̄o

(Spanish translation of Francisco de Madrid, *De los remedios contra la prospera y adversa fortuna,* Valladolid, 1510.)

Did Núñez de Reinoso draw upon Petrarch as well as events from his own life when he supplemented the unfortunate adventures supplied in Tatius's tale?

49. In *De casibus,* Boccaccio espouses the causal theory.

envidiosa is one of the epithets most frequently applied
to Fortuna;[50] Reinoso makes use of this precedence in
order to relate the novelistic events to social circumstances
within Spain. Envy is first presented as operational in
the court, and, as such, is a standard example of the
"menosprecio de corte" theme. The episode is of importance because it is one of Reinoso's earliest interpola-
tions and because it is the first time that any of his
characters suffers a reversal.[51] The Caballero Constan-
tino, Altayes de Francia (or Arquesileo in his pastoral
disguise), the object of this envy, is accused of treason
and of having committed adultery with the queen:

> . . . aquellos pastores, que con la infanta quedaron,
> habiendo grande invidia al pastor por pensar dañarle,
> le levantaron que él era traidor, y habia cometido
> traicion en el palacio real y casa de la infanta; y esto,
> con tener no honesta ni lícita conversacion con la reina
> Sagitaria . . . (434a)

In Núñez de Reinoso's novel, a key passage, essential
to an understanding of the work itself and its relevance
to the author's life, is a lengthy commentary on the
workings and effects of envy. The scene is a confrontation
between Isea and her long-lost husband, but the circumstances neither call for nor measure up to the words

---

50. Patch, p. 38.
     Also cf.:
> Fortuna, invidiosa a lor quiete,
> Ruppe ogni legge e pieta misé infundo.
>   Poliziano, *Stannze . . . Lorenzo de Medici*
51. The incident is similar to one recounted by both Silva and Ribeiro.
One of the rumors circulated as the cause of Ribeiro's supposed banishment from court, his subsequent melancholy, madness, and death was his
attentions to a noble lady. Because of the paucity of data dealing with
Ribeiro's life, it is impossible to ascertain whether this fictional account
was based on reality or whether it was the basis of the rumor. Vasconcelos
in both *Obras* and *Poesias* supplies a reasonable reconstruction of
Ribeiro's life, though there are few facts available for verification.

employed, for Isea is merely trying to appease her irate
husband who has returned to find her involved in a
seemingly adulterous relationship. Fundamental differ-
ences between Reinoso's treatment and that of Tatius and
of his seventeenth-century imitator, Ágreda y Vargas,
serve to point up the originality of Reinoso's handling
of the situation. In Tatius's work, Melitte (Isea) was
plainly lying to her spouse; Ágreda y Vargas focuses
upon the husband's rage and his physical attack on
Clitophon (Clareo) and plays down Melita's part.
Núñez de Reinoso, however, treats Isea as a sympathetic
victim, even though she is only technically telling the truth
—as we remember, she had ardently pressed for the
consummation of her second "marriage." But she is not
passive; instead, Reinoso transforms her defense of her
actions into an eloquent attack on *envidia*.

The passage begins as a translation of some lines from
Dolce's version, themselves an imitation of Virgil's
famous flight of "fama" (rumor) :[52]

> . . . comienza la fama á volar, y á correr mas que
> saeta, y hiere las orejas de aquel á quien se endereza,
> y derrámase después por todas las cortes, villas y
> ciudades. (448a)

By linking rumor ("fama") with *envidia*, Núñez de
Reinoso will proceed to hispanize and personalize the
situation. The force of Isea's words becomes directed
toward the *malsín*. As Domínguez Ortiz remarks about

52.
> Ex templo Libyae magnas it Fama per urbes—
> Fama, malum qua non aliud velocius ullum;
> ....
> luce sedet custos aut summi culmine tecti,
> turribus aut altis, et magnas territat urbes.
> *Aeneid*, IV, 173–74, 186–87.

the manner of gathering information for inquisitional *procesos*:

> El defecto radical de las informaciones estribaba en que estaban basadas . . . en declaraciones orales de testigos que no solían aducir más pruebas que *la pública voz y fama*.[53]

And as Núñez de Reinoso observes in one of his poems, the result of rumor, or unfounded oral accusation, is the public proclamation uttered by the town crier as the condemned went to his death: "A otro vuelves cosarios y ladrones / en pena de lo cual pierden su vida / *por las públicas calles con pregones*"[54] (no. 16; italics mine). In the novel, Reinoso also attests to the connection between oral accusation and official denunciation; his description of the scene preceding Clareo's impending execution is alien to the Byzantine setting:

> Dada pues la sentencia contra el sin ventura de Clareo, lo llevaron desnudo *por las calles públicas,* atado con duras sogas y *con grandes pregones*, en los cuales decian la causa de mandalle dar aquella triste muerte. (451a; italics mine)

As can be seen, Reinoso transcribes Clareo's journey to the place of execution in terms of circumstances surrounding an *auto-de-fe* (the fact that Clareo was pressured into a false confession of a crime he never committed helps support such an interpretation). Again, in the confrontation between Isea and her husband, he

---

53. Domínguez Ortiz, *La clase social de los conversos en Castilla en la edad moderna,* Madrid, 1955, p. 75. (italics mine).
54. Cf. Petrarch, *De Remediis.*
De la Infamia
Dolor—Por las calles y encruzijadas me menosprecia el pueblo.

forgets or ignores what is appropriate to a Byzantine tale. Indeed, Reinoso becomes so preoccupied with his message that he quite loses the thread of his story and the events that precipitated the crisis. Leaving behind literary imitation and the fictional situation, Reinoso, through the voice of his narrator, begins to talk about conditions in what would seem to be sixteenth-century Spain:

> . . . *destruyen hoy dia á muchos,* porque si un falso con *falsa acusacion* acusa á uno delante de su señor ó delante de su príncipe, y trata mal dél, suele imprimir tanto aquella falsa y perversa acusacion, que aunque después el pobre acusado se quiera defender ó desculpar no le aprovecha, . . . lo cual no es justo: . . . *envidia . . . es destruicion de las honras,* y causa que la virtud no sea honrada, ni los virtuosos favorecidos, ni los grandes vistos ni conocidos; y el mal es que la envidia roe y come á los ánimos de los envidiosos; . . . esta envidia reina mas contra los grandes y en las casas grandes, destruyéndolas y despedazándolas, y poniéndolas en *pleitos, discordias, trabajos, desventuras, poco ó ningun reposo ni sosiego,* y es causa de que muchos bajos suban, y otros de mayor suerte anden abatidos; porque la envidia sigue la naturaleza del sol, el cual escurece las cosas claras . . . Y ansí yo creo bien que algun envidioso, porque nos vió valer y subir, por destruir esta nuestra casa y abajalla, . . . ha metido discordia y odio entre nosotros . . . (448a; italics mine)

As applied to the novelistic events, the meaning of the last line, at least, is clear: Isea is saying that some envious person is trying to destroy her marriage and the family name. The implied reference to the wheel of fortune contained in the antithetical expressions "suban"-"anden abatidos" and "subir"-"abajalla" lends thematic importance to the speech. The use of the word "discordia" intensifies such an interpretation, as it is one of Fortuna's functions to sow discord.

Neither Tatius nor his translators, however, had dealt with the problem of "envy"; nor do the fictional circumstances justify such a digression or sustain the charge of envy as a motivating factor. Lexical emphasis indicates that Reinoso's is more than the standard complaint against fortune for the leveling of estates; Castro has suggested that the words "envidia," "honra," "reposo," and "sosiego," had special significance for Golden Age Spain, meanings that sprang from the historical reality and the tensions of the period.[55] In his Hispanization of Isea's defense, Reinoso supplies the legal consequences of envious attacks—"pleitos," records the emotional response —"ningun reposo," and relates the total situation to "destruicion de las honras." The virulence of the words in contrast with their inappropriateness to the novelistic situation intimates Reinoso's personal involvement. And in addition to conveying the idea of personal disaster, Reinoso implies civic or national distress, the exact nature of which is not clear: either the Office of the Inquisition has sown discord and engendered hate among people of the various faiths who had previously been living more or less harmoniously in Spain, or Peninsular *conversos,* divided in their response to the assault, have turned upon each other, thus hastening their destruction (the latter suggestion arising from the expression "destruir esta *nuestra casa,*" which may be to say "temple".[56]

---

55. For Castro's ideas on this subject, see *La realidad histórica de España, passim.*

56. In his *Consolaçam,* Usque refers to the destruction of the first temple as "Lamento de Ysrael sobel perda da primeira *casa*" (I, lxvii-v; italics mine).

It is then possible to conclude that this digressive diatribe, which does little to advance the plot, not only supplies the cause of Isea's eventual fall from fortune but also reveals the reasons for Reinoso's leaving Spain. The passage would seem to summarize the agonizing existence of a *converso*, falsely accused, denounced to the authorities, embroiled in legal battles, threatened in a thousand ways, living in dread of the consequences.

It is of importance that the speech about "envy" is uttered by Isea, for her suffering does not cease when the adventures borrowed from Tatius's work come to an end. In the passage that marks the transition between the two parts of the novel, she announces her decision: ". . . yo, viéndome . . . sin familia, y *sin honra y sin ningun descanso,* parecióme dejar mi tierra y natural, y irme por ese mundo" (452a; italics mine). After saying goodby to a hitherto-unmentioned sister (presumably a reference to Reinoso's farewell to his own sister Isabel),[57] Isea's exile begins. Part two deals with her efforts to find "reposo" and "sosiego." "Peregrina, perdida, acosada y estranjera" (453b), the "sin ventura" Isea wanders through the world.

The Travails of a "peregrino"

The definition of the word "peregrino" that most easily comes to mind is the one listed second in the *Diccionario de la lengua española:* "Dícese de la persona que por devoción o por voto va a visitar un santuario."[58] This is the meaning that Covarrubias emphasizes: "El que sale de su tierra en romería a visitar alguna casa santa o lugar

---

57. As noted in Chapter 2, Isabel, the only relative whose name he disclosed, remained in Spain. Reinoso acknowledged missing her.
58. Decimoctava edición, Madrid, 1956.

santo."[59] Just as Berceo had compared man's life on earth
to a pilgrimage, "todos somos romeros que camino
andamos," Gracián conceived of a "peregrino" as one
whose earthly terminus was Rome and whose celestial
terminus was La isla de la inmortalidad.[60] However, for
Núñez de Reinoso and others like him, a "peregrino"
did not anticipate arriving at a holy destination, earthly
or heavenly. Reinoso's use of the word coincides with
the first dictionary meaning, and is closer to its etymological derivation (*per* + *agrum*): "Aplícase al que
anda por tierras extrañas." In other words, a "peregrino"
is not a "pilgrim" but a "traveler," or more precisely,
a "wanderer." Rather than having a goal toward which
he strives, Reinoso's "peregrino" is a wanderer who is in
flight from his homeland, an outcast who finds himself
without honor in his native land, an exile pursued by a
relentless foe, the Inquisition in the guise of Fortune.

Núñez de Reinoso was not alone in his interpretation
of the word "peregrino." A "pobre e afanado pelegrino"
is the manner in which Usque's Ycabo first identifies
himself (I, ii-v); later he likens his exile from the Land
of Canaan and the joys of the pastoral life to Adam's
banishment from Eden. A century later, Enríquez Gómez,
yet another Spanish *converso* in self-imposed exile to
avoid religious persecution, composed a work entitled
La culpa del primer peregrino, dealing with Adam's expulsion from Paradise.[61]

Being an exile means spending a great deal of time

---

59. Covarrubias, p. 863.
60. Life as a pilgrimage was standard fare: Rome as a sacred city
gave rise to the words "romería" and "romero": "Romero. El peregrino
que va a visitar los cuerpos santos de San Pedro y San Pablo y los demás
sanctuarios y besar el pie al Papa," Covarrubias, p. 913.
61. Ruán, 1644. There was a strong *marrano* colony in Rouen and an
active press for the publication of works by New Christian authors.

on the road, and Peninsular literature of the period is replete with references to the Senecan warning about the discomforts of travel. We have previously commented upon the similarity of a prophecy contained in the poems of Ribeiro and Sá de Miranda and fulfilled in those of Reinoso, when, for example, he says, ". . . ya no espero / salir de tierras agenas," and complains that he is condemned to a peripatetic existence, "Biviendo por los mesones, / Durmiendo por los passares / Sin plazer." In Senecan fashion, he includes lack of friends ("no tengo solo acá / Ni amigo, ni amiga") and of appetizing food ("El manjar es desabrido") as contributing to the misery of the traveler's life. In the novel, Reinoso reiterates the charge; Isea laments that she is "viviendo aquí sin ser usada á estos cielos, ni á las aguas, ni manjares destas tierras; sin tener persona ninguna á quien pueda contar mis males" (467b-468a). In Rojas's work, Celestina projects a similar attitude toward life on the road when she counsels Pármeno:

> . . . has tantas partes vagado é *peregrinado* . . . Que, como *Séneca* nos dize, los *peregrinos* tienen muchas posadas é pocas amistades . . . Ni puede aprouechar el manjar . . . , ni ay cosa que más la sanidad impida, que la diuersidad é mudança é variación de los manjares.
> (I, 100-101; italics mine)

She concludes by advising him to "reposa[r] en alguna parte" and Pármeno decides to "yrme al hilo de la gente." As previously demonstrated, advice of this nature— "settle down, conform"—was rejected by Núñez de Reinoso and his fictional counterparts.[62]

---

62. Cf. "Que yr al hilo como siento / Trabajo cierto me diera / Menos fuerte" (Reinoso, No. 5) and "Que em fim a verdade era / Ir polo fio de gente" (Sá de Miranda, 388).

Travel as travail was more than a literary theme of the epoch: for the "gente peregrina" received by doña Gracia (No. 1), for those who suffered "desuenturas e pelegrinaçoes"—in short, for the thousands displaced by the Second Diaspora—it was a living reality; and it was an essential component of the exile's lament.

4

THE EXILE'S LAMENT

Por qué dexaste triste
e solo in hac lachrymarum
valle?   *La Celestina*
(II, 212)

Melancholy

Setting out on her endless journey Isea remarks:
". . . me comencé á entregar á la tristeza, como la
pasada no me hubiese bastado" (452a). Indeed, a
mood of melancholy pervades the entire work. And while
Núñez de Reinoso borrowed certain portions of his plot
from Tatius, via Dolce's translation, for the literary tech-
nique of projecting melancholy, he is indebted to Boccaccio
and Ovid, as well as to his friend Ribeiro.[1] In *Fiammetta*,
he evidently saw a method suitable for expressing unhappiness in love, his concern in the first part of the book; in

---

1. As stated earlier (Chapter 2), critics generally concede that Ribeiro's
novel was published some years after his death. Vasconcelos, *Obras,* is
of this opinion; she even suggests that Reinoso brought the manuscript
of *Menina e moça* to Italy. Therefore, the fact that *Menina e moça* bears
the date of 1554 does not obviate the possibility that Ribeiro influenced
Reinoso. It is, however, impossible to determine whether or not Reinoso
drew directly from Boccaccio's *Fiammetta,* because Ribeiro was obviously
indebted to the Italian work and both men could have read the Spanish
translation of 1497.

Tristia, a manner of describing the agonies of exile; and in *Menina e moça,* a way of creating an atmosphere in which the physical world responds to the emotional state of the protagonist. As in *Fiammetta,* the action is concluded before the work begins; it is, then, a retrospective recounting of the events that led up to the narrator's present hopeless plight, a literary confession in which she examines and imparts her subjective response to adversity. And like the nameless narrator of *Menina e moça,* Isea has retired to an isolated pastoral area; there, in seclusion, she begins to write the book in order to divert herself from her sorrows. The work she composes might well have been called "Isea's Lament."

The novel opens and closes on a note of sadness. The first words uttered by Isea,

> Si mis grandes tristezas, trabajos y desaventuras, por otra Isea fueren oidas, yo soy cierta que serán no menos lloradas que con razon sentidas . . . de quien leyere esta obra que escribo, no pido remedio, sino piedad, si para mí hay alguna . . . (433a)

are reminiscent of Boccaccio's Fiammetta,

> Adunque acciò chè in me volonterosa più che altra a dolermi, di ciò per lunga usanza non menomi la cagione, ma s'avanzi, mi piace, o nobili Donne, . . . narrando i casi miei, di farvi, s'io posso, pietose. (1)[2]

who reiterates the thought at the conclusion of the work: "là dove io ti mando, e co'miei infortunj negli animi di quelle, che ti leggeranno, destare la santa pietà" (226).

---

2. Giovanni Boccaccio, *La Fiammetta,* Parma, 1800. All further references to the work imply this edition; its orthography has been followed.

Ribeiro's "heroine" also expresses the desire that her book arouse pity in female readers:

> Se em algum tẽpo se achar este libro de pessoas alegres, nã ho leã, . . . hos tristes ho poderã leer mas ahi nã hos ouue mais depois q̃ nas mulheres ouue piedade . . .
> (5-6)

Ovid, too, seeks a sympathic reader: "Invenies aliquem, qui me suspirit ademptum, / Carmina nec siccis perlegat ista genis" (I-l, 27-28).

However, the narrators in the books of both Reinoso and Ribeiro claim that they write only for themselves:

Núñez de Reinoso	Ribeiro
Esta mi obra, que sola-mente para mí escribo . . . *(433a)*	*. . . poys nam auia de escreuer pera ninguem se nam pera mi soo.* *(5)*

Isea then goes on to mention that her work conforms in appearance to its sad subject: "Esta mi obra . . . es toda triste, como lo soy; es toda de llanto y de grandes tristezas, porque ansí conforme con todas mis cosas, y tenga el hábito que yo tengo" (433a). Ovid expresses a similar thought when he addresses his book: "Vade, sed incultus; qualem decet exsulis esse. / Infelix, habitum temporis hujus habe" (I-l, 3-4). And Fiammetta looks upon her work as the misshapen offspring of her distress:[3]

---

3. This disclaimer, and indeed that of all four authors under discussion in this chapter, pertains to the tradition that Curtius (pp. 410ff.) calls "protestation of incapacity," here transformed from the inability to deal with the mysteries of being (i.e., man's awe of the godhead and his incapacity to speak of it) to the inadequacy of words to transmit a hyperemotional experience. Also, our authors draw upon traditional literary tropes; i.e., in his discussion of personal metaphors, Curtius, pp. 132-33, illustrates the conceit of the book-as-child through a quotation from Ovid.

E tu, o picciolo mio Libretto, tratto quasi della
sepoltura della tua donna . . . la tua fine é venuta, o con
più sollecito piede, che quella de'nostri danni; adunque
tale quale tu se'dalle mie mani scritto, e in più parti
delle mie lagrime offeso . . . (225)

Tu dei essere contento di mostrarti simigliante al tempo
mio, il quale, essendo infelicissimo, te di miseria veste,
come fa me . . . A te si conviene d'andare rabuffato
con isparte chiome, e macchiato, e di squallore pieno . . .
(226)

All four authors apologize for the lack of order in the
composition. Ovid blames the storms at sea, which made
it difficult for him to write:[4]

Quo magis his debes ignoscere, candide lector,
  Si spe sunt, ut sunt, inferior tua.
Non haec in nostris, ut quondam, scribimus hortis:
. . . .
Jactor in indomito brumali luce profundo;
Ipsaque coeruleis charta feritur aquis.
                                   (I-ll, 35-37, 39-40)

Fiammetta imputes her emotional state ". . . tue parole
rozzamente composte . . . però che li parlari ornati richieg-
gono gli animi chiari, e li tempi sereni e tranquilli" (229).
The narrator of *Menina e moça* explains that the disorder
results from both emotional turbulence and constant

---

4. See Chapter 3 for a comment in Núñez de Reinoso's use of Ovid's
description of storms; cf. these lines spoken by a narrator describing his
flight from Portugal:

> A las estrellas subian
> Y subiedas abaxavan
> A la tierra.
> . . . .
> En creçiendo la tormenta
> El marinero no sabe
> Que azer. (No. 5)

physical movement. She also comments upon the fact that events in life do not occur in a schematic fashion:

> porque escreuer algũa cousa pede alto repouso, e a mi as minhas magoas oras me leuã para hum cabo oras para outro e trazẽme assi que me he forçado tomar as palauras que me ellas dam . . . , das tristezas nam se pode contar nada ordenadamente: por que desor-denadamente acõtecem ellas . . . (7)

Isea mentions the matter twice, at the opening and at the close of the novel: ". . . [el libro] no lleva estilo, ni orden" (433a), and ". . . no uso mas estilo de aquel que mi desventurado y triste hado me enseñó" (467b). In his introductory poem Reinoso also begs forgiveness for any poetic lapses because of the circumstances under which the verses were composed and because they accurately reveal his internal distress and disorder:

> De las faltas que tenia.
> Y tristezas que sentia
> Es razon no me culpeis.
> Porque quando la escrevia,
> Enfermo y mas descontento
> Sin ningun plazer bivia
> Teniendo por compañia,
> Tristezas y gran tormento.
> . . . .
> Estos tiempos considrad:
> Y ninguna culpa dad,
> A los versos de mi musa.
> . . . .
> Yo triste de males lleno
> De contino affano y peno
> Desseando de morir.   (No. 1)

Later Reinoso reemphasizes the correspondence between life and work, when in a manner analogous to Isea's initial statement, he identifies himself to Feliciano de Silva as "Reinoso el sin plazer sin alegria / Que bive ausente assi de su mudança," adding that "Es la vida que bivo muerta vida / Y aquesta Elegia llena de borrones / No va limada ni menos polida" (No. 15).

As has been indicated, Núñez de Reinoso changed the focus, in his adaptation of Tatius's novel, so that he might make Isea the central figure and stress her misfortune and melancholy. Not only does the book open with her words, but she also reintroduces herself and explains her pertinence to the plot when she enters the action in the place appropriate to her involvement in the loves of Clareo Y Florisea. Such was not the case in Tatius's work, where Melitte (Isea) is first introduced indirectly: i.e., we hear that she has been pursuing Clitophon (Clareo) before we actually meet her. In Reinoso's work, sadness is always emphasized when Isea is present. Accordingly, at the beginning of the book, she views her past, present, and future as unhappy: ". . . que hallándose en tan triste tiempo, aun el que vendré será peor, y todas mis cosas como las pasadas han sido" (433a). She repeats this thought when she reappears in Chapter VIII: "¡Oh triste de mí! ¡Qué triste era yo! Y triste busqué, y triste vivo, y triste viviré siempre" (436b). Like the narrator in *Menina e moça*, Isea yearns for death to put an end to her suffering:

Núñez de Reinoso	Ribeiro
. . . *mis trabajos, los cuales no quiero yo que en esta tierra tengan remedio, porque ansi no se detenga la muerte de mí tan deseada.* (468a)	. . . *nẽ remedio nẽ cõforto ouue ahi. Para morrer, azinha me pudera ysto aproueytar* . . . (7)

Often Isea complains of her survival; part of the following example is in imitation of Ovid, although its often-repeated last line is used in a reverse sense:

Núñez de Reinoso	Ovid
¡Oh triste de mí, y quién nunca partiera de aquella tierra, ó ya que partia muriera ahogada en la brava y alta mar, y fuera tragada y comida de los peces della . . . (444a)	Nec letum timeo: . . . . . . , mors mihi munus erit. . . . . In solida moriens ponere corpus humo: Et mandare suis aliquid, sperare sepulcra, Et non aequoreis piscibus esse cibum. (I-2, 51-52, 54-56)

Tears and Laments

Accompanying Isea's laments are torrents of tears. Tears are a normal component of the sentimental novel; indeed, Fiammetta's outbursts are always accompanied by tears: ". . . li dilicati visi con lagrime bagnerete, le quali a me, che altro non cerco, di dolore perpetuo sieno cagione" (3). Accordingly, early in the book Isea comments, ". . . solo conmigo lloraba mi gran pena y trabajo, sin tener otra compañía mas que la de mis lágrimas" (436b). And resorting to the common medieval device, a dream sequence,[5] for exploring the psyche of a fictional

---

5. There is a dream sequence in *La Fiammetta,* wherein the heroine imagines herself to be in a meadow, the typical *locus amoenus,* where she is bitten by a serpent—and the beautiful, sunlit day turns dark. The episode serves, 1) as a premonition of her capitulation to unbridled passion; and 2) as a reminder to the reader that carnal sin caused the fall of Adam and Eve and their expulsion from the Garden of Eden and brought the first Christian Golden Age to an end.

character, Reinoso permits Isea to describe her lachry-
mose condition in terms of an Ovidian metamorphosis:

> Y aquella noche dormimos en el campo, riberas de
> un manso arroyo, que por debajo de un sombrío
> arboreado pasaba . . . y parecíame después que me
> mudaban en aquellos árboles que dicen Júpiter haber
> mudado á las hermanas de Faeton, cuando lloraban
> riberas del rio Eridamo [sic], las cuales están siempre
> allí vertiendo vivas lágrimas. (464a)

As in the dream, Isea can be found in the typical
pastoral landscape where she lets loose her flood of tears.
She finds the bucolic setting suitable for exhibiting her
unhappiness; the natural world, at least, responds to her
tears: ". . . mis tristes lágrimas ablandaron y enter-
necieron las duras piedras" (433a). In the contemporary
work so analogous to that of Reinoso, Usque's *Consolaçam*, Ycabo begins his lament with a comment on
the appropriateness of the natural setting for the expression of his grief:

> Conveniente lugar pera chorar meus males, e sobir
> ao derradeiro çeu meus gimidos. Vos outros soos
> aruores, e mansas agoas, despostas ame ouuir, ouui,
> e doeiuos de minhas lastimas: dessalesçidos espiritos,
> lassos equebrantados membros, graue peso de soster,
> esforçaiuos: olhos cansados da jaa tam seca vea soltai
> mil a mil lagrimas de sangue . . . (I, i-r)

Seeking refuge from the troubled world, Isea, at her
journey's end, finds the perfect place:

> . . . aporté una mañana á una tierra que la ínsula
> Pastoril tenia por nombre . . . aporté á unos valles
> sombríos, á los cuales unas altas sierras cercaban, y

dellas claras aguas corrian, y los valles eran todos
llenos de altos árboles, debajo de los cuales pasaban
unos mansos arroyos y habia muchas fuentes que de
verdes y floridas ramas estaban cubiertas y de blancas
pedrezuelas ornadas. (467a)

. . . aporté á un hermoso y deleitoso prado, ornado
de gran copia de flores, entre las cuales estaba mezclada
una ordenada compañía de árboles y de plantas; los
árboles eran espesos, . . . y hacian una hermosa sombra
y cobertura á las flores; hallábanse allí muchos lirios
y rosas y mirtos, debajo de los cuales el agua corria.
(467b)

However, Isea immediately transforms this *locus
amoenus* to conform with what could be termed her own
interior emotional landscape:

Yo, viendo tan deleitoso lugar, acordé de quedarme
allí, haciendo otro prado de mis trabajos, siendo los
árboles mis grandes sospiros, y los arroyos las lágrimas
que de mis ojos salen, y las rosas mis penas, y las flores
mis cuidados, y las sombras mis tristezas, y las yerbas
mis enojos. (467b)

The description is reminiscent of the spot where the
narrator of Ribeiro's *Menina e moça* spends her days:

. . . de aruoredos grandes e verdes eruas e deleitosas
sombras cheo he, por onde hum pequeno ribeiro de
aguoa de todo año . . . onde eu vou muitas vezes
deixar as minhas lágrimas . . . (9-10)

Usque's Ycabo, too, speaks of adding his tears to the
waters of rivers:

O mundo mundo, jaa que tuas racionaes creaturas

nam consentes se doiam de minhas tribulações e
lazeiras, se nas insensiueis influirom os çeos algum
modo secreto de piadade, daa liçença aos rios . . . com
manso e lamentoso roido, acompanhem o cõtinuo
cursso de minhas lagrimas . . . (I, ii-r)

Rivers, then, are an essential feature of the pastoral
landscape where Isea, Ycabo and others tearfully utter
their laments. In his article "¿Melancolía renacentista o
melancolía judía?" Bataillon has suggested the relationship between the shedding of tears that swell the waters
and the Twenty-third Psalm ("Super flumina Babylonis")
as a manifestation of what he calls the "multisecular
herencia de la melancolía del pueblo judío, criado en la
amargura del destierro. . . ."[6] Although Avalle-Arce
dismisses Bataillon's theory, ". . . creo no hay que hacer
hincapié en el judaísmo de Montemayor, en especial en
lo que se refiere a la concepción de su novela pastoril,"[7]
it would seem that Núñez de Reinoso's novel is yet
another example of the type of Peninsular literature
whose melancholic tone separates it from the pastoral
works of other nations. Since the concluding chapter of
this study will demonstate the almost simultaneous development of two different tendencies within the *genre*,
at the moment suffice it to say that the evidence at hand—
Isea's weeping into brooks and rivers, indeed, her dream
of being changed into a poplar forever rooted to the
riverbank and shedding tears into its waters—links
Reinoso's work with other Hispanic pastorals exhibiting
Diasporic discontent.

Reinoso's novel could have been entitled "El llanto

6. *Estudios hispánicos. Homenaje a Archer M. Huntington,* Wellesley,
1952, pp. 39–50.
7. *La novela pastoril,* pp. 58–59.

de Isea." It is literature of exile. As such it bears correspondence to those Biblical works written when the
people of Israel were held captive in Babylon. Isea seems
to have been modeled upon the figure of the "Viuda
Israel" from Lamentations, who is "vuelta muy descon-
solada, cargada de luto . . . llorando a la continua su
gran desdicha. . . ."[8] Isea early identifies herself as a
widow and a foreigner:

> . . . me viese tan presto viuda; siendo tan moza y de
> pequeña edad, con gran pena podia sufrir mi nueva
> y triste adversidad; y como fuese estranjera, sola
> conmigo lloraba mi gran pena y trabajo, sin tener otra
> compañía mas que la de mis lágrimas y continuos
> suspiros . . . (436b)

Commenting upon her widowhood and exile, she com-
pares herself to the turtledove of the old *romance,* "Fonte
frida": ". . . parece que me convertian en tórtula,
diciendo: 'tu vida será siempre como es la desta sin
ventura ave, la cual viéndose viuda no posa en ramo
verde'" (464a).[9] The resemblance to the widow Israel
of "Las lágrimas de Jeremías" (Lamentations) is not
accidental. In the poem purportedly written by "Thomas
Gomez," the narrator make note of Núñez de Reinoso's
unhappy frame of mind during his Italian exile; and
after observing that Reinoso cannot eat, but rises from
the table midway through a meal, cannot sleep, and
avoids company, Gómez chastizes Reinoso for his constant complaints:

---

8. *La Sacra Biblia.*
9. The subject of the *romance* is the inconsolable turtledove's faithful-
ness to the memory of her dead mate; her self-imposed mourning is
stressed.

De vuestras penas y males
Escrivis noches y dias
Y las pintais mas mortales
Que el planto de Ieremias. (No. 11)

Now while Joseph Gillet observes that "reference to Jeremiah in poetical *lamentaciones* seems to be 'de rigueur,'"[10] Wilson and Blecua, in their introduction to Quevedo's *Lágrimas de Hieremías castellanas,* contend that "casi todas las traducciones españolas de los Trenos [i.e., Lamentations] entre los años 1550-1600 son heterodoxas."[11] Attitudes toward this Biblical book, written during the Babylonian captivity and dealing with the causes of the destruction of the first temple, can be divided into those held by *conversos* who looked upon the work as expressing the grief of the forsaken,[12] and by others, like Quevedo, who assumed that it depicted the suffering justly inflicted upon the people of Israel for their sins.[13] Indeed, in the section called "Aphorismos morales sacados del primer alphabeto de Ieremias," Quevedo equated the Horatian aphorism[14] concerning transference with the perpetual wandering meted out as punishment by God to those of Jewish faith:[15]

---

10. *"Propalladia" and other Works:* III, *Notes,* Pennsylvania, 1951, p. 35.

11. P. xi.

12. Two who could be considered proponents of the *converso* interpretation are Casiodoro de Reina, a Protestant *morisco* who essayed a version of Lamentations in his translation of the Bible (Basilia, 1569), and Cipriano de Valera, whose modified version of the previous Protestant Bible is the text cited in this study (first published in Amsterdam in 1602). Both men are mentioned by Ménéndez Pelayo in *Historia de los heterodoxos españoles,* II.

13. A spokesman for the Catholic point of view was Francisco de Borja, who delivered an ascetic sermon in 1553 directed toward Israel as a sinner (later published by Nieremberg in his *Vida del santo padre Francisco de Borja*).

14. See Chapter 2, n. 36, for a discussion of this aphorism as either Senecan or Horatian.

15. The attitude expressed by Quevedo and others like him coincides with the then contemporary belief in the Wandering Jew (in Spain called

GIMEL

Necio es quien siendo malo y vicioso peregrina por uer si muda con los lugares las costumbres. El que así lo haze está, si peregrina, en otro parte, pero no es otro . . . al que castiga Dios en Ierusalem por malo, también le castigará donde fuere, si lo fuere: y assí es bien mudar de vida y no de sitio.[16]

It is not, therefore, unreasonable to hypothesize that not only translations of Lamentations, but also references to the work itself can be associated with those embroiled in Spain's religio-social struggle.

While Núñez de Reinoso does not explicitly state that he has fashioned the figure of Isea (his fictional self) upon that of the widow Israel, the hint supplied in one of his poems, the structure and tone of his novel, the prevailing preoccupation with Lamentations during his times, and the outline of his life combine to suggest that such was his intent. Like the young widow Israel, Isea sits and weeps and reviews the events that contributed to her present disconsolate state. Her lament is similar to those composed by other contemporary *converso* authors in that it is not one of amatory suffering; rather, like Pleberio—"Del mundo me quexo, porque en sí me crió" (II, 211), like Ycabo—"O mundo pera q̃

"Juan de voto a Dios") as one punished for insulting Christ on the day of his crucifixion. See Bataillon "Nouvelles recherches sur le *Viaje de Turquía,*" *Romance Philology,* V, 1951-1952, pp. 77-97, where he comments: "Juan est celui qui reste ici-bas, qui est condamné à une immortalité vagabonde. . . ." For amplification of this topic as it relates to the *Buscón,* see C. H. Rose, "Pablos' *damnosa heritas,*" *Romanische Forschungen,* LXXXII, 1970.

16. P. 36. Cf. the ending of the *Buscón,* p. 280, ". . . pues nunca mejora su estado quien muda solamenta de lugar, y no de vida y costumbres." Quevedo insinuates that Pablos is a *converso*; his father is a barber, and his mother is called "Aldonza de San Pedro, hija de Diego de San Juan y nieta de Andrés de San Cristóbal," names that recall the one assumed by the converted rabbi of Burgos, Pablo de Santa María. Quevedo further states: "Sospechábase en el pueblo que no era cristiana vieja."

criaste em ti quem tanto auias de aborrecer e engeitar?"
(III, xli-v), and like Fenicio—"voy del mundo muy
quexoso, / porque vn poco de reposo / nunca en él pude
hallar" (364-366), Isea's complaint is directed toward
a hostile society and an indifferent universe. Reinoso,
speaking in his own right, gives vent to his outrage against
a world that has no place in it for him:

> *Por qué, dime, traydor mundo engañoso,*
> *En qué para todo lo que tú vendes*
> . . . .
> *Por qué, o mundo falso, nos offendeses*
> *O mundo, manjar de duros gusanos,*
> *Y di por qué no sueltas los que prendes.*
> . . . .
> *Por lo qual te quiero ya dexar*
> *Llorando de mis ojos, cara el çielo,*
> *Y a Dios todas mis culpas confessar. (No. 16)*

Pastoral Ambivalence

The Ínsula Pastoril, to which Isea has retired, does
not offer her true consolation, does not relieve her
melancholy, for she is in exile. In the harmonious setting
only her grief is out of order. The impediment to internal
peace is memory, which she is not able, indeed, does not
try to still. She is given the opportunity to erase the
past, but unlike the shepherds in Montemayor's *Diana*,
who willingly accept Felicia's curative "agua de olvido,"
Isea rejects the remedy:[17]

---

17. In the *Diana,* the drinking of the water that obliterates memory
makes possible new amorous alliances based on more practical criteria
such as correspondence, proximity, etc. In *Clareo y Florisea,* Isea does
not bathe in the water because she is unwilling to relinquish her memory
of the "gran Señor" (Gracia Nasi, Reinoso's Jewish patroness). Is it
possible that this magic water is a symbol for baptism, that Isea is

. . . un rio que del Olvido se llamaba, porque quien
bebia de aquellas aguas, luego se olvidaba de todas las
cosas pasadas, sin de ninguna tener memoria. Y siendo
así llegados, aquel gran sabio dijo que allí estaba
nuestro remedio, si lo queriamos tomar . . . Yo, viendo
el gran bien que de aquello se me seguia, porque en
las cosas sin esperanza y sin ningun remedio, el
olvidallas es la propia medicina, quise beber de aquellas
aguas leteas; pero por otra parte, pareciéndome que si
dellas bebia, que me habia de olvidar de las grandes
mercedes y beneficios recebidos de aquel gran señor
de Egipto, no lo quise hacer . . . (465b)

In his pastoral eclogue, Reinoso depicts a scene in which
an end to suffering is similarly declined. Baltheo comes
upon a group of shepherds and shepherdesses, former
friends, who chorus: "En las cosas sin remedio / El
olvido es mejor medio." At first he mutters to himself,
"Yo no supe que juzgar / Y dixe no puede aver / En mi
olvido." But he is sorely tempted. However, he resolves
to leave the country ("Acordé de me passar / A los
Alpes de Alemaña / A bivir") like ". . . los que desaman /
El remedio a sus dolores" (No. 5). For Reinoso, it
would seem, suffering and exile are preferable to denying
one's past.

---

unwilling to change her faith, but Montemayor's characters are willing,
and do so? Sireno, as a result of this conversion, is left in an "anes-
thetized" state so that he feels nothing in the presence of his former
love, Diana, but can form no new attachments; his condition suggests
the state of mind of those *conversos* who had left one religion but were
unable to embrace another. Similarly, in Feliciano de Silva's *Amadís de
Grecia,* the hero and company come to the river "Olvido" and observe
those immersed in the water who "con el favor olvidaron el conocimiento
que a Dios debian." They are subsequently denied entrance to a palace
they wish to enter until the knight is able to prove his "limpieza." In
her supplement to a work by Patch (*El otro mundo en la literatura medieval,* trad. de J. Hernández Campos, Buenos Aires, 1956), María Rosa
Lida remarks, "La escena tiene un fuerte carácter de parodia sacropro-
fana," p. 415. Indeed, the scene did not escape the eye of the censor and
it was suppressed in the 1586 edition.

While the pastoral world does not release Isea from her sorrows, it does offer her temporary refuge from her troubles. For it is a static world where men are not subject to the mutations of fortune. There are no actions, no events, that take place in the bucolic setting. All action governed by fortune has taken place in the past and has led up to Isea's profoundly unhappy condition. If Isea were willing or able to forget, she might be content to dwell on the Ínsula Pastoril, for her period of persecution is over. Her description of country life emphasizes its peacefulness as harmonizing with the natural setting:

> Habia por aquellos valles muchos pastores, que tañendo sus flautas rodeaban sus ganados, sin de otra cosa ninguna tener cuidado, mas que de levantarse cuando el sol salia, y guardar sus ovejas, y pasar el dia en honestos ejercicios; y, venida la noche, . . . comiendo de aquellos sus pastoriles manjares, y después recogerse en sus cabañas. . . . (467a)

And in a prose reworking of Horace's ode "Beatus ille qui procul negotiis," she catalogues the joys of the bucolic life:[18]

> ¡Oh bienaventurados y venturosos pastores, á los cuales cupo por suerte tan venturosa y sosegada vida; . . . os podeis llamar dichosos y bienaventurados, pues tan dulce y sosegadamente en estos valles vivís . . . ! ¡Oh cuán dulces y mas sobrosas os son aquí á vosotros las claras y naturales aguas . . . ¡Oh cuán de mejor sabor es aquí la fresca y blanca leche . . . cuán mas suave olor os es este, que destas flores nace, . . . cuán mas dulce y alegremente canta aquí un pájaro de su

---

18. "Trozo es éste que no me parece muy inferior al celebrado discurso de don Quijote sobre la edad de oro." Menéndez Pelayo, *Orígenes,* II, p. 79.

natural, ... cuán mayor contento recebís aquí vosotros,
metidos en la pastoril cabaña ... ! (467b)

Employing the same formula as Reinoso, that outlined
in the manuals of rhetoric available to Renaissance
authors, Usque, too, eulogizes the pastoral world:

Ora assi viçosamente passando a fresca manhãa:
quando jaa o Sol e sua seca calma embebido auia nas
verdes eruas o orualho, se abalauão e punhã en camiñho
com o rebañho de suas mãsas ouelhas, a busquar as
deleitosas sombras, onde a fresca e tẽperada viração os
recrease: e laa ao cabo de hũ alegre vale hum fermoso
e muy basto aruoredo os recebia, regado e viçoso coas
doces agoas dhũa fonte que ao pee dhũ altissmo
acipreste a borbolhões e con alegria rebentaua. . . .
(I, iv-r—v)

He then summarizes the activities of a typical Virgilian
day: the shepherds rest from their chores at noon, playing flutes, wrestling, dozing, while birds sing; at night
they gather their flocks, return contented to their simple
cottages, and peacefully sleep. Usque, however, equates
the classical Golden Age to the idyllic life in the land of
Canaan. He devotes a chapter to explaining the significance of what he calls "esta ydade douro, debaxo do
cajado do summo pastor" (I, vi-v). The land of Canaan
was God's gift to man, a terrestrial paradise, leading to
the Garden of Eden, a portent of heavenly bliss:

... bẽ auenturados os que com suor de suas palmas
comem seu pam ... Eram as deleitosas sombras que
sentiam jaa da bem auenturança celeste: Esta era
afresca e tẽperada viraçam q̃ a alma de contentamento
recreaua; Estes os sóbrios e alegres vales onde vi-
çosamete pasciã e ocupauam seu tẽpo. . . . E gozando

daquelle verdadeiro mel, rezente e branco leite de
doçura e deleite sem fim nem termo, pasto dos justos,
fruto e mantimento da quella mais certa terra santa,
Propia naturaleza e erãça dos filhos de Ysrael, e do
treslado desta caa baixo, verdadeiro original. . . . Esta
era aarmonia dos namorados e musicos rufinoes, das
gentis melroas, dos outros graciosos pasarinhos, alta
melodia, diuinas Proporções, . . . Estes os frescos ares,
os apraziueis e verdes campos, os graciosos e felices
vales, onde as ouelhas e seus pastores sahiam, . . .
Estahe a fermosa varzia . . . que tee o *orto de deleite*
. . . dereita se estendia. . . . (I, x-r-xi-r; italics mine)[19]

But the children of Canaan sinned and turned away
from God who punished them by scattering them throughout the World:

Lançarteha o señor entre todolos pouos do cabo da
terra a te o fim da terra, e seruiras aly outros deuses
que nam conhecias tu nem teus padres, ec. e entre
aquellas gentes nam descansaras, nem sera repouso A
planta de teu pee, mas aly te dara o señor continua
ynquietud no coraçam, e os olhos sumidos e tristeza
nalma. (III, lvii-r)[20]

Usque states that Moses's prophecy has been fulfilled
because Spain and Portugal are at the ends of the earth:[21]

. . . e sobre todalas outras ja padecidas estas vas tãbẽ
agora vltimamente padecendo na ynquisiçam de

19. The English translator, M. A. Cohen, subtitles the section called
"Origẽ de Ysrael e fabrica do templo," "The Explanation of the Metaphor
Entitled 'Pastoral Life.'"
20. The fulfillment of the prophecy from Deuteronomy is the crux of
Usque's argument; he likens the apostasy of Spanish and Portuguese
conversos to the worshiping of false gods, a repetition of the transgres-
sions that caused the original expulsion from Canaan.
21. Cf. Núñez de Reinoso's statement: ". . . Y así comencé de caminar
acia el fin de Europa, porque allí queria descansar. . . . Y ansí habiendo
caminado mas de un año aporté en una ciudad de España." (466b)

Espanha e Portugal que he dito fim da terra (e de feito o he) õde elle disse que se auiam de comprir.
(III, lvii-v)

And Usque concludes that the time for the return is at hand. An early Zionist,[22] he believed that God would punish the enemies of Judah and would restore the faithful to the land where they would once more pursue the idyllic pastoral existence:

> Guay dos pastores das gentes que perdem e desbaratam o rabanho do meu pasto que he ysrael diz o Señor pastores q̃ mal pascem o pouo meu . . . ; e apanharei as reliquias de meu rabanho de todalas terras onde os lancey; e tornalas ey a trazer a seus pastos viçosos que sohiam ter . . . De maneira que farey tornar os catiuos do meu pouo ysrael e yehuda ha terra que dey a seus padres e posuyla am. (III, lxi-r-v)

Consoled by the words of Numeo and Zicareo, Ycabo accepts the remedy proffered by the divine healer, God:

> E pois assi he ja agora qu todas minhas chagas vos ey mostrado, e com tam preciosos ynguentos as vntastes, peçouos que as acabeis de curar com particulares nouas se as trazeis da calidade que minha verdadeira meizinha ha de ter, e quando aquella tam desejada ora arribar que bẽs sam os que ey de possuyr cujos effeitos espero que tanto e mais descubertos am de ser ao mundo e a mi, quanto estes que conmigo vsa o señor ao presente lhe sam escuros. (III, lvii-v-lviii-r)

> Celestes sam as palauras que ouuẽ minhas orelhas yndinas, e bem parece ser mensage dos ceeos porque como eccelente triaga quanto veneno ate este tempo auia englutido a matou. (III, lxii-r-v)

---

22. Usque's patrons, Gracia and Joseph Nasi, did establish a homeland in Tiberias.

Ycabo leaves his rural retreat, the *locus amoenus* that he had found appropriate for uttering his lament—appropriate because of the solitude, the sympathetic natural environment, the rivers that he could flood with his tears, and, perhaps, the solace supplied to his troubled soul by the vestigial memory of the perfect pastoral land of his ancestors, the land of Canaan. With renewed faith he leaves for the Promised Land.

But Alonso Núñez de Reinoso was not sustained by a firm faith, as was Samuel Usque; he could envision no land of permanent peace. His Isea may yearn for the pastoral life, but it is for others, not for her. In such a setting, she is a figure apart; in solitude she sits and weeps. Resentful and bewildered, she allows her mind to dwell on the ills that afflict society. Turning from her panegyric of country life where simple shepherds enjoy the fruits of nature without perverting her gifts in pursuit of material gain, Isea transforms the usual negative litany[23] into an indictment of the inverted system of values of what would seem to be Reinoso's homeland:

> . . . sin tener cuenta con las cortes de los altos
> príncipes y poderosos señores, ni de sus mudables
> favores, . . . no les dando pena la hambre grande,
> que los que sirven á los señores de privar tienen, ni
> menos trabajo las galas de la agracida y superba dama,
> ni las mudanzas que en sus favores suele haber. No les
> quitaba el sueño si los [sic] naos cargadas de merca-
> dería . . . se podrian perder, ni si los bancos gruesos y

---

23. There is a lengthy discourse on the Golden Age, including the standard negative litany, in *La Fiammetta*. The speech begins: "Oh felice colui, il quale innocente dimora nella solitaria villa, usando l'aperto cielo" (130ff.), in which Fiammetta contrasts the corruption of the city with the innocence of the country and equates life in the spatial pastoral landscape (the *locus amoenus*) to the temporal pastoral age before the reign of Jupiter.

de gran crédito, quebrarian, . . . No temian que los
príncipes los arruinasen, ni de todo destruyesen; no les
daba pena sufrir aquellos, á quien los oficios hace malos
y contrarios a toda virtud; no les daba cuidado el con-
quistar reinos, adquirir ciudades, vencer batallas, de-
sear señoríos, querer mander, buscar las Indias, servir
al mundo, perder la vida, destruir el alma. (467 a-b)

Isea does not look forward to a return to Byzantium;
she looks back toward Spain. She foresees no solution
to her problems, no end to her suffering; she even rejects
any remedy: "los cuales [trabajos] no quiero yo que en
esta tierra tengan remedio" (468a). Her closing remark
shows her concerned with vindicating her reputation in
Reinoso's Spain: "Bien sé que si esta mi obra en algun
tiempo aportare á las riberas del rio Henares, que
piadosamente será leida, y mis penas sentidas y con
razon lloradas" (468a). Before the pastoral landscape,
Isea exhibits that Peninsular reaction of "soledad," for
what she sees directly before her eyes only serves to fill
her with nostalgia for the land she has left or lost. This
feeling, "soledad," is more clearly displayed in the poetry.
At first Reinoso, in autobiographical fashion, declares
that he willingly abandoned family and country and
attached himself to the wandering household of his
patroness in order to devote himself to the task of
writing:

> Que si las musas amar
> Que si mi tiempo perder
> Fueron causar de buscar
> Quien me quiso vida dar
> Y por suyo me tener
> Yo doy por bien empleado
> El gastar mi tiempo mal,

Y lo doy por bien gastado,
Y tengo por bien dexado
A mi padre y natural.
(No. 1; emphasis mine)

However, he does have regrets; he misses Spain:

Soledad de España siento
. . . .
Aqui en esta çiudad
Adonde peno en ausençia
Y muero con soledad. (No. 2)

And just as the exiled Reinoso writes from Italy, "Grito, peno, lloro, clamo, / Y por mis amigos llamo" (No. 2), from her pastoral retreat Isea cries out

¡Oh triste de mí, y quién nunca partiera de aquella tierra, . . . y no haberme venido á vivir en aquestos valles, adonde á todas horas lloro, á todas horas sospiro, á todas horas peno, á todas horas me quejo, á todas horas muero, á todas horas cuido, á todas horas grito, á todas horas rompo con sospiros los cielos, los valles y montes, y ablando las peñas, detengo los ganados, y espanto á los pastores, y ningun remedio hallo! (444a)

Such is the dilemma of the Spanish *converso,* Alonso Núñez de Reinoso. He could not accept the remedy offered by man nor could he foresee one proffered by God. By converting and conforming he would annihilate the past. Yet if ancient loyalties caused him to accept exile, his was a dual heritage and he could not deny the country that had forsaken him or that he had forsaken. Indeed, he counsels fellow *conversos* ("otras Iseas") to stay in Spain; Isea, he says, demonstrates "quan bien

estan los hõbres en sus tierras, sin buscar a las agenas"
(5). Immobilized by conflicting sentiments, Reinoso was
an exile in a total sense, spiritually and socially, as well
as geographically. And so he composed a lament without
end; feeling herself abandoned by God and by man, his
Isea sits and weeps "in hac lachrymarum valle."

CONCLUDING REMARKS

Yo deviera de bivir,
. . . .
Y tener el pensamiento
Sossegado en escrevir
(No. 1)

Que las letras den sossiego,
Ninguno ay que no diga.
(No. 15)

Núñez de Reinoso's voice was not the only one lifted in lament. His work is of interest precisely for its relevance to that of other Peninsular exiles of the period. As previously indicated, his novel most closely resembles Usque's *Consolaçam*; each is an exile's lament uttered in a pastoral setting and consisting of a retrospective catalogue of woes. Or to transcribe Reinoso's achievement in terms of the developing novelistic *genre, Clareo y Florisea* is primarily a Byzantine tale[1]

---

1. For the present study the chivalric portion of Reinoso's novel is unimportant because of 1. the impenetrability of its allegory other than the interpretation postulated, that it deals with events in the life of Feliciano de Silva, 2. its lack of generic novelty, and 3. its thematic repetitiveness—i.e., it depicts Isea as *errante,* wandering, thus duplicating her situation in the Byzantine portion.

set in a pastoral framework. And while Reinoso was neither an isolated phenomenon nor a precursor, an examination of his work is valuable for illuminating the factors that led him to select certain fictional forms for the telling of his sad tale.

The Pastoral

In Chapter 4 I indicated that his choice of the pastoral for expressing his anguish was shared by others of his condition, fellow *conversos* who sought refuge from the vicissitudes of life in the melancholic recreation of a static land free from the mutations of fortune, fellow exiles who considered their situation somewhat analogous to that endured by the Israelites during the Babylonian captivity. Like Usque, Ribeiro, and Montemayor, Reinoso found a brief measure of relief from his troubles through the creation of a sympathetic natural world where one might weepingly record the causes of one's grief. But unlike the zealous Usque, Reinoso, a confused *converso,* could foresee no return to a terrestrial paradise, no renascent Golden Age. Rather, Núñez de Reinoso transforms the *locus amoenus* into a vale of tears.

Peninsular pastoral made its debut almost simultaneously in two different locations. However, the poetic production of Núñez de Reinoso and his friends would seem to antedate that of Garcilaso by a few years. In Chapter 2 I spoke of Ribeiro's Italian sojourn (1522-24), his return to Portugal and retirement to the Basto, where, until 1536, he, Sá de Miranda, and Núñez de Reinoso engaged in the writing of pastoral eclogues. Their chief concern was in transmuting their emotional life into poetry. Desirous of imparting their *Welt-*

schmerz, they made use of the pastoral eclogue to conceal contemporary events and identifiable people. Subjective content rather than objective form was of paramount interest to these bards. It is significant that they were not metrical innovators. Ribeiro's eclogues are in traditional meters; Sá de Miranda did not essay the hendecasyllable until his contact with Garcilaso;[2] Núñez de Reinoso, until his residence in Italy.[3] They looked upon pastoral poetry as a vessel for the outpouring of their grief or their bitter dissatisfaction with the society from which they had fled. The bucolic world they created represented a poetic retreat in the here and now, where they could enjoy some respite from their torment.

A further contribution by this Hispano-Lusitanian group to Peninsular *belles lettres* was the creation of the indigenous pastoral novel, with its prevailing melancholic tone, whose tentative beginnings can be seen in *Menina e moça,* probably written before 1536. The climactic moment, when fortune seemed to smile on these authors, was also the final phase; the decade of the 1550s opened with the publication of Núñez de Reinoso's work in 1552, followed by Usque's in 1553 and Ribeiro's in 1554, and

---

2. Sá de Miranda's eclogue entitled "Nemoroso," written in hendecasyllables, is thought to have been composed on the first anniversary of Garcilaso's death. Doña Carolina remarks, "É possivel que Miranda tratasse, durante as suas viagens, com Boscan e Garcelaso, e se declarasse, tambem por influencia de Andrea Navagiero, e ao mesmo tempo que os visinhos hespanhoes, pelas novas formas italianas." She goes on to suggest possible points of contact between the poets. Vasconcelos, *Obras,* pp. 831–32.

3. Núñez de Reinoso acknowledges essaying the hendecasyllable while still in Spain, when he writes to Juan Hurtado de Mendoza: ". . . algunos versos que van escritos al estilo italiano, tienen y llevan la misma falta que vuestra merced les solia hallar" (432). However, the few examples of his venture into Italian verse form that remain to us were clearly written from Italy, as two are letters to friends at home in Spain and the third is a gloss of some lines from Ariosto, who was, it must be remembered, connected with the court at Ferrara.

closed with the appearance of Montemayor's *Diana* in 1559. And just as it had been the source of formal inspiration, Italy, with possibly one exception, was the land where each work was printed.[4] With the death of Montemayor in Italy in 1561, this literary movement came to an end; the lamenting voice of the exiled Peninsular *converso* ceased to be heard.

Conversely, other Peninsular practitioners of the pastoral, submerged in an international atmosphere of more purely aesthetic ideals, emphasized the formal aspects; for example, in his "Égloga primera" Garcilaso utilized the Virgilian eclogue together with Italian metrics and versification to elevate and dignify Spanish poetry. The successful solution to the aesthetic problem of synthesizing art and nature may be illustrated by his "Égloga tercera." The pastoral subsequently entered the domain of the preceptors. In his *Galatea* Cervantes was to invoke the Golden Age *topos* as an example of creativity; he visualized a land of perpetual spring where

> . . . la industria de sus moradores he hecho tanto, que la *Naturaleza*, incorporada con el Arte, es hecha artífice y connatural del Arte, y de entrambas a dos se ha hecho una *tercia Naturaleza*, a la qual no sabré dar nombre.[5]

The idea of the pastoral world as resulting from the union of art and nature, the concept of the shepherd-poet as the creator of a supranatural region ("tercia natu-

---

4. The first edition of the *Diana* is thought to be that printed in Valencia; there is an early Italian edition (Milan) without date; but it is probably the second printing, for Montemayor in his dedication says of his novel: "Ella salio a luz en España (a ruego de algunas Damas y Cavalleros, que yo deseava complazer").

5. Edition of Schevill and Bonilla, *Obras completas de Miguel de Cervantes Saavedra*, Madrid, 1914, II, pp. 188–89.

raleza"), a fictional, yet earthly Golden Land, was articulated by Sir Philip Sidney:

> Only the poet . . . lifted up with the vigour of his own *invention*, doth grow, in effect, into *another nature*, . . . so as he goeth hand in hand with Nature. . . . Nature never set forth the earth in so rich tapestry as divers poets have done; neither with pleasant rivers, fruitful trees, sweet-smelling flowers, nor whatsoever else may make the too-much-loved earth more lovely; her world is brazen, the poets only deliver a *golden*.[6]

Another demonstrable difference between the two literary streams is that there is a chronological gap of almost thirty years that separates pastoral poetry from similar prose fiction in the creation-conscious group; whereas, among Núñez de Reinoso and his friends, eclogue and novel had appeared simultaneously. The popularity of the *Diana* caused it to be viewed as the archetypal pastoral novel and the plethora of pastoral romances in the second half of the sixteenth century can be seen as further elaborations on Montemayor's work, but neither inspiration, tone, nor aim was the same for the post-Tridentine pastoral where literary form took precedence over subjective matter. With the ascension of Felipe II to the throne in 1556, followed by all the repressive measures that the years 1558 and 1559 imply—the Index, prohibition of foreign study, and the first statutes of *limpieza de sangre,* all hopes were extinguished. When a cure for Spain's religio-social ills was no longer possible, it was useless to examine the patient, useless to divulge the symptoms. And so literature took on a different tone; gone was the melancholy, gone the desire to communicate

---

6. *Defense of Poesie,* 1583 (?), published posthumously in 1595.

personal anguish. Those who remained in Spain were a different breed from "los que desaman el remedio." The period of the exile's lament had come to an end.

The Byzantine Novel

Núñez de Reinoso's selection of Dolce's *Ragionmenti* as a means of setting forth his continuously assailed state perhaps helps to explain the popularity of the Byzantine novel among Spanish Erasmians, many of whom were *conversos*. Hitherto, critics have limited their explanation of the rising interest in this fictional form to strictly literary considerations, paying scant attention to the socio-historical circumstances.

Bataillon focuses his attention on the *genre* for its potential as a justification for the existence of imaginative literature, a solution made possible through the discoveries of this period of intellectual exploration, the Revival of Learning. Therefore, he underscores Erasmian concern with verisimilitude and intellectual substance as an antidote to the "mentirosímos" chivalric romances:

> Esta novela [bizantina] les agrada por mil cualidades que faltan demasiado a la literatura caballeresca; verosimiltud, verdad psicológica, ingeniosidad de la composición, sustancia filosófica, respeto de la moral.[7]

On the other hand, López Estrada manifests critical interest in novelistic structure. He has proposed that the Byzantine tale

ofreció un camino para ayudar a la creación de un

---

7. *Erasmo y España*, traducción de Antonio Alatorre, México, 1966, p. 622.

> nuevo sentido del relato de ficción, diferente de los caballerescos y aun de los sentimentales, más complejo que la novela italiana . . .[8]

and that in addition to offering ways of complicating the simple plot development of the Italian *novella,* it provided the necessary means of transforming the pastoral eclogue into prose. However, Sannazzaro had already written the *Arcadia* (1502) and Peninsular authors, such as Silva and Ribeiro, had essayed the proto-pastoral in prose before the diffusion of the Byzantine novel in Europe. With the discovery of Heliodorus' manuscript in 1533, the Latin edition of 1534, and its subsequent translations into various European languages, beginning with Amyot's work in 1547,[9] it is obvious that it was chronologically impossible for the Greek romance to have had any stylistic influence on the early pastoral novel. López Estrada's remarks would seem to be more applicable to the second stage of development of the *genre,* its post-Tridentine period.

In addition to the stimulation through the exercise in literary suspense provided by the complex, sinuous plots, and to the re-creation of an adventurous atmosphere corresponding to the excitement generated by the voyages of discovery, the Byzantine novel helped to supply the need for new material to the expanded reading public created by the printing press, and to satisfy the demand for knowledge of far-away places or ancient times in a world of newly discovered temporal and geographical relation-

---

8. Quoted from his introduction to Mena's Spanish translation (1587) of Heliodorus's *Historia etiópica de los amores de Teágenes y Cariclea,* Madrid, 1954, p. xx.

9. It was once again the Giolito press that was responsible for an early Italian translation: *Historia delle cose ethiopiche,* trans. L. Ghini, Giolito, Vinegia, 1556.

ships. The reasons set forth thus far could account for the appeal of the Byzantine novel in general throughout Europe, but do little to explain why it held such interest specifically for Erasmians in Spain. And once more the real impact of the literary potential of the *genre* was delayed to the post-Tridentine period when authors and preceptists alike—Lope, Cervantes, Gracián, and El Pinciano—concerned with literary justification for the epic in prose, or in exploring new forms of prose fiction, invoked the name of Heliodorus.

Erasmian interest in the Byzantine novel in Spain occurred in their years of waning power, after their fall from favor. Francisco de Vergara, brother of the famed Hellenist Juan de Vergara (tutor, incidentally, of Juan de Valdés), died in 1545 before completing his translation of Heliodorus' romance. He seems to have undertaken the task after he was threatened with, and his brother underwent, a lengthy *proceso*.[10] The first completed Spanish edition, Antwerp, 1554, was that of an Erasmian, evidently living in exile and unwilling to reveal his name.[11] Perhaps the early Spanish translators of Heliodorus' *Aethiopica* were drawn to the work for the resemblance it bore to the social situation they shared with a certain portion of potential readers. The Byzantine tale with its thematic insistence on the workings of adverse fortune must have seemed remarkably analogous to the historical predicament in which they found themselves. Peninsular *conversos* could equate their own plight with the problems of those fictional characters who were con-

---

10. In *Erasmo y España,* Bataillon goes into the *proceso* in great detail, pp. 438–70.

11. López Estrada discusses this translation. The volume, printed by the Martín Nucio press the same year that it published the *Lazarillo,* was dedicated to Alonso Enríquez, Abbot of Valladolid and author of *Defensiones pro Erasmo Roterodamo,* a work placed on the Papal Index.

stantly subject to the arbitrary acts of the fickle goddess. The very lack of causality in the fictional events could be likened to the often irrational and absurd functioning of the Office of the Inquisition. In Chapter 3 I indicated that it was the possibility of applying the fortune theme to his own situation that prompted Núñez de Reinoso to make use of the Byzantine tale.

In addition to thematic insistence on the role of fortune, perhaps setting and structure contributed to the suitability of interpreting the Byzantine novel in terms of contemporary events. The Near Eastern locale held special associations for some *conversos*: it not only offered potential refuge to the troubled wanderer of the sixteenth century but also recalled the homeland from which his ancestors had been expelled during the first Diaspora and to which he emotionally longed to return. Such was the case of Núñez de Reinoso's associates, the Nasis and the Usques. Also the *anagnorisis*, characteristic of the *genre*, could be looked upon as supplying the longed-for solution to the *converso* problem in that recognition of being and worth prophesied a favorable future. The resultant triumph over fortune could be viewed both as a consolation and an inspiration to those for whom enforced travel or the threat of exile had become a way of life. The appeal of the Byzantine novel to translators and readers alike was that it transmitted a message of hope to a despairing people for whom it depicted fictional characters combating fortune. The reading public could identify with the plight of the hero, agonize over his perils, and rejoice in his victory. His triumph was the substance of their dreams.

Byzantine fiction had its counterpart in life. No novelistic adventures are more incredible than the deeds of

Núñez de Reinoso's patron Juan Micas (Joseph Nasi) who became adviser to the sultan of Turkey and was a legend in his own times. In the seventeenth century, Antonio Enríquez Gómez fled Spain for France, where he was knighted and appointed councillor to the king.[12] Indeed, Enríquez Gómez's dramatization of the *Peregrinaçao* of Fernão Mendes Pinto casts that Portuguese adventurer as a Peninsular exile who has been denied honor in his own country but rises to a position of power in a foreign kingdom.[13] Thus, for two centuries, the dream of many a *converso*, sustained by fact and fiction, was that of finding recognition in a foreign land.

For those *conversos*, however, who did not possess the religious strength of a Juan Micas who openly reverted to Judaism, the Byzantine novel could be seen as a means of merely relating the historical situation, of recounting a life of wandering and personal suffering. As I indicated in Chapter 3, such was the way Núñez de Reinoso employed the *genre* when he dispensed with the usual happy ending. Furthermore, his heroine does not combat fortune, thereby restoring her honor; rather, she flees from country to country as disaster follows upon disaster, forever pursued by adverse fortune. She can find no solace from her actions. Through the life of the unhappy, bewildered Isea, Alonso Núñez de Reinoso sets forth the

12. This assertation on the part of Enríquez Gómez is recorded by Ramón Mesonero Romanos in his introduction to *Dramáticos posteriores a Lope de Vega*, I, Madrid, 1858, p. xxxii. For more recent and more accurate bibliographical information on the life of this author, see I. Révah, "Un Pamphlet contre L'Inquisition d'Antonio Enríquez Gómez: La Seconde Partie de la 'Política Angélica' (Rouen, 1647)," *Revue des études juives* (NS), Ser. 4, I, 1962, pp. 83–168.

13. For elaboration of this theory, see the forthcoming work, *Fernan Mendez Pinto: Comedia Famosa en Dos Partes*, ed. and intro. by Francis M. Rogers, Louise G. Cohen, and Constance H. Rose, where the topic is treated in the section entitled "Enríquez Gómez and the Literature of Exile."

dilemma of the ordinary *converso* to whom greatness of
spirit was lacking and final triumph denied.

The Author

Núñez de Reinoso's work is of importance for what it
reveals of the man. Reinoso offers a number of explana-
tions for the writing of his book. On several occasions
he declares himself to be a lifelong devotee of the muses:

> *Soy amigo de las Musas*
> . . . .
> *Pero a mi entendimiento*
> *Como lo desseo y quiero*
> *Satisfazen segun siento*
> *Las letras que dan contento*
> *Y ser pobre como Homero*
> *Son mas de mi condiçion*
> *A estas solas quería. (No. 15)*

Yet, he was apparently nothing more than an avid dilet-
tante; all his previous endeavors remained unfinished, and
the slim volume published by the Gabriel Giolito de Ferrari press in 1552 hardly testifies to any steadfast dedication on the part of an actively engaged author. And while,
in keeping with literary trends of his times, he promised
a continuation to his novel—"quise poner fin [a esta mi
obra] con propósito de en algun tiempo escrebir la segunda parte" (468a-b)—he seems not to have done so.

According to Reinoso, his book was written to honor
Juan Micas. Both novel and poetry are replete with
presumably sincere vows of devotion to patron and patroness, without whose support the volume could never
have been published in the first place. Reinoso's intention

of proclaiming the greatness of the Nasi family is prophesied in the novel, where Isea and Felisindos arrive at an
Ovidian House of Fame and hear maidens singing. Isea
moves closer to listen to the words of the song:

> . . . y entendí que cantaban la vida y grandezas de
> aquel gran señor de Egipto, en cuya casa yo habia
> estado, y de quien tantas y tan señaladas mercedes habia
> recebido, y holguéme en estremo de oir todas aquellas
> cosas, las cuales yo sabia y hkbia visto. (464b)

While praise for great deeds could be spread by word of
mouth, elevation to the House of Fame could be achieved
only through the celebrative work of a poet. And that
poet is presumably Reinoso himself, because his is the
earliest work to so honor doña Gracia ("el gran señor").
However, at this encomiastic point in the novel, Isea goes
on to bewail her separation from the "gran Señor" and
his household: "acordándoseme de aquella casa, y de la
deuda en que era, hube gran soledad, y pesóme de me
haber partido, no olvidándome jamás" (464b). Thus,
there remains the suggestion that Reinoso's book may
have been written to reingratiate himself with the Nasis,
from whom he had somehow become estranged.

Reinoso also confesses his desire to honor his fellow
poets—[en estas obras de poesía] "se an hallado señalados uarones, y hombres de gran erudicion" (3)—whose
talents he considered greater than his own. But, as Isea
says, ". . . [su libro] cuenta fortunas ajenas, porque mejor
se vea, cuán grandes fueron las mias" (433a). For much
as Reinoso may protest the purpose of his work, the primary justification for its existence rests with its subject
matter, and it is his fictional stand-in, his narrator Isea,
who makes the definitive statement of purpose: first in

order of importance, "esta mi obra, *que solamente para
mí escribo,* es toda triste, como lo soy"; and second, "si
mis grandes tristezas, trabajos y desaventuras por otra
Isea fueron oidas, yo soy cierta que serán no menos lloradas que con razon sentidas" (433a), repeated at the
novel's conclusion, ". . . si esta mi obra en algun tiempo
aportare á las riberas del rio Henares, que piadosamente
será leida, y mis penas sentidas y con razon lloradas"
(468a). While Reinoso (Isea) hopes to arouse the pity
of those with similar troubles who still remain in Spain,
his chief concern is to set forth his suffering, to compose
a journal depicting the hardships endured in exile, and
to distract himself from his *penas.* Isea explains that the
correlative benefit of literary endeavor is to supply the
author with peace of mind: "teniendo mayor necesidad,
en esta vida que paso, de sosiego que de fama ni de loor,
engañando mis trabajos con lo que escribo" (467a), a
thought Núñez de Reinoso repeats in his poetry:

> *Yo deviera de bivir,*
> . . . .
> *Y tener el pensamiento*
> *Sossegado en escrevir. (No. 1)*

> *Que las letras den sosiego,*
> *Ninguno ay que no diga. (No. 15)*

"Sosiego," peace of mind, that elusive state so desired by
Spain's *conversos,* is what Alonso Núñez de Reinoso ultimately hoped to obtain for himself when he sat down
to compose the story of his exile, to create his surrogate
life.

BIBLIOGRAPHY

Ágreda y Vargas, Diego. *Los más fieles amantes, Leucipe y Clitofonte*. Madrid: Iuan de la Cuesta, 1617.

Andrews, James R. *Juan del Encina: Prometheus in Search of Prestige*. Berkeley: University of California Press, 1959.

Antonio, Nicolás. *Bibliotheca Hispana Nova*. I. Madrid, 1783.

Avalle-Arce, Juan Bautista. *La novela pastoril*. Madrid, 1952.

Avendaño, Francisco de. *Comedia Florisea,* 1553. Edited by A. Bonilla y San Martín. *Revue Hispanique,* XXVII (1912), pp. 398–422.

d'Azevedo, Lucio. *História dos Christãos novos portugueses*. Lisboa, 1921.

Balletti, Andrea. *Gli Ebrei e gli Estensi*. Reggio, 1930.

Bataillon, Marcel. *Erasmo y España*. Traducción de Antonio Alatorre. México: Fondo de Cultura Económica, 1966.

———. Introduction to *La vie de Lazarillo de Tormés*. Paris, 1958.

Blecua, José Manuel. (See Quevedo.)

Boccaccio, Giovanni. *La Fiammetta*. Parma, 1800.

Bongi, Salvatore. *Annali di Gabriel Giolito de Ferrari*. Roma, 1890.

Bonilla y San Martín, Antonio. (See Avendaño, Cervantes.)

Braga, Marques. (See Ribeiro.)

Braga, Teófilo. *Renascença*. Lisboa, 1914.

Burckhardt, Jacob. *The Civilization of the Renaissance in Italy*. II. New York, 1958.

Caro Baroja, Julio. *Los judíos en la España moderna y contemporánea*. 3 vols. Madrid, 1962.

Castro, Américo. *"La Celestina" como contienda literaria*. Madrid: Revista de Occidente, 1965.

165

———. *De la edad conflictiva. I. El drama de la honra en España y en su literatura.* Madrid: Taurus, 1961.

———. *España en su historia (Cristianos, moros, y judíos).* Buenos Aires: Losada, 1948.

———. *La realidad histórica de España.* México: Porrúa, 1954.

Catalina García, Juan. *Biblioteca de escritores de la provincia de Guadalajara y Bibliografía de la misma hasta el siglo XIX.* Madrid: Rivadeneyra, 1899.

Cervantes Saavedra, Miguel de. *El ingenioso hidalgo don Quijote de la Mancha.* Edited by Francisco Rodríguez Marín. 7 vols. Madrid, 1927–1928.

———. *Obras completas.* Edited by R. Schevill and A. Bonilla y San Martín. 9 vols. Madrid, 1914–1931.

Clerico, Giuseppe. *Giornale della Biblioteche fondato e diretto da Eugenio Bianchi.* Genova, 1869.

Cohen, Louise G. (See Enríquez Gómez.)

Cohen, Martin A. (See Usque, Samuel.)

Croce, Annibale. *Narrationis amatoriae fragmentum e graeco in latinum conversum, Annibale Cruceio interprete.* Lugduni: S. Gryphium, 1544.

Croce, Benedetto. *La Spagna nella vita italiana durante la Rinascenza.* Bari, 1917.

———. Editor of *Alfabeto Cristiano* by Juan de Valdés. Bari, 1938.

Curtius, Ernst Robert. *European Literature and the Latin Middle Ages.* New York: Bollingen Foundation Inc., by Pantheon Books Inc., New York, 1953.

Diges Antón, Juan, and Sagredo y Martín, Manuel. *Biografías de hijos ilustres de la provincia de Guadalajara.* Guadalajara, 1889.

Dolce, Ludovico. *Amorosi Ragionamenti. Dialogo nel quale si racconta un compassionevole amore di due amanti, tradotto per Ludovico Dolce, dal fragmento d'uno antico Scrittor Greco . . .* Venezia: Gabriel Giolito de Ferrari, 1546.

Domínguez Ortiz, Antonio. *La clase social de los conversos en Castilla en la edad moderna.* Madrid: Consejo Superior de Investigaciones Científicas, 1955.

Enríquez Gómez, Antonio. *La culpa del primer peregrino.* Ruán: Maurry, 1644.

————. *Fernan Mendez Pinto: Comedia Famosa en Dos Partes.* Introduction and edition by F. M. Rogers, L. G. Cohen, and C. H. Rose.

————. *La política angélica.* Ruán: Maurry, 1647. (See Révah, Periodicals . . .)

Gillet, Joseph E. *Propalladia and other Works.* II. *Collected Plays;* III. *Notes;* IV. *Torres Naharro and the Drama of the Renaissance* (Transcribed, edited, and completed by O. H. Green). Pennsylvania: Bryn Mawr, 1946, 1951, 1961.

Gilman, Stephen. *The Art of "La Celestina."* Madison: University of Wisconsin Press, 1956.

Goris, Johannes Albertus. *Les colonies marchandes méridionales à Anvers.* Louvain, 1925.

Green, Otis H. Spain and the Western Tradition. 4 vols. Madison: University of Wisconsin Press, 1962.

————. (See Gillet.)

Guillén, Claudio. Editor of *El Lazarillo de Tormes y El Abencerraje.* New York: Dell Publishing Co., Inc., 1966.

Guimarães, Delfim. *Bernardim Ribeiro (O Poeta Crisfal).* Lisboa, 1908.

Hadas, Moses. *An Ethiopian Romance: Heliodorus.* Introduction and translation. Ann Arbor: University of Michigan Press, 1957.

Hare, Christopher [Mrs. Marian Andrews]. *A Princess of the Italian Reformation: Giulia Gonzaga 1513–1566: Her Family and her Friends.* New York, 1912.

Herculano, Alexandre. *História de origem e estabelecimento da Inquisição em Portugal.* Lisboa, 1867.

[Hurtado de Mendoza, Diego.] *Carta del Bachiller de Arcadia. Sales españoles o Agudezas del ingenio nacional.* Recogidas por A. Paz y Melia. Primera serie. Madrid, 1890.

Hurtado de Mendoza, Juan. *Buen plazer trobado en treze discátes.* Alcalá: Ioan de Brocar, 1550.

Hurtado de Mendoza y Bobadilla, Francisco. *Tizón de la Nobleza.* Edited by A. Luque y Vicens. Madrid, 1849.

[Laguna, Andrés.] *Viaje de Turquía.* (Attributed to Cristóbal de Villalón.) Edited by Manuel Serrano y Sanz. *Autobiografías y memorias.* (N.B.A.E. II.) Madrid, 1905.

Lando, Ortensio. *Dialogo di M. Ortensio Lando nel quale si ragiona della consolatione e utilità, che si riporta leggendo la Sacra Scrittura, e si tratta eziandio dell'ordine da ternersi nel leggerla, mostrandosi esser le Sacre Lettere di vera eloquenza e di varia Dottrina alle Pagane superiori.* Venezia: Segno del Posso, 1552.

————. *Due Panegirici nuovamente composti de quali l'uno é in lode della S. Marchesana della Padulla et l'altro in comendatione della S. donna Lucrezia Gonzaga da Gazuolo.* Venezia: Gabriel Giolito de Ferrari e fratelli, 1552.

————. *Lettere di Lucrezia Gonzaga da Gazuolo con gran diligentia raccolte à gloria del sesso feminile nuovamente in luce posto.* Vinegia: Scotto, 1552.

————. *Sette Libri de Cathaloghi a'varie cose appartenenti, non solo antiche, ma anche moderne: opera utile molto alla historia et da cui prender si po materia di Favellare d'ogni proposito che ci occorra.* Vinegia: Gabriel Giolito de Ferrari e fratelli, 1552.

Lapesa, Rafael. *Historia de la lengua española.* Madrid: M. Escelicer, 1959.

Layna Serrano, Francisco. *Historia de Guadalajara y sus Mendoza en los siglos XV y XVI.* 4 vols. Madrid: Consejo Superior de Investigaciones Científicas, 1942–1943.

Lázaro Carreter, Fernando. (See Quevedo.)

Lewis, C. S. *The Allegory of Love: A Study in Medieval Tradition.* New York: Oxford University Press, Inc., 1958.

Lida, María Rosa. *La visión del trasmundo en las literaturas hispánicas.* Supplement to Spanish translation of Patch, *El otro mundo en la literatura medieval.* Translation by J. Hernández Campos. Buenos Aires, 1956.

López Estrada, Francisco. Introduction to Mena's translation (1587) of Heliodorus's *Historia etiópica de los amores de Teágenes y Cariclea.* Madrid, 1954.

————. (See Montemayor.)

————. (See Villegas.)

López Pinciano, Alonso. *Philosofia antigua poetica.* Edited by A. Carballo Picazo. 3 vols. Madrid: Consejo Superior de Investigaciones Científicas, 1953.

Machiavelli, Niccolo. *El Principe.* Introduction by Federico Chabod. Torino, 1927.

Madrid, Francisco de. (See Petrarca.)

Márquez Villanueva, Francisco. *Investigaciones sobre Juan Álvarez Gato*. Madrid: Academia española, 1960.

Menéndez Pelayo, Marcelino. *Historia de los heterodoxos españoles*. 2 vols. Madrid: Biblioteca de Autores Cristianos, 1967.

————. *Orígenes de la novela*. 4 vols. Santander: Consejo Superior de Investigaciones Científicas, 1943.

Michaëlis de Vasconcelos, Carolina. (See Vasconcelos. See also Ribeiro; Sá de Miranda.)

Montemayor, Jorge de. *Los siete libros de la Diana*. Edited by F. López Estrada. Madrid: Espase-Calpe, 1946.

————. *Los siete libros de la Diana de Jorge de Montemayor*. Milano: Andrea de Ferrari.

Moreno Báez, Enrique. *Lección y sentido del "Guzmán de Alfarache"*. Madrid: Consejo Superior de Investigaciones Científicas, 1948.

Netanyahu, Benzion. *The Marranos of Spain from the Late XIVth to the Early XVth Century According to Contemporary Hebrew Sources*. New York: Kraus Reprint Corp., 1966.

Núñez de Castro, Alonso. *Historia ecclesiastica y seglar de la muy noble y muy leal Ciudad de Guadalaxara*. Madrid, 1653.

Núñez de Reinoso, Alonso. *La historia de los amores de Clareo y Florisea y de los trabajos de la sin ventura Isea*. (B.A.E., III.) Edited by Carlos Arribau. Madrid, 1846.

————: *Item. Algunas rimas*. Venezia: Gabriel Giolito de Ferrari, 1552.

————. *La plaisante histoire des amours de Florisée et de Clareo, et aussi de la peu fortunée Isea, trad. du castillan en françois par Jacques Vincent*. Paris: Kerver, 1554.

————. *Historia dos trabalhos da sem ventura Isea natural da Cidade de Epheso & dos Amores de Clareo & Florisea*.

Ortíz, Andrés. "Romance No. 287." *Romancero general*. (B.A.E., XVI). Edited by Augustín Durán. Madrid, 1851.

Patch, Howard. *The Goddess Fortuna*. Cambridge: Harvard University Press, 1927.

————. (See Lida.)

Petrarca, Francesco. *De remediis*. Translated by Francisco de

Madrid. *De los remedios contra la prospera y adversa fortuna.* Valladolid: Diego de Gumiel, 1510.

Quevedo Villegas, Francisco de. *Lágrimas de Hieremías castellanas.* Edited by E. M. Wilson and J. M. Blecua. Madrid: Consejo Superior de Investigaciones Científicas, 1953.

———. *La vida del Buscón llamado Pablos.* Edited by F. Lázaro Carreter. Salamanca, 1965.

Reznik, Jacob. *Le Duc Joseph de Naxos: Contribution à l'Histoire Juive de XVIᵉ siècle.* Paris, 1936.

Ribeiro, Bernardim. *Bernardim Ribeiro e Cristovão Falcão "Obras".* Introduction by Carolina Michaëlis de Vasconcelos. Edited by Anselmo Braacamp Freire. 2 vols. Coimbra, 1923.

———. *Éclogas de Bernardim Ribeiro.* Edited by Marques Braga. Lisboa, 1923.

———. *Trouas de dous pastores. Feytas por Bernarldim Ribeyro* . . . 1536.

Rodrigues Lapa, Manuel. (See Sá de Miranda.)

Rodríguez Marín, Francisco. (See Cervantes.)

Rogers, Francis M. (See Enríquez Gómez.)

Rojas, Fernando de. *La Celestina.* Edited by Julio Cejador y Frauca. 2 vols. Madrid, 1963.

Rose, Constance H. (See Enríquez Gómez.)

Roth, Cecil. *The History of the Jews in Italy.* Philadelphia: The Jewish Publications Society of America, 1946.

———. *The House of Nasi: Doña Gracia.* Philadelphia, 1948.

———. *The House of Nasi: The Duke of Naxos.* Philadelphia, 1948.

———. *Personalities and Events in Jewish History.* Philadelphia, 1953.

de Rougemont, Denis. *L'amour et l'occident.* Paris, 1962.

Ruscelli, Girolamo. *Delle Lettere di Principi le quali o scrivono da principi, o a principi, o ragionan di principi.* Venetia: G. Ziletti, 1562 (1564–77).

———. *Del Tempio alla divina Signora Donna Giovanna d'Aragona, fabricato da tutti i più gentili spiriti, e in tutte le lingue principali de mondo.* Venetia: Giovana Pietrasanta, 1555.

Sá de Miranda, Francisco. *Poesias de Francisco de Sá de Miranda.* Edited by Carolina Michaëlis de Vasconcelos. Halle, 1885.

————. *Sá de Miranda "Poesias"*. Introduction by M. Rodrigues Lapa. Lisboa, 1942.

Salinas, Pedro. *Jorge Manrique o tradición y originalidad.* Buenos Aires: Suramericana, 1948.

Santa Biblia. Edición de Cipriano de Valera. Revisada y corregida. Nueva York, 1881.

Salveraglio, Filippo. *Catalogo d'una raccolta di opere stampate di Giolito di Ferrari in Venezia,* Milano, 1890.

Schevill, Robert. (See Cervantes.)

Sidney, Sir Philip. *Defense of Poesie.* 1583 (?).

Silva, Feliciano de. *La coronica de los muy valientes e esforçados e invencibles cavalleros don Florisel de Niquea y el fuerte Anaxartes, hijos del muy excelente Principe Amadis de Grecia* . . . Valladolid, 1532.

————. *Cuarta parte de D. Florisel.* Salamanca, 1551.

————. *Lisuarte de Grecia.* Sevilla, 1514.

————. *El noveno libro de Amadis de Gaula, que es la cronica del muy valiente y esforçado Principe y cauallero de la Ardiente Espada Amadis de Grecia, hijo de Lisuarte de Grecia, emperador de Constantinopla y de Trapisonda,* . . . 1530 (?).

————. *Parte tercera de la Crónica de D. Florisel.* Medina del Campo, 1535.

————. *Segunda comedia de Celestina.* Venezia, 1536.

————. (See Thomas.)

Thomas, Henry. Introduction to *Dos Romances Anónimos del Siglo XVI. El Sueño de Feliciano de Silva. La Muerte de Héctor.* Madrid, 1917.

————. *Portuguese and Spanish Romances of Chivalry.* Cambridge: The University Press, 1920.

Toda y Güell, Eduardo. *Bibliografía espanyola d'Italia dels origens de la imprempta fins a l'any 1900.* 5 vols. Barcelona: Castell de Sant Miquel d'Escornalbou, 1927–31.

Torres Naharro, Bartolomé de. *Comedia Jacinta.* (See Gillet.)

Urrea, Jeronimo de. *Don Clarisel de las flores.* (1550?) Sevilla: Sociedad de Bibliófilos Andaluces, 1879.

————. *Orlando Furioso . . . traduzido en Romance Castellano por don Ieronymo de Urrea.* Anvers: Martín Nucio, 1549.

Usque, Salomon. *Sonetos canciones, mandriales sextinas de gran*

POETA y orador *Francisco Petrarca, traduzidos de toscano por Salomon Usque, Hebreo.* Venezia: Nicolao Bevilaqua, 1567.

Usque, Samuel. *Consolaçam ás tribulaçoens de Israel.* Edited by Joaquim Mendes dos Remedios. 3 vols. Coimbra, 1906–08.

———. *Consolation for the Tribulations of Israel.* Edited and translated by M. A. Cohen. Philadelphia: The Jewish Publications Society of America, 1965.

Vasconcelos, Carolina Micaëlis de. *Nótulas relativas á "Menina e moça" na edição de Colónia (1559).* Coimbra, 1924.

———. *Novos estudos sobra Sá de Miranda.* Lisboa, 1911.

———. (See Ribeiro, Sá de Miranda.)

Villegas, Antonio de. *Auscencia y soledad de amor.* Medina del Campo, 1568. Edited by F. López Estrada. "Estudio y texto de la narración pastoril 'Ausencia y soledad de amor' del 'Inventario' de Villegas." *Boletín de la Real Academia Española,* XXIX (1949,) pp. 99–133.

Vossler, Karl. *La soledad en la poesía española.* Translated by R. de la Serna y Espina. Buenos Aires: Losada, 1946.

Wilson, Edward M. (See Quevedo.)

Archival Material

Archivio di Stato. Venezia. *Santo Uffizio.* "Ebrei anonomi." Bustamento 1, 39.

———. Conciglio di Dieci. *Secreta, Criminales.* 1553.

Archivo Histórico Nacional, Madrid. *Inquisición.* "Pleito, sobre el mayorazgo de Diego de Reinoso y de las Salas y su mujer Petronila de Reinoso."

———. *Inquisición.* "Proposiciones escandalosas." Leg. 22 (9).

Archivo de la Universidad de Salamanca. *Libros de claustros.* VIII–XI (1526–1533).

Biblioteca de la Real Academia de la Historia, Madrid. *Collección de Don Luis de Salazar y Castro.*

Periodicals and Collected Studies

Asensio, Eugenio. "El *romance* de Bernardim Ribeiro 'Ao longo da ribeira.'" *Revista de Filología Española,* XL (1957), pp. 1–19.

Avalle-Arce, Juan Bautista. "Espionaje y última aventura de José Nasi 1569–1574." *Sefarad,* XIII (1953), pp. 157–286.

Bataillon, Marcel. "Alonso Núñez de Reinoso et les marranes portugais en Italie." *Revista da Faculdade de Letras,* III, No. 1. *Miscelánea de estudos em honra do Prof. Hernâni Cidade.* Lisboa, 1957, pp. 1–21.

————. "¿Melancolía renacentista o melancolía judía?" *Estudios Hispánicos: Homenaje a Archer M. Huntington.* Wellesley, 1952, pp. 39–50.

————: "Nouvelles recherches sur le *Viaje de Turquía.*" *Romance Philology,* V (1951–1952), pp. 77–97.

Bonilla y San Martín, Antonio. (See Avendaño, primary sources.)

Cotarelo, Emilio. "Nuevas noticias biográficas de Feliciano de Silva." *Boletín de la Real Academia Española,* XIII (1926), pp. 129ff.

Cortés, Narciso Alonso. "Feliciano de Silva." *Boletín de la Real Academia Española,* XX (1933), pp. 382–404.

Durham, Donald Blythe. "Parody in Achilles Tatius." *Classical Philology,* XXXIII (1938), pp. 19ff.

Foulché-Delbosc, Raymond. "Remarques sur 'Lazarille de Tormes,'" *Revue Hispanique,* VII–VIII (1900–1901), pp. 81–97.

Fraker, Charles F. "The Importance of Pleberio's Soliloquy." *Romanische Forschungen,* LXXVIII (1966), pp. 515–29.

Gallina, Anna Maria. "Un intermedio fra la cultura italiana e spagnola nel sec. XVI: Alfonso de Ulloa," *Quaderni Ibero-Americani.* XVII (1955), pp. 4–12.

Gilman, Stephen. "The 'Conversos' and the Fall of Fortune." *Collected Studies in honor of Américo Castro's Eightieth Year.* Oxford, 1965, pp. 127–136.

————. "The Fall of Fortune from Allegory to Fiction." *Filologia Romanza,* IV (1957), pp. 337–54.

————. "Fortune and Space in 'La Celestina.'" *Romanische Forschungen,* LXVI (1955), pp. 342–61.

————. "Retratos de conversos en la *Comedia Jacinta* de Torres Naharro." *Nueva Revista de Filología Hispánica,* XVII (1966), pp. 20–39.

Lida, María Rosa. "Dido y su defensa en la literatura española." *Revista de Filología Hispánica,* IV (1942), pp. 209–52, 313–82.

López Estrada, Francisco. (See Villegas, primary sources.)

Palamo, Robert J. "Una fuente española del *Persiles.*" *Hispanic Review,* VI (1938), pp. 57–68.

Randall, Dale B. J. "The Classical Ending of Quevedo's *Buscón.*" *Hispanic Review,* XXXII (1964), pp. 101–8.

Révah, Isaac. "Un Pamphlet contre l'Inquisition d'Antonio Enríquez Gómez: La Seconde Partie de la 'Política Angélica' (Rouen, 1647)". *Revue des études juives* (NS), Ser. 4, I (1962), pp. 83–168.

Rivers, Elias. "The Horatian Epistle and its Introduction into Spanish Literature." *Hispanic Review,* XXII (1954), pp. 174–94.

Rose, Constance H. "New Information on the Life of Joseph Nasi, Duke of Naxos: The Venetian Phase," *Jewish Quarterly Review,* LX (1970), pp. 330–44.

————. "Pablos' *damnosa heritas.*" *Romanische Forschungen,* LXXXII, (1970), pp. 94–101.

Roth, Cecil. "Salusque Lusitano." *Jewish Quarterly Review* (N.S.), XXXIV (1934), pp. 65–85.

————. "Les Marranes à Venise." *Revue des études juives,* LXXXIX–XCI (1930–31), pp. 201–223.

Wardropper, Bruce. "Hacia una historia de la lírica a lo divino." *Clavileño,* V (1954), pp. 1–11.

Williams, Robert H. "Notes on the Anonymous Continuation of 'Lazarillo de Tormes,' " *Romanic Review,* XVI (1925), pp. 223–35.

Zimic, Stanislav. "Alonso Núñez de Reinoso, traductor de 'Leucipe y Clitofonte.' " *Symposium,* XXI (1967), pp. 166–75.

Reference Works

Almeida de Carvalho, Carlota. *Glossário das Poesias de Sá de Miranda.* Lisboa, 1953.

Biographie universelle ancienne et moderne. Nouvelle édition. Paris, 1854.

Corominas, Joan. *Diccionario crítico etimológico de la lengua castellana.* 4 vols. Madrid, 1954–1957.

Covarrubias, Sebastián de. *Tesoro de la lengua castellana o española.* Madrid, 1611.

Diccionario de autoridades. Madrid, 1726–1739.

Diccionario de la lengua española. Decimoctava edición. Madrid, 1956.

García Carraffa, Alberto and Arturo. *Enciclopedia heráldica y genealógica hispano-americana.* Madrid, 1948, 1951.

APPENDIX

7

SYGVENSE LAS
OBRAS EN VERSO Y EN
ESTA PRIMERA HABLANDO
CON VNA SEÑORA SV PRI=
MA.DESCVLPA LOS YER=
ROS DE SVS OBRAS.

I uos esta obra mia
Señora prima leeis,
De las faltas que tenia
y tristezas que sentia
Es razon no me culpeis.
Por que quando la escreuia,
Enfermo y mas descontento
Sin ningun plazer biuia
Teniendo por compañia,
Tristezas y gran tormento.

Y pues uuestra gran bondad:
El guardar la razon usa,
Estos tiempos considrad:
y ninguna culpa dad,
A los uersos de mi musa.
Con el animo sereno
Los uersos suelen uenir
yo triste de males lleno
De contino affano y peno
Desseando de morir.

A   iiii

8 -

E *stos tiempos tristes son*
   Muy *oscuros para mi*
   Biuiendo *nesta region* ,
   Tan *lexos de mi naçion*
   Y *tierras do yo nasci.*
   Los *uersos quieren contento*
   Y *del bien no ser ausente* ,
   Y *ser libre el pensamiento* ,
   Mas *ami la mar y uiento*
   Me *siguen continuamente.*

E *l cauallero criado*
   En *exerçitos de guerra*
   Rescibe *graue cuidado*
   Quando *ue que les forçado*
   De *biuir en otra tierra*
   El *pastor que su ganado*
   Es *usado de guardar*
   Con *enzina coronado*
   Llora *uiendosse quitado*
   De *a quel sabroso lugar.*

El *cortesano brioso*
   La *corte auiendo perdida* ,
   No *tiene ningun reposo* ,
   Mas *biue siempre quexoso*
   Por *a quella dulce uida*
   Ansi *yo siendo apartado* ,
   De *uuestra connersaçicon.*
   Con *razon biuo penado* ,

Y mi uerſo ua forçado,
Y creçe, mi gran paſsion.

Que no ſoy acoſtumbrado,
 A los çielos deſta tierra
Ni aſus aguas uſado,
Con tener a prego nado,
Contra mi los males guerra.
Sin tener quien me conſuele,
Ni mis penas quiera uer
Pero quien de miſe duele,
Por offiçio, tener ſuele,
El de todos ſe doler.

A quien ſy la muſa mia
 Agora loar quiſsieſſe,
Con gran trabajo podria:
y meneſter le ſeria
 Que fauor ella le dieſſe.
El bien que en ella ſeſmalta,
No lo digo ni lo toco:
Por que lo tengo porfalta,
Por quen coſa ques tan alta
De zir mucho es dezir poco.

Quado en trabajos ſe ue-
 El ſu roſtro mueſtra manſo,
Que pues tan claro lo ſe
Flega a dios preſto le de
Como mereſçe, descanſo

Su trabajo, en alegria
Mudado preſto lo uea:
La coſa que bien queria
Pues tan gran ualor tenia
La uea como deſſea.

M as tornando a lo primero,
De la uida que tenia,
A qui daros cuenta quiero,
Para que ſepais que muero,
Dela ſuerte que biuia,
Q uando Crinito ſe ue
Con ſus rayos tan galanos
Con dolor que no ſe cre
Lloro por que nada ſe
De mi padre ñi hermanos

Y trabajando de uer,
Si ami puedo engañar,
Comienço uerſos hazer
Pero como puede ſer
Mi natural oluidar
Ado paſſe mi niñez
Y lo mejor de mis años
Sin ganar honrra ni prez,
Con que agora en la uejez,
Me deſpida de mis daños.

V na hermana que tenia,
Con tan gran amor amaua

1 1

Y tanto yo la queria,
Que de noche ymas dedia,
En ella siempre pensaua
Y contanto yo querella,
Mingun ora ni momento
Passa que no piense en ella,
Y con solo pensar uella,
Biuiria yo contento.

Con ella yo hablo ausente,
Y con lagrimas dezia,
Si uos fuessedes presente
Biuiria alegremente
Hermana querida mia.
En suenos os represento,
Y hablo Como queria,
Pero como sea uiento
Luego torno ami tormento:
Y a la pena que tenia.

Con amor limpio y humano
Vos dezis segun yo creo
Que se hyzo de mi hermano
Que si es biuo muerto o sano,
Yo saber cierto desseo.
Yo biuo, mas no contento,
Yo biuo, mas con cuidado
Yo biuo, mas descontento.
Yo biuo, mas de tormento.
De contino acompañado.

12

E s uerdad que siruo: aquien;
  Es justo que el mundo alabe,
  Pues atantos haze bien,
  Pero mis males nouen
  Remedio que no los sabe,
  Que si mi razon supiesse,
  Pues razon nunqua torçio,
  Soy cierto que se doliesse,
  Y que culpa no me diesse,
  Pues ninguna tengo Yo;

L os ryos han de tornar,
  Para tras con sus corrientes
  Y los, cielos se han de harar
  Y la tierra, estrellas dar
  Y llamas biuas las fuentes,
  El Sol ha de caminar
  Sin cauallos su camino
  Pero yo jamas dexar,
  De querer, ni de amar
  Muy grato siendo contino.

Q ue si las musas amar
  Que si mi tiempo perder.
  Fueron causa de buscar
  Quien me quiso uida dar
  Y por suyo me tener
  Yo doy por bien empleado
  El gastar mi tiempo mal,
  Y lo doy por bien gastado,

13

Y tengo porbien dexado
Ami padre: y natural.

Y si los hados quißieren
Lleuarme de tierra eſtraña
Y si tal dicha tuuieren
Mis ojos triſtes que uieren;
A quellas tierras deſpaña
Alla tengo de querer
A quien soy tan obligado
Sin ingrato nunqua ser
Y pues mas no puedo hazer
No deuo deser culpado.

Que si la suerte tuuiera
Como tengo uoluntad
Muy claramente se uiera
Que deſſeos yo no diera
Sino obras de uerdad,
Pero pues quiso faltar
Mi uentura y nada soy
No me deuen de culpar
En coſas grandes nodar
Pues que lo que tengo doy.

Los otros seruiços dan
De trabajos que paſſado
En seruilla siempre han,
Otros le comen su pan
Por sus manos trabajado
Que perlas orofulgente

14.

Ninguno yamas le dio
Ni riquezas del Oriente,
Antes peregrina gente,
Della siempre rescibio.

Otros nombre de pariente
Alegaran, segun creo:
Con seruicios juntamente,
Pero yo tan solamente,
Mi uoluntad con desseo.
Ansi con esto contento
Yo deuiera de biuir,
Y perder todo tormento
Y tener el pensamiento
Sossegado en escreuir.

Pero la gran soledad,
Que de mucchas cosas tengo:
No me dan tal libertad,
Ansi con mi uoluntad,
yo me auengo y desauengo
Orden no puedo guardar:
Si comienço alguna cosa
En otra uoy a saltar
Sin poder tino tomar
Mi alma que no reposa.

Firmeza no se tener,
Ora biuo, ora me mato,
Ora no quiero plazer

25

Ora no se que me hazer,
Pues no ato ni desato :
En nada tengo sentido
En nada puedo acertar ,
De mudanças combatido ,
En el mundo ando metido
Y queria me saluar.

Fin.

Comienço, de considrar
El orbe tan bien formado
Y con gracias a dios dar
De alli me uoy a hallar
En los uicios engolfado ;
Anda muerta mi razon
Sin cabeça, ni sin pies ,
Finalmente en conclusion
Estas obras mias son
Tales qual el tiempo es.

CARTA A LA SEÑORA
DONNA MARIA,
DE GYZMAN

ERMOSA Doña Maria
Si de mi quereis saber,
Sabed que ya mi alegria
Con la dulce gloria mia
Son ydas con el plazer

16

Ya no soy quien ser solia
Cercado de males canso
Sin plazer sin alegria
Pues que uida no tenia
Ni reposo ni descanso.

Ha consentido mi hado
Ymi muerte mecondena
Ha que biua desterrado ,
Y que muera sepultado
Sin plazer entierra agena
A donde todo medaña
Donde mi muerte seue
Pues morando en tierra estraña
Con la memoria despaña
Como biuayo no se.

Las gentes desta region,
Malas mas que el mismo mal
Barbaras y sin razon
Como diamantes son
De su mismo natural
Fortuna mes enemiga
y no tengo solo aqua
Ni amigo, ni amiga ,
Ni persona que me diga
O hombre como te ua

Y si conestos enojos
Soledad despaña siento
Luego

27

Luego rebientan los ojos
Con las lagrimas despojos
Del cansado pensamiento,
Las aguas, que aqua auia
En lo que mi dolor ued
Aunque en oro las beuia,
No me matan la sed mia,
Mas quedo muerto de sed.

E l manjar es desabrido,
Pues se come con tormento,
Que quien como yo se uido,
Y su bien ue ya perdido
Como biuira contento,
Y con tal desassossiego
Yo confiesso mi biuir,
Pero ser alegre niego
Ni poder tener sossiego,
Para poder escreuir.

E l reposo que se pinta,
Para bien dezir es cruel
Que pues todo se despinta
Hago de lagrimas tinta,
Y de sospiros papel:
Los hombres de aquesta tierra
Son mas falsos que Medea
Hazen assi mismos guerra,
A quel que los busca ierra
Y mas quien uellos dessea,

B

48

Que eſtoy en çiudad Rodrigo,
   Muchas uezes finjo aqua,
   Y comigo mismo digo
   Eſte camino que ſigo
   A los alamos yra.
   Y digo contento hufano
   Y Alegre podre llegar
   A caſa de Feliçiano.
   A donde contino gano,
   Por tal ingenio tratar.

Vere a doña Iſabel,
   Quexoſa de la fortuna,
   Por le ſer tan dura y cruel:
   Vere ſi tiene de aquel,
   Su eſpoſo nueua alguna,
   Y despues con gloria igual
   Con temor, que lleuo digo
   Ana de carauajal.
   Mi enemiga capital,
   Vere que riñe comigo.

Pero como claramente
   La uerdad ſe uea clara
   Y me uea claro auſente,
   Soſpiro menudamente
   Lexos de Guadalajara
   Soſpiro por doña juana
   Ramirez muy ſin repoſo,
   Y por ſu bondad tan ſana

Y sospiró por mi hermana.
Doña Isabel de Reynoso.

Y con este pensamiento
Ando con pensar cansado;
Tan triste tan descontento,
Que ninguna cosa siento
Que no sea de cuidado.
Las cosas oscuras amo,
Sin saber do estoy, ni donde
Grito, peno, lloro clamo,
Y por mis amigos llamo:
Pero ninguno responde.

A qui en esta çiudad,
A donde peno en ausençia,
Y muero con soledad
Dizen que tratar uerdad
Es no saber de conçiencia
Hazen todo con despecho
Lo falso tienen por çierto
Vsan iustiçia de hecho
Lo tuerto llaman derecho
Y ael derecho llaman tuerto.

A nsi con pena creçida
Es cosa de no creer,
Qual ando por esta uida
La uoluntad ia perdida
El seso para perder

B   ii

No puedo conualeçer
Con ualeçen mis enojos,
Y sin nadie me querer
Las piedras tienen poder
Para quebrar moles ojos.

Fin.

Y pues que señora ansi
Destos males soy catiuo
Con dolor suplico aqui
Tengan memoria de mi
Que en estrañas tierras biuo,
Pues que mi uida prestada
Otra cosa ia no quiere
Que pues la muerte es llegada
En el fin de la jornada
Pagare como pudiere.

OTRAS GLOSANDO ESTE
VILLANCICO.

Pues que biuo en tierra agena
Muy lexos de donasçi
Quien aura dolor de mi.

Quien sera tan piadoso,
Que se duela de mi mal
Perdido mi natural
Mi descanso, y mi reposo

21

Pues biuo siempre dudoso
Y lexos de donasçi
Quien aura dolor de mi .

Fuertes mi mal y tormento,
Y cansado mi desseo
Ya ninguna cosa ueo
Que me pueda dar contento
Muerto ya mi pensamiento
Muy lexos de donasçi
Quien aura dolor de mi .

S i con tanto mal no muero
Señora de uos ausente
Es por que ueros presente
Y gozar de uos espero,
Mas pues falta lo que quiero
Muy lexos de donasçi
Quien aura dolor de mi .

S i alguno piedad
Tiene desta uida dura
Estan poca mi uentura
Que se muda su bondad
Pues creçe mi soledad
Muy lexos de donasçi
Quien aura dolor de mi .

A quellas fuentes despaña .
A quellos campos de gloria
Me lastiman la memoria

B   iii

22

Y penfar nellos me daña
Que pues biuo en tierra eftraña
Muy lexos de do nafçi
Quien aura dolor de mi.

A l Sol que ua caminando
Quando nafçe io le pido
Que de mis males ueftido
Mi mal uaia pregonando
Continuamente penando
Mui lexos de do nafçi
Quien aura dolor de mi.

N inguno a qua nc me quiere
No fe yo lo que les hize
Solo mi dolor me dize
Que ningun plazer efpere
Que pues mi uentura muere
Muy lexos de do nafçi
Quien aura dolor de mi.

D e dos primas que tenia,
La una ia me falto,
Y la otra me quedo,
Donde uella no podia,
Sin plazer: fin alegria,
Muy lexos de do nafçi
Quien aura dolor de mi

Q uien come eftraño maniar
Y quien beue agua agena,

23.

Que crezca siempre su pena,
Es iusto por mas penar,
Ya muerto con sospirar
Muy lexos de do nasçi
.Quien aura dolor de mi.

Quien me puede remediar
Entre mi fortuna y guerra
Andando de tierra en tierra
I de lugar en lugar
Sin mis amigos tratar
Muy lexos de do nasçi
Quien aura dolor de mi.

Fin.

Pues que sin lo meresçer
Aqui todos me combaten
A puñaladas me maten
Sin de mi mal se doler
Perdido ia mi plazer
Muy lexos de do nasçi
Quien aura dolor de mi.

MVERTE DE LAGRIMAS
Y DE DIANA.

Entre tajo, y guadiana,
Vna pastora biuia,
A quien lagrimas seruia,
Por nombre tiene Diana
Diana por nombre auia

B   iiii

24

.L agrimas por su uentura
Sin ella guarda ganado
Por campos deftremadura
Do prefente su hermofura
Nunqua muere su cuidado.

A nda aufente delas gentes
Sus bienes todos paffados
Sus males todos prefentes
Sus ojos tornados fuentes
Sus fentidos en cuidados
Su fortuna lo deftierra
Para moftrar su firmeza
En aquella sola tierra
Cercada toda de fierra
Y de campos de trifteza.

C onforme con su penar
Aquellas fierras bufco
Para de fi se uengar
Donde no puede dexar
De penar el que peno
En cabaña de afficion.
Recogia su tormento
Forjado de la paßion
Nafçido del coraçon
Criado del penfamiento.

Y por do apaçentaua
El paftor fin alegria

El rico tajo paſſaua,
Que los ſoſpiros lleuaua,
Por do Diana biuia
No deſcanſa, con cuidar
Ni ſin cuidados deſcanſa,
Con todo ſiente peſar,
Quando pienſa deſcanſar,
En tonces mucho mas canſa.

Quando la tarde uenia
Venia pena mayor,
Y como ſu mal creſçia
Entre cuidados dezia
La cauſa de ſu dolor
Las claras aguas corriendo
Se quexaua de ſu ſuerte,
Y de todo ya muriendo
El echo eſta reſpondiendo
Penaras haſta la muerte.

Aguas puras que hare
Que ſufro males de amor
Sufridos ſobre mi fe,
O aguas adonde ire:
Que no uaia mi dolor.
O ſin uentura paſtor,
O ſin uentura ganado:
De triſteza acompañado,

268

Quanto te fuera mejor
No naſcer ni ſer criado.

Mis ſoſpiros anſi uan,
Tan cercados de dolores,
Que en eſte contino afan,
Poco remedio da pan
Nueſtro Dios de los paſtores
Paſſando mi uida anſi,
Entre triſteza, y triſteza,
Deſpues que a Diana ui,
Poco aprouechan ami,
Mis ganados y riqueza.

O paſtor deſuenturado
Solo morir te conuiene,
Pues eres tan mal hadado
Que ſi ſe parte un cuidado
Otro por la poſta uiene,
Por ſolo querer la paga,
Ha ſido ſiempre penar:
No ſe que diga ni haga
Pues que adonde que pa llaga,
En mi cuerpo no ay lugar.

Con eſte mal, y dolor,
Ando de mi tan ageno,
Que penar es lo mejor,
Mas Floreſindos paſtor,
No pena como yo peno.

27

Conforme al dolor que tengo,
Muy liuiano es su tormento,
No siente lo que yo siento,
Que me auengo y desauengo,
Yuntamente en un momento.

Cabras mias yos: yos,
Ganado mio sabroso,
En otro tiempo dichoso,
Yd a buscar otros rios,
Do pazcais con mas reposo.
Y por mas pena me ser,
De uentura y su reues:
Yamas os uere pasçer,
Ni que uengais a beuer
Lagrimas: de quien lo es.

Lagrimas ansi biuia,
En su tristeza contina,
Mas quando su mal dezia,
Diana linda uenia,
Por una uerde campina.
Vnas Oueias traia,
Entre las quales sospira,
Vestidos blancos uestia,
Hermosa bien parescia,
A ojos de quien la mira.

Ansi uiene tan galana,
Que qualquier nascido hombre,

28

La siruiera de su gana
Y por que sirue a Diana
Diana tomo por nombre,
Su uida passa en guardar,
Vnas cabras que heredo,
Con esto quiere passar
Y de nunca se casar
A Diana prometio.

o traye çarçillos de plata,
No tray çintas encarnadas,
No trae gorgueras labradas,
Mas con solo mirar mata
Sin estas cosas contadas
Baxando por una cuesta,
Su lindeza mas descubre
Y la pastora dispuesta,
Con toca muy mal compuesta,
Sus roxos cabellos cubre.

Quando lagrimas la uio,
Y uio su gesto diuino,
No se yo lo que sintio,
Pero pues que no murio,
Muera y pene de contino.
Y esforçando su sufrir
Sin perder punto ni hora,
Començo la de seguir
Pero comierça de huir
Por los montes la pastora.

S us dedos todos torçiendo ,
   Corre el paſtor ſin uentura ,
   Mas Diana ua huiendo ,
   Y·los uientos descubriendo ,
   Blancas carnes de hermoſura ,
   Anſi ſin orden corria ,
   Lagrimas tras ſu ſerrana ,
   Y grande dolor ſentia ,
   En penſar que ſe hiria ,
   En ſus blancos pies Diana .

Y como yua corriendo ,
   Tal pena leua conſigo ,
   Que del todo ia muriendo ,
   No huyas le ua diziendo ,
   Pues no te ſoy enemigo .
   Que pues a ſeruir te uoy ,
   O paſtora adonde uas
   Mira quan rico, que ſoy ,
   Y quanto tengo te doy
   Pues me tienes lo que es mas .

T anto tras ella corrio ,
   Tan turbado tan ſin rienda
   Qui çerca della llego ,
   Mas ella quando lo uio
   A las aguas ſe encomienda ,
   Y por el tajo ſe entro ,
   Por de lagrimas huir ,
   Y tan a dentro ſe hallo ,

E I   30

Que con las aguas murio,   2
O muerte para sentir.

A ssi Diana acabo,
Y como con su desseo,
A Diana çelebro,
Ella misma la lleuo
Con la madre di Aristeo
En una casa de Flores
De tan superba grandeza,
Que segun es su lindeza,
No tiene tantas colores,
La misma naturaleza.

A donde Nimphas biuian,
Hermosas de gran beldad,
Que cantauan, y tañian,
Y todas juntas dezian:
Es casa de castidad
Alli passauan su uida,
Aquellas castas donzellas,
Sin auer pesar entrellas,
A donde fue rescebida,
Diana de todas ellas.

D espues que lagrimas uido,
Tal dolor, ansi quedo.
Tan ajeno de sentido,
Como queda el ques herido,
Que no sabe quien lo hirio,

32

Bien conoſçe que mas muerte,
   Le ſeria ſi biuieſſe,
   Pero con anſia muy fuerte
   A las aguas deſta ſuerte
   Habla antes que murieſſe.

A guas claras que cauſaſtes,
   En uos Diana acabar,
   No uno mas dos mataſtes,
   Que ſi uida me dexaſtes,
   No puede mucho turar.
   La uida tengo por dura,
   Reſçibo gloria en muriendo,
   Pero quiere mi uentura,
   Que muera ſin ſepultura,
   De los peçes maniar ſiendo.

E n las hojas de mi hado,
   Por las parcas ſe eſcriuio,
   Que no muera ſepultado,
   Por que paſtor tan penado,
   La tierra no conſintio.
   O aguas por que tardais,
   O tarda uueſtra creçida,
   Por que ſi no me matais
   No por tanto me dexais,
   O aguas claras la uida.

M uero con firme firmeza,
   No tengo ia que eſperar.

· 3 2

Quedad con dios mi tristeza,
La muerte con su crueza,
De uos me quiso apartar
En la uida con amor,
Biuimos siempre los dio
Mas direis con gran do or,
A Floresindos pastor,
Que no se oluide de uos.

Estando para morir,
Pues la muerte lo condena
Vna trença uio uenir,
De cabellos que sentir
Le haze doblada pena,
Por que luego conoçio,
Los cabellos de Diana,
Que quando en tajo salto,
Paresçe que se cayo,
A la defunta serrana.

La qual despues que tomo
Tomando mayor cuidado,
Despues que bien la miro:
Con sospiros le hablo,
De llorar ia bien cansado.
O trença dexada aqui
Para mal de mayor mal,
Ventura lo quiso ansi,
Quien te lleuo lleua ami,
O trueque tan desigual.

O trueque

33

O trueque para morir,
O trueque para llorar,
O trueque de no sufrir,
O trueque para sentir,
O trueque para penar
Trença de roxos cabellos,
De mirarte nunca canso :
Pues eres trença de aquellos,
Que solamente con uellos,
Se sentia gran descanso,

Fin.

Tan graue pena sintio
El pastor que con llorar,
El rio tanto cresçio :
Que la uida le quito,
Por la pena le quitar
Las Nimphas, lo recogieron,
Y por que murio de amores ;
Con amor lo resçibieron,
Y desta suerte murieron,
Aquellos dos amadores.

C

34

COMIENCA
LA EGLOGA DE
LOS DOS PASTORES
BALTHEO Y ARGASTO.

 V a n d o la noche uenia
Repofando alos mortales,
No repofando a mis males,
Y la luna alta Regia,
Los cauallos Noturnales.
Baltheo trifte paftor
Lamentaua fus querellas,
Es Amor la caufa dellas,
Y la pena es fu dolor
Son teftigos las eftrellas.

S olo llora y fin confuelo,
Solo fin confuelo uiene,
Solo lamenta fu Duelo,
Los ojos tiene en el cielo,
Y el alma con Delia tiene,
Pero como no biuia
Triftezas fin orden hecha,
Y como ya no fentia,
Ni fabe lo que dezia,
Ni que fepa no aprouecha.

·3 5

Aßi solo en los defiertos
Se huelga por mas penar
Y con el claro lunar
Los ojos tiene defpiertos
Defpiertos par llorar.
Todos los otros paftores
En fus cabañas eftan
Contentos con fus amores
Pero el con fus dolores
Que uienen y nunca uan.

A y Delia dezia el,
Que ningun remedio en ti
Hallar fpero,
Que fi hermofa eres cruel
Y fi cruel trifte de mi
Que me muero.
Ya no puedo eftar aufente,
Que me muero en tu aufençia
Con triftura,
Ni puedo fufrir prefente
Ay Delia tu gran prefençia
Ni hermofura

A y Delia nunca fentifte
Mi dolor ni mi triftura
Defigual,
Por que fi te ui quefifte
Que miraffe tu hermofura
Por mi mal.

36

Por mi mal que me parti
Por contino trifte fer
En aufençia
Pero fi ami ofendi
Partieme por no ofender
Tu prefençia.

A ffi con pena crefçida
Biuen mis males prefentes
Y cuidados,
Si puede llamarfe uida
La uida delos aufentes
Defterrados
Affi uan las penas mias
Metidas en atahud
Donde ueo,
Yr fepultados los dias,
Defta trifte Iuuentud
Que poffeo.

E s tan fuerte mi dolor
Y tan contrario el reues
De mi allaga
Que fi aquesto no es amor
Yo no fe trifte que es
Ni que haga
Ami mal no hallo cura
Por que me ueo llagado
De tal mal
Que me tray mi desuentura
De cuidado en un cuidado

37

Desigual.

Assi biuo en esta tierra
Donde soledad mi amiga
Me persigue
Padezco contino guerra.
Y ninguno me fatiga.
Ni me sigue.
Mis ojos tornados fuentes
Mas quien otros me prestasse
Por pensar
Que con lagrimas corrientes
Mi corazon se hartasse
De llorar.

O Delia que tu no sabes
Que muero por te seruir
Y amar,
Mas porque mi se alabes
Yamas te osare dezir
Mi penar
Assi biuire muriendo
Muriendo con tal contienda
Biuire,
Que mi dolor no lo entiendo
Ni aunque triste lo entienda
Que hare.

Que aunque Delia quissiesse
Aeste mal que no siente
Dalle medio,
No puede ni que pudiesse
                    C iii

38

Su grandeza no confiente
Mi remedio
O Delia que hare fin ti
Pues la muerte que no uiene
Es lo mejor
Que hare trifte de mi
Que ningun remedio tiene
Mi dolor.

O Delia que fer feñora
De todo merescimiento
Dios te dio.
Yo paftor tu no paftora
Que hare quel penfamiento
Me engaño,
Que hare con pena fuerte
Para mi gloria uenida
Pues es tal,
Que no me quiere la muerte
Ni yo puedo con la uida
Por mi mal.

O mi penfamiento uano
A tu mal tan crudo fuerte
No ay falida,
Sino fanas por la mano
Que te pudo dar la muerte
Y la uida
O mi gloria que en dolor
Mi nueua gloria tornafte

3 9

Y puſiſte
Tan preſto, como la flor
O mi gloria te ſecaſte
Y buiſte.

Pero pues queſiſtes uos
Ojos ponerme en el mal
Que padezco,
Plazeres andad con Dios
Pues que eſta uida tal
Yo merezco.

AVTHOR.

Aſſi Baltheo Acabo,
Su triſteza no acabada,
Y tanto el triſte lloro
Que con el llorar quedo.
La tierra toda mojada
Aſſi ſu pena creſça
Sus ojos de agua llenos
Deſpiertos pues no dormia
Pero phosphoros uenia.
Paje de la Dioſa Venus

Aſſi con ſu mageſtad
Salia Phebo dorado,
Y con ſu gran claridad
Cubria con oſcuridad
El mundo que era eſtrellado.

                    C iiii

40

Y quando ya se mostraua
Por entre los dos hermanos
Su carro phebal guiaua
Y la uida començaua
El que biue por sus manos
Ya salian los pastores
Con sus hermosos ganados .
Y a los sacan por los prados,
Vnos no tienen dolores
Otros padeçen cuidados .

V nos salen a cantar
Otros lloran su mal fuerte.
Que no se puede escusar
A quien tiene triste suerte
Su triste pena llorar .
Ya comiençan asaltar
Los cabritos por el prado,
Ya salia sin pesar
El labrador para harar
La tierra con su harado.

Y como ya se mostraua
El claro y sereno Dia ,
Cada uno despertaua ,
Y con fuerças procuraua
La causa porque biuia ,
Ya gradiuus floreszia
Y su animo mostraua
El que las armas queria

41

Y Minerua ya uenia
Que los espritus cansaua.

Y Paphia ya se esmaltaua
Con las damas que floresçen
Que la uoluntad robaua
Yel oro se procuraua
A quien todos obedesçen
Ya se empieça la jornada
Del caminar por tener
Y la justiçia quebrada
Y de todos desseada
Mostraua su gran poder.

Y a los mares demostrauan
Las fuertes naos que uenian,
Y los que ya despertauan
Vnos gimendo cantauan
Otros llorando tañian
Vnos uan a Alexandria,
En riquezas su cuidado,
Otros uan do se ponia
Crenitus phebal Dorado
Quando cansado uenia.

O tros por su desuentura
Do gente nunca se uio
A buscar uan su uentura
Quando la razon no cura
A lo que el tiempo curo
Assi neste tiempo tal

42

A somaua otro pastor
Soriano es natural
Su uestido es de sayal
Y de pardilla color .

S us males uiene cantando
Males deuen ser de amor
Triste uiene y sospirando.
Y Baltheo esta llorando
La causa de su dolor.

ARGASTO CANTADO.

D esauenido cuidado ,
Me a tomado entresi
Nunca tal cuidado uj .

Y o nunca ui tal cuidar
Ni lo entiendo nilo se ,
Pero mi mal ni mi fe
No se pueden ya mudar ,
Pero pues para penar ,
Me a tomado entresi
Nunca tal cuidado ui .

HABLA.

Y o canto porque me muero
Para que mi gran cuidado
Menos sienta ,
Como haze el marinero

43

Quando uee que esta cercado
De tormenta
Por que crezca mi dolor
Y mi mal tan uerdadero
Me de guerra,
Mas ay Argasto pastor
Que haras siendo estrangero
En esta tierra.

Que haras con este mal
De que te uees combatido
Y llagado
Quien te truxo a Portugal
En Soria siendo nascido
Y criado.
O ualles do los pastores
Guardan por esta uerdura
Su ganado,
Que hare pues mis dolores
Me truxeron tan sin cura
Desterrado.

O sierra de mi conquista
Pues uengo con mis enojos
A buscarte,
A qui se ciega mi uista
A qui se ciegan mis ojos
En mirarte
O amarga y triste uida
Ala qual el mal que uiene

44

No falto

Toda la cosa nacida
Por tiempo remedio tiene
Sino yo
Sino yo que por mi suerte
Padezco pena doblada
Y crecida
Y no me quiere la muerte
Por que ue ques desseada
Y querida

P   ero pues ningun plazer
Ventura quiere que espere
Ni lo ueo
No quiero nada querer
Pues no sera lo que quiere
Mi desseo
Mas Baltheo esta durmiendo
Y no duerme su cuydado
Ni su fe,
Ni ael ni ami entiendo
O pastor triste cuitado
Que hare.

O   quan flaco y triste ueo
Alcuitado que no tiene
Ya plazer
Mas o Baltheo Baltheo
Ves aqui Argasto uiene
A te uer

45

BALTHEO.

O Argasto mi amigo
De los males que posseo
Propio dueño,
Es possible que comigo
Hermano Argasto te ueo
O lo sueño
O Argasto, Argasto, Argasto
Es assi o yo no creo
Lo que digo
Que uiniesse auer abasto
Argasto al triste Baltheo
Su amigo.

Quien te truxo por aca
Quien te truxo Argasto aqui
A tal sierra
Mas o quan mal que me ua
Despues que parti de ti
Y tu tierra
Tu seas muy bien uenido
Por que no puede faltar
Mi Amor,
Pero seras Rescebido
De mi solo con llorar
Mi dolor.

Y a perdida mi alegria
Quiere Amor que con firmeza
Me consuele
Que no soy quien ser solia

46

Y aßi del trifte trifteza
Venir fuele.
Biuo la uida que uees
Pues otra gloria ninguna
Ya merezco,
Por lo qual mi uida es,
Conforme con la fortuna
Que padezco

L os bienes que ya me uifte
Alegrias y plazer
Y dos fon,
Por que yo feyendo trifte
Todo trifte deue fer
Con Razon
En otro tiempo paffado
Con quanto plazer yo ui
Alos dos
No lo tengo aun oluidado,
Pero quanto pefe a mi
Sabe dios.

P ero pues hallas aßi
A tu Amigo Baltheo
Tu diras
Quiente uio como te ui,
Y te uee come te ueo
Que haras.
Que haras con efta pena
Paftor desdichado herrido

47

Y llagado,
Que haras en tierra agena
Tu buen tiempo ya perdido
Y passado.

H allarasme sin sentido,
Do contino en soledad
Biuire,
Que pues ya mi tempo es ydo
Y passado en esta edad
Que hare,
Que hare triste de mi
Y dos mis dias hufanos
Tan ayna,
Mas dame cuenta de ti
Y de tu padre y hermanos
Y corina.

ARGASTO.

O Baltheo amigo amado
O Baltheo ay de ti
Que es aquesto,
Como te ueo mudado
Como te mudaste aßi
Tan de presto
Tan ajeno de los bienes,
Como podras tu cuidado
En cubrillo
La barba cumplida tienes

48

E l gesto todo arrugado
   Y amarillo

O Baltheo como feno
Despues que de nos partiste
Te secaste
Y passosse el tiempo Bueno
Que con mudança tuuiste
Y passaste
El bien todo se passo
Y todo el plazer tornaste
En pesar
Y mudanza se mudo
Pero tu no te mudaste
Depenar

Ella se goza sin ti
Y se burla y se burlo
De tu pena,
Y a andres dixo de si
Pero el no que a ti quedo
La condana.

BALTHEO.

A rgasto pues mi esperança
   Della remedio no espera
   Assi sea
   No me da pena mudança
   Que si uerde es la Ribera
   Verde sea.

Yo

4 9

Yo confieſſo que ſu amor
Me cauſo pena creçida
Y cuidado,
Mas eſte nueuo dolor
Es tan alto que ſe oluida
Lo paſſado.

Ella enfin mudo ſu fe.
Pero yo por quien no uia
Siempre caſſo,
Mas plega a Dios que le de,
Hourra, riqueza, alegria
Y descanſo,
Quando yo lo oy contar
Solo eſto me eſpanto
Y no al
En ſaber poderſe hallar
En mudança un ſino
Siendo tal.

Perineo ſer deſpoſada,
Y biuir con dulçe gloria
Me conto,
Mas como coſa oluidada
Argaſto por la memoria
Me paſſo
Por que ya Argaſto ſigo
Otra nueua pena y uida
En eſta ſierra,
Pero cuentame amigo

D

La razon de tu kenida
Enesta tierra.

ARGASTO.

La causa de ser llegado
Mi morir triste adiuina
Cada hora,
Por que uengo condenado
Por sentençia de corina
Mi señora,
Que en pago de mi penar
Por que mi gloria passasse
Y se fuesse,
Me mando yr a buscar
Tierra agena do morasse
Y biuiesse.

Y que luego me partiesse.
Porque la pena de ausençia
Me cercasse,
Y que nunca paresçiesse
Do jamas su gran presençia
Yo mirasse
Y que biuiesse contento
Con la pena que sin ella
Passo aqui,
Y que no sienta tormento
Ni con ella ni sin ella
Ni sin mi.

5 2

> Y que por mas mal queria
> Que sufriesse siempre mal
> Y gran pena,
> Y la sentencia dezia
> Argasto por desleal
> Se condena,
> Aßi ago mi camino
> De descanso y de plazer
> Alongado
> Solo uoi y peregrino
> Por mejor obedecer
> Su mandado.

B A L T H E O.

> A rgasto en sufrir dolor
> Yo confiesso que soy uiejo
> Exprementado,
> Pero con todo en amor
> Solamente dar consejo
> Me a quedado
> Y. pues que llagado uienes
> Sin poder tu firme fe
> Ya mudar,
> Mi consejo es que tu penes
> Por que yo siempre pene
> Por amar,
> Que es tan graue este dolor.

52

Que la vida toda gasta
Segun uiste,
Por que en los casos de amor
Ninguna cordura basta
Ni resiste.

Y deste crudo ladron
Que en sobre nombre cruel
Es llamado,
Las palabras dulçes son
Pero guarda guarda del
Que es maluado.
Y guarda no te Acometa
Por no quedar tan perdido
Como yo,
Que do llega su saeta
Quien de muerte queda herido
Bien libro.

Pero pues que mi penar
En mi alma esta imprimido
Y de buxado,
Dexolo por te contar
Lo que despues de partido
E passado,
En noche clara y gentil
Quando todos los pastores
Reposauan,
Enel mes era de Abril
Quando con Phebo las flores

35

Se esmaltauan.

A buscar prouinçia agena:
   Començe de caminar
   Sin consuelo,
   En la noche mas serena
   Que se podia pintar
   Enel cielo.
   Y como ya la sperança
   No remediasse el partir
   Tanto fuerte
   Al 's casas de mudança
   Començe triste a dezir
   Desta suerte.

O casas pues fuistes uos
   La causa de mi paßion
   No mortal,
   A hora quedad con Dios
   Pues que uuestro galardon
   Me fue tal
   Aßi despues de dexar
   Alas uelas y uentura
   Mi gran fe,
   Para de mi me uengar,
   Bien lexos de estremadura
   Camine.

Y cresçiendo en mi el tormento
   Como en firmes Amadores

                              D iii

134

Que bien aman,
Acorde de hazer assiento
En lugar que los pastores
Basto llaman,
Era solitaria tierra
Conforme para mis males
No contrarios,
De una parte cerca sierra
Y de otra tercanuales
Solitarios.

Y ansi con libertad
Tan ageno de sperança
Yo me ui,
Que tenia soledad
Del dolor que por mudança
Ya sufri,
Y con gloria que passaua
Por las dehesas diuinas
De hermosura,
Con los ganados andaua
Por los prados y campiñas
De uerdura.

Hufano por los collados
Cogiendo contino flores
Por la sierra,
Me holgaua por los prados
Amigo con los pastores
De la tierra.

55

C onmigo todos holgauan
   Y delo que ellos tenian
   Yo gozaua
   Y si solo me dexauan,
   Como las aguas corrian
   Contemplaua;
   Pero una noche a hora
   Que la luna era salida.
   Por mi suerte,
   En figura de pastora
   Yo pienso que ui la uida
   O la muerte.

Q uando la ui tan galana
   Y que su resplendor daua
   Por la sierra,
   Yo pense que era Diana
   Que del cielo se abaxaua,
   A la tierra,
   En fin yo no me entendia
   Confuso quando e nel suelo
   La miraua,
   Pero ui que oscurçia
   Con su beldad la del cielo
   Y sobraua.

Y como mas la mire
   Esforçado con mis males
   Todos juntos,
   Ay Argasto tal quede
   Quales quedan los mortales

56.

Ya defuntos

No fabia lo que hazia
  Bien fabia que era amor
  De amores
  Y que bien claro veys
  La caufa de mi dolor
  Y dolores,
  Y moftro alli cupido
  Su poder y fu mandar
  Sobrenos
  Pues de fu faeta herido
  Qual yo quede en la mirar
  Sabe Dios.

Mis bienes todos mudados
  De los males hecho alarde
  Ya oluidaua,
  A mudança y fus cuidados,
  Y por que fuera tan tarde
  Me pesaua
  Eftando fufpenfo anfi
  Y penfando en lo que yo
  Pienfo ahora,
  La paftora pufo en mi
  Sus ojos y luego huyo
  Ala ora.

Yo quando la vi partir
  Si en ella me caufo.

57

Algun mal
Pues que no lo se dezir
Sientalo el que sintio
Pena tal,
Que si no es bien contado
Mi dolor ser bien sufrido
Yo lo se,
Y que fue sin causa dado
Y que no fue meresçido
De mi se.

En fin la empieço a seguir,
Pues lo quiso ansi amor
Siendo esento,
Y perdiosse mi sentir
Hufano con mi dolor
Y contento
Y tomando por mi guia
Fuerças que de voluntad
Yo sacaua,
Con dolores la seguia
Y con poca libertad
Caminaua.

Y siendo partido el dia
Quando a buscalla parti
Sin demora,
La ursa Arcadia boluia,
De su exe segun ui
A tal hora.

i

58

Y empeçando a caminar
Por lugar que parecia
Horcomeo,
Vn uerde y solo lugar,
Ado Pan pastor biuia
Triste ueo

Entre dos rios estaua,
Y de todas partes flores
Con sus fuentes,
A donde ui que moraua.
Este Pan dios de pastores
Y sus gentes.
Paresçiome ser diuina
Vna r.bera que alli
Se hazia,
Que de fuente cristalina
Con aguas claras yo ui
Que salia.

Que muy dulçe gloria dauan
A los ojos que las uian
Estilar,
Y muchas casas estauan
A do pienso que deuian
Demorar,
Todas de Laurel y flores
Las estauan ordenando
Segun ui
Y pastoras y pastores

59

En estando las mirando
Conoçi.

V i Siluestre y Amador
    Con Agrestes pastor bueno
    Que murio,
    Con Andres aquel pastor
    Que la dicha de Fileno
    Heredo,
    Vi Dirçeo, y mas Rosano
    Contento con el tormento
    Que hallo
    Vi Panflores y uijano,
    A quien solo el pensamiento
    Acabo.

V i Melibeo y Siluano,
    Vi Titiro y Coridon
    Desdichado,
    Vi a Perseo y ui a Fauno
    Hufano con su passion
    Y cuidado,
    Lagrimas y penamor
    Vi tambien eneste cuento
    Con firmeza,
    Floresindos el mayor
    Que no tiene ya descuento
    Su tristeza.

6 0,

V i Armenia , y ui Clarinda
 Y ui Silua la pastora
 Que biuia ,
 Con la serrana Florinda
 Y ui la Nimpha que Mora
 Se dezia
 Vi Eufrosina y Siluana
 Que ojos con que mataua
 Tien de fuero ,
 Y mas ui la linda juana
 La que las patas guardaua
 Por el duero .

V i tambien otra pastora
 Y que a todas las sobraua
 Segun ui
 Sola de todas señora
 Y que Delia se llamaua
 Conocci
 A esta todas seruian
 A buel tas de mis dolores
 Y passion,
 Y cantauan y tañian
 Las pastoras y pastores
 Tal cançion .

E n las cosas sin remedio
 El oluido es mejor medio

61

Y o no supe que juzgar
  Y dixe no puede auer
  En mi oluido,
  Mas con el dulçe cantar
  Del todo senti perder
  Mi sentido,
  Pero como me oyeron
  Sintieron alteraçion
  Por yo uellas
  Y sin uellas se me fueron
  Pero fue mi corazon
  Ay tras ellas.

Y como mas se altero
  A quella mas principal
  Mi señora,
  Vna flauta le quedo
  Que llora y canta mi mal
  Cada hora
  Esta flauta dexo alli
  Para pena mas mortal
  Yo sentir,
  Y lleuome el alma ami
  O trueco tan desigual
  De suffrir.

Pero uiendola partir
  Mi alma uiendo lleuar
  Su partida,
  Yo la quißiera seguir

62

Pero nunca pude hallar
La salida.
Aßi solo me quede
Negando para penar
El morir
Dolo que triste passe
Se dize sin se contar
Ni dezir.

Y   para mas me uengar
De la uida y pena estraña
Yo sufrir
Acorde de me passar
Alos Alpes de Alemaña
A biuir,
Y como los que desaman
El remedio a sus dolores
Yo me fue,
Y en una ciudad que llaman
Viana los moradores
En barque.

Pero el mar con su furor
Y tormenta ansi de suerte
Nos cerco,
Que fuera cierto mejor
A todos la amarga muerte
Que falto
La tormenta leuantada
El remedio era morir

61

Solamente,
Porque el agua falada.
Nos comiença a combatter
Brauamente.

Y a fe embraueçen los uientos
Y la mar esquiua y braua
Ala qual,
La fuerça de mis tormentos
Con fu tormenta ayudaua
Por mi mal,
Montes de agua uenian
Con el uiento noto ayrado
En furor,
Y con Auftro combatian
Ala nao de mu cuidado
Y dolor.

Y con fuerças nos forçauan
Pues que la fuerça uenia
A pefar,
Y con pefar nos lleuauan
Ado uentura quería
Caminar,
Y las ondas que uenian
Que las uelas nos lleuauan
Como en guerra
A las eftrellas fubian
Y fubiedas abaxauan
A la tierra.

64

Ya la uida se cansaua
  Y quedara en acabar
  Bien contenta,
  Por que ya nada miraua
  Que no fuesse brauo mar
  Y tormenta.
  Tierra ya no parescia
  Para mas mi mal crecer
  En tormentos
  Y la onda no sabia
  Aquen pueda obedescer
  De los uientos.

E uro en pieça a combatir
  Por que mas me combatiesse
  Pena estraña
  Y por que no pueda yr
  A tierra do jamas uiesse
  Nuestra España
  Y por que mas penas sienta
  Y mi uida ássi acabe
  Por querer
  En creçiendo la tormenta
  El marinero no sabe
  Que azer.

Quando yo esto dezia
  Era la noche passada
  Ya talhora
  La mañana, ya uenia

                              Y parescia

65

Y parescia encarnada
El aurora
Yl a tormenta amanso
Y con el dia Phebal
Segun ui
Vna çiudad paresçio
Que fer Lisboa triumphal
Conoçi.

E ra tan clara al mirar
Con esmalte en perfiçion
Tan hermoso
Que pudiera alli ceffar
El templo de Ioue Amon
Arenofo
Tan hermofa que uentura
Paresçia que afu guifa
La formara
Do la rica fepultura
De la fuperba Artemifa
Bien callara.

Quando la ui tan galana
Con el animo confufo
La miraua
Por que a Memphis y Diana
Con el templo que compufo
Las fobrana
Quanto era de triumphante
Podello bien dezir yo

E

66

Cierto me go,
Po juntar a Thimante
Quando con uelo cubrige
Al rei Griego.

Y alli desembarcamos
Puestos yan en libertad
Y poder
Y por Coymbra passamos
Do cresçio mi soledad
Por la uer.
Y uoluime en fin argasto
Como de la mar sali
Por el duero
A uiuir eneste basto
Donde triste Delia ui
Por que muero.

Donde mi uida no entiendo
La muerte buena seria
Siendo assi
Pero pienso que muriendo
Sepultura faltaria
Para mi
Ando assi de sierra en sierra
Con mi pensamiento uano
Y sin camino
De una tierra en otra tierra
Como si fuesse gitano
Peregrino.

67

Por lo qual yo desespero
  Con mis males en mis penas
  Tan continos
  Por que Argasto ya no espero
  Salir de tierras agenas
  Ni caminos
   Sepultado en las passiones
   De la mar de mis pesares
   Y querer
    Biuiendo por los mesones
    Durmiendo por los passares
    Sin plazer.

Todo lo causa el amor
  Todo lo veo acabar
  Y perdi
  El tiempo que es lo mejor
  Que no lo podre cobrar
  Ay de mi
  Mis padres uiendome assi
  A dolerse de mi mal
  Ya no ay modo.
  Pero poco pena ami
  Que muerto lo principal
  Muera todo

Mueran todos mis plazeres
  Muera todo mi descanso
  Y holgar
  Ellos gozen sus aueres

68

Que yo Argasto no canso
Con penar
Ellos uistan terçiopelo
Coman su leche y su trigo
A plazer
Que yo solo me consuelo
Con esta uida que sigo
Por querer.

Y pues nada les penaua
No usar humanidad,
Poco ua
Que Dios que esta donde estaua
Conforme con la uerdad
juzgara
Mi pena nada les pene
No curen ya de sentir
Mis cuidados,
Que tiempo tras tiempo uiene
Argasto suelen dezir
Los penados.

Y no piensen que de todo
Mi buen tiempo sea ydo
Y acabado
Por que Dios me dara modo
Por do uean de perdido
Ser ganado.

69

ARGASTO.

B altheo tus males fon
   Tan fubietos a querer
   Y penar
   Que cordura ni razon
   Ya no bafta a refponder,
   Ni hablar
   Pero en cofas que no ay cure
   No fe deue auenturar
   Mi querella
   Ventura que desuentura
   Se·puede defpues llamar
   Sin tenella.

N o te feas tan contrario
   De un dia-en otro dia
   Efperando
   Ni biuas tan folitario
   Tan folo y fin compañia
   Lamentando
   Haz en tu uida mudança
   Y en lo que as de feguir
   Sin tardar
   No biaus en efperança
   Del tiempo que ha de uenir
   Ni legar.

Q ue por fuerte de tus fuerte
   Tan tarde puede lle gar

                    · E   iii

Algun medio
Que ni el tiempo ni la muerte
Ni razon te puedan dar
Ya remedio.

BALTHEO.

Aunque Argasto se detenga
El remedio por quien canso
Poco ua
Que puede ser quando uenga
Entonçes menos descanso
Me dara.
Que en este mar de tormentos
Es la uida ya tan cruel
Sin guarida
Que todos son descontentos
Los con descanso y sin el
En esta uida.

Todos bien sin plazer
Pero en cueto no me meto
Peligroso
Mas quien pudiesse saber
En que ua este secreto
Tan dubdoso
Que no ay cosa en esta uida
Por que diga solo esto
Me contenta
Yo la tengo comprehendida

71

Ay de mi que ui tan presto
Su tormenta.

Que yr al hilo como siento
Trabajo cierto me diera
Menos fuerte
No ua mal quien ua contento
Quien ahora aßi yr pudiera
Desta suerte
Tu me reprehendes Argasto
Por que biuo en soledad
En esta sierra
Pero fuera deste basto
Ves tu mas seguridad
En tu tierra.

A questos grandes segnores
Que quitan entendimiento
A uosotros
Fridalgos o regidores
Tienen mas contentamiento
Que nosotros
Los medianos olos chicos
Que ueen solo el sol nascer
Tan hermoso.
Con los pobres olos ricos
Vees les tu quiza stener
Mas reposo.

Que en este mar de tormento
A anadie falta cuydado

                    E   iiii

72

Ni triſtura
Pues nadie biue contento
Con la ſuerte que le ha dado
ſu uentura
Los que biuen en caſtilla.
Tienen ya en Portugal
Su ſentido
Lo que no me marauilla
Que eſte mal de otro mal
Me ha uenido.

Mis males yo no los niego
Pues que mi uida ſe ue
A cabar
Pero mi desſaſosſiego
En la leche lo mame
Sin dudar
En fin que coſa que quadre
En aqueſte mundo uano
No ſe halla
Que es el hijo contra el padre
Y el hermano contra hermano
En battalla.

Pero no ſe que penſamos
Pues el mundo todos es guerra
Y ſon tales
Los ſeñores y los amos
Que ſon luitos de la tierra
Principales

71

Comen trigo y dan auena
Beben y nos sudamos
Sin caudal
No les duele pena agena
Y quieren que nos dolamos
De su mal.

Comen de nuestros sudores
El como no digo yo
Pues no ai cura,
Son en todo mandadores
Por que en fin todo les dia
Su uentura.
Todo pudiera passar
Pues que la dicha cayo
Sobre nos
Pero quieren nos quitar
El entender que nos dio
Solo Dios.

Assi que nada se ue
Ni se halla alla en tu tierra
Sin reues
Por loqual yo me aparte
A biuir en esta sierra
Como uees.
Adonde ueo nascer
Encarnado y mas hermoso
Claro Apolo
Ado lo ueo poner

No querria mas reposo
Queste solo.

Aqui lloro con mi pena
Y canto con mi penar
Y tristeza
Aqui ueo la luna llena
Y ueo tambien menguar
Su grandeza.
No ay aqui quien me deseche
Aqui mis ojos yo çeuo
En mirar
Aqui como fresca leche
Y las claras aguas beuo
Al lunar.

Y llora mi tiempo bueno
Aquin por estas montañas
Mi uentura
Aqui como Pan,çenteno
Con bellotas y castañas
En artura
Estas sierras de plazer
Y de descanso son llenas
Sin afan.
Y contino ueo correr
A las aguas que serenas
Aqui uan.

Ningun juego de perder
Seguro que en esta sierra

- 71

Iamas halles
Como lo suelen hazer
Los pastores de la tierra
Que tu sabes
Pues se fingen uerdaderos
Hasta que de todo acaben
Los aueres
Mas ganados los dineros
Tan solamente no saben
Quien tu eres.

Ni aqui Reyna Cupido
Ni biue mal ni passion
Sino en mi.
Y Dios salue muy cumplido
Con un claro corazon
Ay aqui.
Aqui no biuen ladrones
Ni cossarios desleales
De uerdad,
Sino claros corazones
Con piensamientos boçales
De maldad.

No moran aqui traydores
Desseosos de los males
De tu tierra,
Ni saben, aqui de olores
Si no son los naturales
De la sierra.

76.

Aßi que entre estas ouejas
Ageno mas de tormento
Biuo yo
Por que bien dizen las uiejas.
A quel rico que es contento
Y otro no.

ARGASTO.

En tu plazer ni en tu pena
Consejo ni parescer
Puedo dar
Por que uoluntad agena
Yamas se puede entender
Ni mudar.
En tu mal no ueo modo
Ni yo se adonde uo
Ni en que ando
Pero como passa todo
A hora pensaua yo
Tu hablando.

Y la uida delos dos
Tan dulçes y uerdaderas
De passar
Quando nos yuamos nos
Por las huertas y riberas
A holgar,
Mas a hora ya no se
Que te pueda remediar

7 7

Siendo uiejo,
Mas quan bien te aconseje
Si tu quisieras tomar
Mi consejo.

Mas con Dios puedes quedarte
Pues me parto de cuidado
Combatido,
No que parta de lleuarte
En mi alma atrauessado,
Y metido.

BALTHEO.

Pues que te quieres partir
Y dexar tu natural
Do quies yrte
Pues adonde puede sir
Que no uaya alla tu mal
A seguirte
Ya deuias reposar,
Pues sera buscar peor
Tierra agena,
Que aunque mudes lugar
No mudara tu dolor
Ni tu pena.

Andaras muchos lugares
Sin saber tu solo aquien
Tu mal cuentes,
Por que lo que no passares,

78

No pienses sabello bien
Por las gentes.
Mira tu lo que ganado
En andar y a mu uer
Inzgaras,
Como quedas auisado
Para poder escoger
Lo que haras.

A R G E S T E.

No quiere con solo Amor
Ni lo quiera mi fermeza.
Por que es buena
Ni lo quiere mi dolor
Ni lo quiere mi tristeza
Ni mi pena.
En fin no puedo escusar
Esta jornada tan fuerte
Yo hazer
Por que uoluntad forçar
Es la misma cruda muerte
Ami uer.

B A L T H E O.

Argasto pues que te uas
Solos Dios uaya contigo
Y no al,
Pero no se si ueras

79

Al trifte Baltheo amigo
De fu mal.

Pero fi nunca lo uieres,
  Por que lo querra aßi
  Amor ciego,
  Ado quiera que oftuuieres,
  Que tu te acuerdes de mi
  Yo te ruego.

Que yo quedo en'efta fierra
  Conteno por todos modo
  Me quexando,
  Mas fi fueras a tu tierra
  Encomendame a todos
  En llegando.

O con luego me comendar
  A mis padres fin tardança
  Y a Luzia,
  Con tambien me faludar
  A la hermana de mudança
  Y a fu tia.

Y pues has de caminar
  Vete antes que no ouedes
  Con la calma,
  Pero quiero te abraçar
  O abraço como quedas
  En mi alma.

8 0
AVTOR.

A braçados los pastores
Sospirauan y gemian
Y en las cosas que dezian
Bien mostrauan los dolores
Que de partirse tenian
Tristes lagrimas uertian,
No se pueden apartar,
Ni se uan ni se partian,
Por que en se partir sentian
Su coraçon se quebrar.

E ra la stima los uer
Tristes con triste partida,
Partida de no creer
Pues que no pierden la uida
Perdiendo todo plazer.
En fin que el remedio da,
El partir al mal presente,
Vase enfin Argasto ya,
No se qual mas pena siente,
Si el que queda o el que ua.

Que el partir no es partir,
Sino muerte ami pensar
Ni partir se a de nombrar,
Porque cierto que morir
Se deuiera de llamar.

                                        Por

81.

P or fer pena mas crefçida
  Que puede nadie fentir
  Ni que jamas fue fentida,
  Pero la noche uenida
  Comienço Baltheo ha dezir.

B A L T H E O.

O noche que tan ferena
  Te mueftras : pues mi dolor
  No confuelas ,
  No te duelas de mi pena ,
  Pues que mi fera peor ,
  Que te duelas
  O eftrellas pues fentis,
  Que me muero por amar
  Con firmeza ,
  Como todas no uenis ,
  Al penar : de mi penar ,
  Y trifteza .

O trifteza y quan fin orden
  Te hazes de mi feñora ,
  Prinçipal ,
  Por que todo fea deforden :
  El dolor que fiempre mora
  Con mi mal .
  O mi mal pues uerdadero,
  En mi alma eftas metido ,
  Y debuxado

r

82

Contento soy que no muero
Por que no uea perdido
Mi cuydado.

P ero pues que de contino
Me combate cruda guerra
Por que canse,
Ir me quiero peregrino
A buscar alguna tierra
Do descanse.
Campos con Dios os quedad
Pues ordeno, mi partida:
Por mi suerte,
Y me uoy con soledad
Caminando de la uida
A la muerte.

P or Delia si hermosa cruel
Murio el pastor Darinel.

N o ay cosa de mas locura
Ni pena mal ni tormento
Que poner el pensiamiento
Do no basta la uentura
Assi por su desuentura
Por Delia si hermosa cruel
Murio el pastor Darinel.

A lo matado la muerte
Por que el pastor desdichado

8 3

Quiſo poner ſu cuidado
Do no baſtaua ſu ſuerte
Aſſi con pena muy fuerte
Por Delia ſi hermoſa cruel
Murio el paſtor Darinel.

T odos los otros paſtores
A quien fortuna deſtierra
Se juntaron en la ſierra
Como firmes amadores
Cantan con triſtes dolores
Que por Delia hermoſa cruel
Murio el paſtor Darinel.

V ino Celſio y uino Iano
Vino Silueſtre y panſtor
Y Saliçio y Amador
Y Nemoroſo y Montano
Diziendo todos con Fauno
Que por Delia hermoſa cruel
Murio el paſtor Darinel.

Y empeçando de llorar
Con açipreſes cubierto
En aquel ualle deſierto
Lo acuerdan denterrar
Y el doloroſo cantar
Es por Delia hermoſa cruel
Murio el paſtor Darinel.

84

Y cafi ya fe muriendo
No me pefa con morir
Sino por no te feruir
El echo efta refpondiendo
Van en fin todos diziendo
Que por Delia hermofa cruel
Murio el paftor Darinel.

T odo el prado trifte eftaua
El ganado no pafçia
Mas pues Delia lo queria
Ventura lo confirmaua
Anfi fortuna moftraua
Que por Delia hermofa cruel
Murio el paftor Darinel.

L os paftores efcriuian
En los Robles fu hiftoria
Y por que quede memoria
Epitaphios le ponian.
Les quales todos dezian
Que por Delia hermofa cruel
Murio el paftor Darinel.

Y pues Delia fue feruida
Muere contento el paftor
Que nunca falto dolor
Mientras no falto la uida
Anfi con pena crefçida
Por Delia fi hermofa cruel
Murio el paftor Darinel.

85

Murio por no poder uella
Matolo amor y locura
Pero folo fue cordura
Perder la uida por ella
Anfi dize en fu querella
Que por Delia hermofa cruel
Murio el paftor Darinel.

El Poftrer punto llegado
Su alma con Dios embia
Y el coraçon que tenia
A Delia lo ha mandado
En el qual ua debuxado
Que por Delia hermofa cruel
Murio el paftor Darinel.

Y quando ya fe partia
De la uida al çielo mira
Y por Melifeo fofpira
A quien mas que affi queria
Y con lagrimas dezia
Que por Delia hermofa cruel
Murio el paftor Darinel.

Pero enfin murio contento
La muerte tuuo por uida
Que pues Delia fue feruida
Dichofo fue fu tormento
Anfi con fu penfamiento
Por Delia fi hermofa cruel
Murio el Paftor Darinel.

               Fin.   F   iii

86

P ues uuestra graçia perdi
Por querer lo que quereis
Defacordado de mi
A mi mismo aborresçi
A quien uos aborresçeis
A mi mismo mismo sigo
Con el pago que me distes
Peleo mismo comigo
Soy me mortal enemigo
Despues que mal me quesistes.

C laro estaua mi penar
Mi señora si os mirasse
Mas no por eso pensar
Que solo por os amar
A mi mismo desamase
Mis ojos solo por uer
Ni son mios ni ya uen
Ved en fin mi padesçer
Que solo por os querer.
Nunca mas me quise bien.

Y a no soy quien ser solia
A mi mismo ando matando
De mi mismo huyr querria
Los dias passo llorando
Las noches sin alegria
Trocose por mal mi bien
Que pues uos lo consentistes
Dolor a dolor me den

8 7

Que no espero bien conquien
Vos señora aborrescistes.

P rometieron me los ojos
Mi señora de nos uer
No lo quieren mantener.

M i uoluntad y sentido
Mi bufano pensamiento
Viendo cresçer na tormento
Y mi bien todo perdido
A mis ojos en pedido
Que jamas os quieran uer
No lo quieren mantener.

P or que todo lo uedado
En los males de affiçion
En cresçiendo la pasion
Vemos ser mas desseado
Ansi que cuiendo jurado
Mi señora de nos uer
No lo quieren mantener.

C on os uer por su uentura
No hallan ningun remedio
Si nos uer mueren sin medio
Y no basta su cordura
Ansi por mi desuentura
Iurando de nunca os uer
No lo quieren mantener.

F   iiii

88

Quando crefçe el mal que fiento
No pudiendolos forçar
Van los triftes a bufcar
Con es uer algun aliento
Y haziendo juramento
Mi feñora de nos uer
No lo quieren mantener.

Fin.

De los males el mayor
Que enel mundo puede fer
El con neçios entender.

El fufrir mal con amor
El querer fin fer querido
Haze perder el fentido
Y caufa graue dolor
Pero trabajo mayor
Segun que puedo faber
El con neçios entender.

El tener poca uentura
En las armas en los dados
No fon pequeños cuydados
Ni pequeña defuentura
Mas otra pena mas dura
Sin dudar deue de fer
El con neçios contender.

89 ·

E l paſſar la loca mar
    Por oro fino tener
    Y deſpues aca boluer
    Con perder y no ganar
    Coſas ſon para llorar
    Mas mayor mal deue ſer
    El con negios entender.

E l ſalir ha tornear
    Delante de gente alguna
    Y ſer contraria fortuna
    Con honrra poca ganar
    Es cierto graue peſar
    Mas mayor deue de ſer
    El con negios entender.

Q ue no baſta ſufrimiento
    Ver una mala crianza
    Vna vana confianza
    Vn hablar ſin ningun tiento
    Biuira con mas contento
    Con los getas ami uer
    Que con negios entender.

C ierto que pequeña pena
    Con razon no deue ſer
    Sufrir aquel reprehender
    Contratar de uida agena
    A graue mal ſe condena
    Quien por ſuerte ha de tener
    El con negios contender .

90

Qual es el mayor pesar.
Sufrir neçios con furor
Qual es el mayor dolor
Con un neçio conuersar
Al desabrido çelar
Algun mal puede exçeder
El con neçios entender.

El que biue desterrado
En estrangera region
El que padesçe prision
Padesçe graue cuydado
Mas ningun mal comparado
E nel mundo puede ser
Ael con neçios entender.
Fin.

Por que uentura me tiene
Con un dolor tan llagado,
Por que la causa do uiene
Satisfaze ami cuydado
Por que mi gran sentimiento
No siente pena mortal,
Por que tan dulçe tormento
No se puede llamar mal.
Por que nunca ami presençia
Aporta ningun plazer,
Por que quien biue en ausençia
Iamas puede alegre ser
Por que no me quexo yo

91

Al amor de mi penar,
Por que aquel que me perdio
Ya no me puede ganar
Por que con grande clamor
No pido fin ami fuerte,
Por que no puede la muerte
Remediar mas quel dolor.
Por que no espero pues ueo
Que merezco fer pagado,
Por que nunca al desdichado
Se le cumple su desseo
Por que ya no ueo aqui
Ami mal ningun amigo,
Por que yo soy enemigo
Continuamente de mi.
Por que no uoy a buscar
La que causa mi tormento,
Por que pienso no a çertar
A dezir el mal que siento.
Por que no busco yo aqui
Algun remedio ami pena
Por que pago en tierra agena
Lo que en otras tierras ui
Por que no huyo affiçion
Pues que contino me mata,
Por que quien assi me trata
Satisfaze ami passion.
Por que mi seso se ua
A buscar mi pensamiento
Por que a tan grande tormento

9 2

Ser cuerdo no baſtara,
Por que tan graue tormento
No me da hora de gloria,
Por que peſa a la memoria
Con tan gran atreuimiento
Por que quiero yo quexarme
Que pareſçe ſer gran mengua
Por que no mas que la lengua
La uentura quiſo darme,
Pues porque muriendo biuo
Sin querer gozo tener
Por que yo no padeſçer
Me ſera dolor eſquiuo,
Pues por que quiero quereros
Por querer mi perdiçion,
Por que ſi dexo deueros
Renunçio mi galardon
Por que renunçio alegria
Y la trueco por paſsion
Por que os ſirua noche y dia
Ami coſta el corazon
Por que querer me deſtierra
A tener guſto de nada,
Por que tienen pregonada
Contra mi los males guerra
Por que pierdo mi ſentido
Sintiendo tal padezer
Por que fue muy atreuido
Mi querer en os querer,
Por que pues que juſto peno

No hago fino llorar
Por que no puede dexar
La memoria al tiempo bueno
Paraque lloro mis daños
Pues no remedio lo echo
Por uer que gafte mis años
Como cofa fin prouecho,
Pues o mezquino por que
No los procuro cobrar,
Por que el tiempo que fe fue
Atras no puede tornar,
Pues por que a tan gran pena
No procuro de dar gloria
Por que folo la memoria
De lo hecho me condena
Por que la grande pafsion
De mi mal dezir no ofo
Por que permite razon
Que dicha no de repofo
Por que pienfo que fi fiento
Otro jamas no fintio,
Por que pueden morir çiento
Del mal de que muero yo,
Por que no uoy a bufcar
Algun defcanfo mas bueno,
Por que dexando el penar
Penare por que no peno,
Por que mi gran penfamiento
No bufca aquien fe quexar
Por que tal atreuimiento

94

No se puede sentençiar
Por que de aquello que espero
Me uiene graue tormento
Por que espero y desespero
Todo junto en un momento
Por que mi uida esta llena
De confusion desigual
Por querer mal ami pena
Y querer bien ami mal
Por que remedia el dolor
Mi triste uida acabar,
Por que a quien mata el amor
No se deue de quexar
Por que pienso que hermosura
Como la suya no sea,
Por que la hizo uentura
Por que su poder se uea
Por que con todo saber
A esta sola no alabo,
Por que pienso no poder
Dar comienço do no ay cabo
Pues por que me quexo della
Pues que uella mereçi
Por que me pago con uella
La libertad que perdi
Por que pues tal pena sierto
La uida quiero tener,
Por que ha de feneçer
Con la muerte mi tormento
Pues por que no siento gloria

95

En penſar en ella aqui ,
Por que eſtoy fuera de mi
Y lexos de ſu memoria
Por que la uida nã engaña
Pues mi bien tan tarde uiene ,
Por rogar a quien me daña
Burlar de quien mi ſoſtiene .
Pues por que quiero rogar
A la que triſte me offende ,
Por mayores gracias dar
A quien mi dolor enciende .
Pues por que a tal dolencia
Triſte no buſco algun medio
Por que los males de auſencia
No tienen ningun remedio
Por que no pienſo alcançar
Bien de quien tanto mal dio ,
Por que no puede dexar
De penar el que peno .

Fin.

96

AL SENNOR
ALONSO NVNNEZ
DE REYNOSO YN SV
amigo y seruidor, el Sr. Tom̄
Gomez

Ve uale amiſtad tener
Señor Reynoſo pregunto,
Sino ſe deue eſtender
Al amigo reprehender
Quando ua fuera del punto?
Aſi yo de puro amor
Sintiendo uueſtro dolor
Por curar uueſtra dolencia
Vſare deſta licencia,
Concedeldo aſi ſeñor.

De contino os ueo andar
Penſatiuo y enojado,
Inquieto en el eſtar
Nel oyr y en el hablar
Como hombre medio apenado,
Tan metido en confuſion
Tan leno de alteracion
Que por las mueſtras de fuera
Mui claro uera qualquiera
Que padeçe el coraçon.

Veo que el ſueño no amais,
Ni guſtais lo que comeis,

Ni de

97

Ni de ueſtiros holgais,
Y ſi alguna uez jugais
Por que no os plaze, perdeis;
Conuerſacion no os contenta,
Que en lo mejor de la cuenta
La compañia dexais,
Y el remedio que buſcais
Se buelue en mayor affrenta.

D el ſoßiego os apartais
Como coſa que no os toca,
Y quando a meſa os ſentais
El primero os leuantais
Con el bocado en la boca
A la ſoledad os his
Con uos miſmo combais
Y bolueis no muy biſaño
A coſejos de temprano,
No ſe lo que alla ſentis:

D e uueſtras penas y males
Escriuis noches y dias
Y las pintais mas mortales
Que el planto de Ieremias
Ni las furias infernales
Mas por no moſtrar ſlaqueza
Las cubris con gentileza
Fingiendo que en Lombardia
Silueno paſtor tenia
Amores con la triſteza.

G

98

Y si a uezes acontece
  Que os mostrais satisfecho,
  Es falso lo que pareçe
  Y tan poco permaneçe
  Como la flor del Helecho,
  Que dende a un rato passado
  Os tornais tan alterado
  A nuestras lamentaçiones
  Mudanças y confusiones
  Como en el primer estado .

Muestranse estos accidentes
  Y otros mil, que es cosa estraña
  Muy mas rezios y aparentes
  Quando açiertan passar gentes
  Que uan o uienen de España,
  Entonçes creçen las penas ,
  Veros en tierras agenas
  Pensando en çiudad Rodrigo
  Y Guadaljara digo
  Por lo qual perdeis las çenas.

Viene os ala fantasia
  La dulçe conuersaçion
  De Guzman doña Maria
  Y de otras damas que son
  En aquella compañia,
  Y de amigos caualleros
  Que contais por uerdaderos ,
  Y con esto os passeais

99

Muy penſoſo, y nos mirais
A todos como eſtrangeros

De alli ſaliendo en leuado
En un canton os meteis
Triſte y lleno de cuidado,
Y del paſtor deſterrado
Vna obra componeis,
Y os uenis a reſoluer
Ningun remedio tener
Pues teneis en eſta uida
La uoluntad ya perdida
Y el ſeſo para perder .

Dizen os los paſſajeros
Que ſeria bueno bolueros
Alos Reynos de Caſtilla ,
Y qualquicra palabrilla
Muy preſto haze moueros.
Y uiendos amutinado
Quien uee que uais engañado
Os exhorta a la uerdad
Y con gran difficultad
Conoſçeis uueſtro pecado.

Aſſi que deſtas razones
Segun puedo comprender,
La cauſa de ſus paſſiones
Males y tribulaçiones
El abſençia deue ſer.

G ij

100

No dexando de penſar
Que me podria engañar
Como a muchos acontece,
Que ſoio a Dios pertenece
El coraçon penetrar.

Mas ſi todos uueſtros daños
Se recreçen del abſençia,
Por que no duren mas años
Conuiene con deſengaños
Curaros eſta dolençia,
Que ſeria gran crueldad
Quien tiene uueſtra amiſtad
Si uee que caminais çiego
No prouuraros ſoßiego
Con deziros la uerdad.

Y pues neſto me he metido
Ruego os me querais dezir
Que bienes haueis perdido
Que males os han ſeguido
Por de Caſtilla os uenir?
Que no puedo penſar yo
Que lo que alla os quedó
Fueſſe de tanto ualor,
Que no ſea muy mejor
Lo que en uenir ſe ganó.

Ni ſee qual hombre de honor
Siendo de lexos partido
Hallando tanto fauor
Como hallaſtes uos Señor

101

No se aya por bien uenido,
Pues casi sin conoçeros
Le plugo de recogeros
Quien os da tal trattamiento
Que podeis biuir contento
Sin a otro someteros.

Y pues en esto se ençierra
Tanta parte de quietud,
No se por que os hazeis guerra
Hallando en aquesta tierra
Quien usa tanta uirtud,
Que el mejor si lo estimais
Y mirad no lo perdais
Es la buena uoluntad
Que os tiene por su bondad
La Señora adonde estais.

D e los suyos sois amado
De parientes bien querido
Y de los mas acatado,
No como hombre desterrado
Mas hermano a qui nascido
Pues las Señoras no oluido
Que assi os han fauorecido
Que podeis dezir de uero
Nunca fuera Cauallero
De Damas tan bien seruido.

A si que Señor Reinoso
Pues tantas cosas sabeis
G iii

102

De hombre muy ingenioso,
Sabed tomar el reposo
Mejor de lo que hazeis.
Que mucho es de reprender
El que sabe componer
Del tiempo la qualidad,
De justicia y de uerdad
Ensi no las conoscer.

Gozad uuestro estado en paz,
Sin traer al pensamiento
Que pudierades ser mas,
Y teniendo sufrimiento
No podreis tornar atras
No conteis con lo mejor
Mas pensad en lo peor
Aque podiades uenir,
Y assi, si os sabeis sufrir,
Verneis a ser muy mayor.

Y por que alguno diria
Que comienço a predicar
Dare fin a esta obra mia,
Mandad señor perdonar
Si fue mucha la osadia.
Y os doi todo mi poder
Que me podais reprehender
Mis deffetos de contino,
Que tambien sera camino
Para me reconoscer.

· 103 ·

ALONSO NVNNEZ
DE REYNOSO AL SEN=
NOR THOMAS GOMEZ
RESPVESTA.

V n que me falta ſaber
(Lo que de mi nunca
niego)
Qviſiera ſeñor tener
Para poder reſponder
Mas repoſo y mas ſoßie=
Eſcriuir uerſo requiere   (go.
En trabajos no penſar,
Y quien eſto no tuuiere.
Ninguna coſa que hiziere
Se podra uer ni mirar.

Mis bienes todos perdidos,
En tal eſtremo me tienen
Mis peſares tan creçidos,
Que unos males partidos,
Otros por la poſta uienen.
Por lo qual yo no eſpero
Coſa buena aqui eſcriuir,
Por que ſe muy bien que Homero
Si muriera como muero
Pudiera menos dezir:
A nſi mi Muſa ueſtida
De triſteza, y mal compueſta,
Su uena toda perdida,

G iiij

104

Descontenta y dessabrida
Os embia la Respuesta,
Pero esta libertad
Concedida Señor tiene
La santa fiel amistad,
Que hablar solo uerdad
Sin mas estillo conuiene.

Descuido suelto es mejor
Sin rodeos ni otra cosa,
Por que adonde hai amor
Vsar tengo por peor
Pesadumbre curiosa
Quien amistad inuento
Bien le puso nombre santo,
Y por mi confiesso yo
Que ningun bien me quedo
Que estime ni precie tanto;

Ni tenga por mas mejor
Ni cosa que mas queria,
Como tener por Señor
A uos, que daros loor
Hurtarlo de uos seria
Es testigo desto Dios
Que yo tuue amigos ya,
Mas ninguno como uos
Y tan solamente dos
Por uos y mi se dira.

Vos me dais siempre fauor
Con contino me mandar

105

Aquello que es lo mejor,
Yo lo pago con amor
Que no tengo mas que dar.
Vos con uuestro gran saber
Emmendais todos mi daños,
Yo dichoso os quiero uer,
Y que no ayais menester
El buscar Reinos estraños.

Vos como bien me quereis
Para biuir me dais medio,
El bien que teneis gozeis,
Y jamas no esereis
Que el tiempo dara remedio,
Vos gran cuidado teneis
Que mi bien por uos ganado
No pierda, pues lo perdeis,
Plega a Dios que no gasteis
Ningun tiempo mal gastado.

Vos que lo cierto sabeis
Que me gane desseais
Y desto pena teneis,
Consejo siempre me deis
Y nunca lo recibais
Y pues uos me reprehendeis
Y mis trabajos sentis,
Las gentes que conuerseis
Sepan como uos sabeis
Y entiendan lo que dezis.

106

En tanto que los uitales
Spritos en mi duraren,
O con bienes o con males
O con tiempos defiguales
Mis años triftes paßaren,
O tenga buena uentura,
O tenga contino llanto
Hafta que la tierra dura
Con fu fuerte fepultura
Me cubra con frio manto,

A uos tendre folamente
Por mi bien tan eftimado
Quel tan deffeado Oriente
Quen riqueçe tanta gente
De ninguno es tan amado,
La madre dulçe al querido
Hijo nunqua quifo tanto,
Ni igual amor fe uido,
Tanto que de andar fentido
De mi mismo yo me fpanto.

Como con fiempre penfar
En uueftro merefçimiento
Tengo tiempo de penar?
Ni de fiempre me moftrar
Tan trifte tan defcontento?
No caufa abfençia mi mal,
Ni menos fer apartado
De mi tierra o natural,
Ni ueftirme de fayal

107

Ni de seda,ni brocado.

Tales cosas no me dan
   Causa de ser descontente ,
   Ni me dan pena ni affan ,
   Por que dizen que de Pan
   No se bive solamente .
   Dame pena que perdi
   El tiempo que no boluiò
   Y no see que fue de mi ,
   Mas pues fue,que sea ansi
   Y que pague quien pecò .

Bien quisiera sufrimiento,
   Pero pues que mi passion
   Es mayor delo que siento,
   Tener ningun sufri miento
   Es falta de coraçon
   Al dexar yo de sentir
   Pudiera dar señor medio
   La muerte con el morir,
   Pero no puede uenir
   Por que es cosa de remedio.

Y pues tan claros se uen
   Mis males con orden tal,
   Todos me maten y den,
   Que quien no espera bien
   No puede suffrir ya mal ,
   No tenga nigun plazer,
   Mi comer sean enojos ,

108

Y tristezas mi beuer,
Las piedras tengan poder.
Para quebrarme los ojos

A nsi mis males doblados
Con razon ser reprehendidos
No deuen sino llorados
Y con razon perdonados
De los amigos queridos
Ni menos biuir contente
No es iusto ni razon
Lo que mas mi alma siente
No se dize breuemente.
Por que cosas de alma son.

E n fin que mi sospirar
Mi perder todo sentido
Mi gemir y mi llorar
Todo lo uereis parar
En tiempo tiempo perdido,
Tiempo de plazer cumplido
A un que para mi cruel
Y tan poco conoscido
Tiempo que despues de ydo
Se me fue mi bien tras el.

F uera desto nada siento
Ni pesar en mi no mora
Por que biuo muy contento
Por uer el buen tratamiento
Que me haze mi señora
Y tantas mercedes son

109

Las que resçibo dobladas
Sin tenerme obligaçion
Que solo con galardon
De Dios le seran pagadas.

Por las quales yo seria
Obligado como digo
Y gran deuda le ternia
Hasta que la tierra fria
Mi cuerpo tenga consigo
Lo qual tengo de dezir
Y ingrato nunqua ser
Y aun despues de morir
Soy obligado á seruir
Si lo puedo a questo hazer.

SIGVESE VN
ROMANCE.

El que nasçio sin uentura
Solo ua sin compañia
Tan altos sospiros dando
Que gran lastima ponia
Solo ua por los desiertos
Que poblado no queria
Al llorar suelta la rienda
Y con lagrimas dezia
Ay de mi mi tiempo ido,
Que atras no bolueria
Todos mis años passados
Vida ninguna tenia
Que en la santa Religion

¶ 1 O

Meterme yo no podia
Que no tengo uoluntad
Ni tenella merefcia
Bufcar los campos de guerra
No fe fi me conuenia
Soy uiejo para Pelea
Armas ufado no auia
Si en Indias me paffaua
No fe fi a Dios feruiria
Y quien es defuenturado
Poca uentura tehia
Algunas letras faber
Aquefto mejor feria
Pero letras de ganar
Mi uoluntad no queria
Soy amigo de las Mufas
Y por fello me perdia
Mas pues foy tan pobre yo
El ganar me conuenia
Y con efta perdicion
A mi mifmo me feguia
Soy me enemigo mortal
A mi mifmo mal hazia
Comigo traigo batalla
A mi mal yo me queria
Agora en aquefta edad
Que haga yo no fabia
En pequeño no ferui
Siendo uiejo lo haria
Quando la barba me crece
Quando ya me encanecia.

111

COMIENZA LA GLOSA
DESTE ROMANCE.

En el tiempo que turbada
    De nubes toda uestida
    Aurora uiene y cansada
    La hoja casi Rasgada
    Por las parcas de su ui
    Por aspera sierra dura
    Do jamas gente biuia
    Con ansia Rauiosa y dura
    El que biue sin uentura
    Solo ua y sin compañia.

Solo ua no de tristeza
    Solo ua su bien passado
    En penar llena firmeza
    Con sospiros en grandeza
    De sus lagrimas bañado
    Consigo se ua quexando
    Consigo su mal sentia
    Y lo que peco pagando
    Tan altos sospiros dando
    Que gran lastima ponia .

Bien mostraua en sus razones
    Quexarse con uoluntad
    Y que sus graues passiones
    A los tigres y leones
    Les pusieran piedad
    Sus trabajos encubiertos

212

Claramente descubria
Y con sus dolores çiertos
Solo ua por los defiertes
Que poplado no queria.

A los duros coraçones
Ablandara çiertamente
Las poffadas o mefones
Son fofpiros a montones
Nasçidos de lo que fiente
Y metido en tal contienda
Viendo que jamas tenia
En fu perdiçion emmienda
Al llorar fuelta la rienda
Y con lagrimas dezia.

S i la uida fe acabara
Quando comiençe mis daños
O quan mejor açertara
Por que agora no penara
Con memoria de mis años
No bafta ningun fentido
A fentir lo que fentia
Porque de todo perdido
Ay de mi mi tiempo ydo
Que atras no bolueria.

E l tiempo que corre mas
Que nadie por mas que ande
No lo ueremos jamas
                        Que

115

Que un paſſo buelua atras
Ni la parca que deſande
Quiſieron aſſi mis hados
Y mi ſuerte conſentia
Que biuieſſe con cuidados
Todos mis años paſſados
Vida ninguna tenia .

M is peccados lo mereſcen
La culpa toda yo tengo :
Quando nis dias feneſcen
Y ſer mortales pareſçen
A buſcar la uida uengo
La diuina ſaluaçion
Como deuo la queria ,
Mas ſiento del coraçon
Que en la ſanta religion ,
Meterme yo no podia .

S i tuuiera por coſtumbre
Dexar los uiçios de gana ,
No me fuera peſadumbre
Buſcar ala clara lumbre
Dexando la uida uana
Engolfado en mocedad ,
Y en regalos cadal dia,
No buſco tanta bondad
Que no tengo uoluntad
Ni tenella mereſçia .

H allone ſin uida aſſi
Sin deſcanſo ſin plazer

H

314

O enimigo de mi
Que pues mi tiempo perdi
Que uida puedo tener .
Ventura comigo yerra
Mas la culpa yo tenia
Y pues todo me deftierra
Bufcar los campos de guerra
No fe fi me conuenia.

No me fe determinar
No me determino en cofa,
En nada pienfo açertar
Mas bueno fuera bufcar
Vna uida tan honrrofa
Aquello que fe deffea
Pocas uezes fe cumplia,
Y menos fe como fea
Soy uiejo para pelea
Armas ufado no auia.

Pues fi quiero nauegar
Para prouar la uentura ,
Y muy lexos me paffar,
Yo fe çierto que la mar
A de fer mi fepultura.
Nada no me contentaua
Lo que haga no fabia ,
Y como dudofo eftaua
Si en Indias me paffaua
No fe fi a Dios feruiria.

285

Fue triste mi nasçimiento
　Por que luego que nasçia,
　Nasçio la pena que siento
　Y luego quiso tormento
　Armar guerra contra mi.
　Han contra mi pregoñado
　En la hora que nasçi,
　Los trabajos y cuidado,
　Y quien es desuenturado
　Poca uentura tenia.

El que conosçe faltar
　Parasi toda uentura
　No la deue procurar,
　Pues quererse auenturar
　Le sera mas desuentura.
　Assi deuo conoçer
　Que todo me faltaria,
　Mas pues me uco perder
　Algunas letras saber
　Aquesto mejor seria.

Que las letras den sossiego,
　Ninguno ay que no diga:
　Ni menos yo no lo niego
　Pero biuiendo tan çiego
　No se triste que me siga
　Ser mejor el studiar
　Claramente conosçia
　Para mas seguro estar
　　　　　　H ij

116

　　　Pero letras de ganar
　　　Mi uoluntad no queria.

E　llas muy honrrosas son
　　　Y segun que claro siento
　　　Son de mucha erudiçion
　　　Pero del monte Helicon
　　　Agenas y de contento,
　　　Mas pues tu mundo las usas,
　　　Cosas tuyas no queria
　　　Ni menos letras confusas
　　　Soy amigo de las Musas
　　　Y por sello me perdia.

A　las letras que son buenas
　　　El loallas le dan solo,
　　　Por que ya passo Miçenas
　　　Que pagaua con setenas
　　　A tus cosas roxo Apollo
　　　Todo lo bueno passo
　　　Y lo malo floresçia
　　　Poesia ya murio,
　　　Mas pues soy tan pobre yo
　　　El ganar me conuenia.

P　ero ami entendimiento
　　　Como lo desseo y quiero
　　　Satisfazen segun siento
　　　Las letras que dan contento
　　　Y ser pobre como Homero
　　　Son mas de mi condiçion

117

A estas solas queria,
Sin oyr otra razon
Y con esta perdicion
Ami mismo me perdia.

Y con esto que yo digo
Muy confuso biuo ansi
Pues que traigo ami comigo
Ami que soy ynimigo,
Tan solamente de mi
Mi uentura enfin es tal,
Que lo peor escogia
Y con aqueste mi mal
Soy me enemigo mortal
Y ami mismo mal hazia.

N inguno me quiere uer
De nadie querido soy
Mas ninguno puede ser
Mas enimigo ami uer
Mio de lo que yo soy
Mi pena no se dexalla
Ni se lo que me queria,
Para mi bien no se halla,
Comigo traigo batalla
Ami mal yo me queria.

Y o bien me supe apartar
D l peligro que temia
Mas como auia de pensar
Que de mi yo me guardar

H iii

118

Era lo que conuenia.
Mi florida moçedad
Gastado contino auia,
A sabor de voluntad
Agora na questa edad
Que haga ya no sabia.

Bien tengo yo conoscido
Que pues no es justo matarme
Que del tiempo que perdido
Era remedio el oluido
Para poder consolarme.
Por quel bien en que me ui
Oluidar mejor seria,
Pero pues que me perdi.
En pequeño no serui
Siendo uiejo lo haria.

Mis fuerças robustas sanas
Por quien yo sospirare:
Emplee en cosas uanas
Agora lleno de canas
En seruir las guastare.
Mi fortuna lo meresçe
Claramente conosçia
Que todo bien me falesçe
Quando la barba me creçe
Quando ya me encanesçia

F I N.

119

ALONSO NVNNEZ
DE REYNOSO AL SEN=
NOR FELICIANO DE SILVA.

Einoso el fin plazer fin alegria
Que biue aufente affi de fu mu
    darça,
Al caualiero de la filua embia
Salud, dulçe fin y buena andança
    De que carezco yo porque mi fuerte
    Me tiene fin uida y fin efperança
Y aun no niego que biuo y que la muerte,
    Como tan fin ley es y defconoçida,
    No me quiere matar por mi mal fuerte.
Es la uida que biuo muerta uida
    Y aquefta Elegia llena de borrones
    No ua limada ni menos polida.
Por quel que la leyere en fus razones
    Conozca bien la pena que padezco
    Y conozca mi mal y mis paffiones.
Conozca lo que fufro y que carezco
    De defcanfo y de plazer y de alegria
    A un paffando mas penas que merezco.
O Feliçiano quien te contaria
    El mal que paffo y fufro por que folo
    Dexe la Mufa tan amada mia.
Que amando de contino el roxo Apollo
    De Horcomuo yo amaua la Corriente
    Mas que nunca a los uientos amo Eolo.
Aquefto amaua yo tan folamente

                    H   iiii

120

A queſto amaua yo tan ſolamente,
    Amaua a Caliope, y ſus hermanas
    Delphico Phebo con Parnaſa fuente .

H olgaua de leer guerras greçianas
    Como ſalia Crenito de encarnado
    Y que fin tuuo la guerra de Canas.

Y donde Nilo burlador criado
    Fue, ſi las gentes de ſu naſçimiento
    Han la cierta uerdad Señor hallado .

P ero deſpues que por tener contento
    Mis caros padres a Iuſtiniano
    Siguo contino con aſaz tormento.

N o leo de Roma ni campo Troiano
    Ni ſe de Triuia ni de Ioue Amon
    Ni los trabajos del cauto Greçiano .

N i ſe do las piramides ſe ſon
    Como en proſa Poliçiano declaro
    Poeta muy fulgente del Helicon.

N o leo en eſtaçio ya que mal ſintio
    El ualeroſo Theſſalo Achileo
    Ni ſe la pena que al baxar paſſo ,

A las eſtigias por Iaſon Theſeo,
    Ni los dolores graues immortales,
    Que ſufrio por mirar a tras Orpheo .

P adezco gran dolor y ſufro males
    En leyes eſtudiar, las muſas dexando,
    Con quien ningunas letras ſon iguales .

A çirçes ya no ueo que engañando
    Paſſa ſiempre ſu uida con engaños
    En leones los hombres transformando.

1 2 1

E n los principios de mis dulces años,
   Alas phebeas musas Yo juraua,
   De no dexallas por ningunos daños,

S ino seguillas como aquien amaua,
   Y que antes hazia tras Tormes yria
   Que dexar a Cecropia a quien adoraua.

Y que antes el olympo dexaria
   La orden que le dio naturaleza,
   Que dexar las Phebales un solo dia.

D exasse de sentir la gran crieza,
   Que uso consigo aquel en flor tornado
   A quien mato su propria gentileza.

S entia descanso dulce y delicado,
   En uer como la biuda griega casta
   Tantos años spero lo desseado.

Y como el caçador por la madrasta
   Ninguna pena siente ni cuidado,
   Aunque ella por su amor se gasta.

Y quan mal a su padre fue otorgado
   De tres el do : postrero prometido,
   Y Hippolito murio despedaçado.

S in el auer tal muerte merescido
   No leo en el Nason el sin uentura
   Las battallas de Apollo y de Cupido.

N i leo la uida triste de amargura
   Que deuio passar Electra ausente
   De Orestes por quien tanto procura,

N i la Parca cruel como consiente
   Quitar al moço rezio de la uida
   Ala dama hermosa y rei potente.

122

Y en fin a qualquier cofa mas querida
   Que cōtra amor fortuna,y cōtra m
   No nos bafta poder ni guarida .

D ichoſo tu dichoſa la tu fuerte
   Naſçido de las Muſas y mas criado
   Y querido tambien de Marte fuerte,

Y de Diana la muy cafta amado ,
   Sigues las letras juaues y queridas
   De la braua Bellona ya enfadado.

Tus horas tienes to das muy medidas
   Leyendo de contino en Ciçeron
   Y lo mas primo de lenguas floridas.

Habitando de contino en Helicon
   Do tu fabroſa Muja tan hufana,
   Canta las cofas altas que en ti fon.

Que la que nos canto guerra Troyana
   No tuuo conel tuyo feſo igual
   Ni tal dulçura de ninguno mana .

Y biue con tigo ſpritu Phebal
   Por que en los figlos todos por uenir
   Sera tu fama eterna y no mortal .

Al fin biues muy lexos de fentir
   Quan poco fatisfaze al fentimiento
   Que ael pofthumo algun tiēpo de biuir

Para que ualer pueda el teftamento,
   Y quan poco fatisfaze degollar
   Cortar manos o pies o dar tormiento.

Que contento al ingenio pueden dar
   Aqueftas cofas Feliçiano di
   Que fe faten folo para ganar

1 2 3

Quiſierá ſer contento y pobre aßi
   Como el ciego de Homero quãdo andaua
   Cantando ſus uerſos a marauedi.
D'choſo pues a ti ſolo ſe daua
   Tratar de letras y de lo que amas
   Cón que todz tu uida ſe paßaua.
Entre las Muſas contemplando damas
   Vees tu hija la hermoſißima Maria
   Que no baſtan a loalla dos mil famas.
Sus galas miras y lo que ueſtia
   Si uiſte azul ſi uerde ſi morado
   Loandole las partes que enſi tenia.
Tales quedan a ti y aßi cuydado
   Que Timante pintor con ſu pinzel
   Sacar no pudo Roſtro tan loado.
Miras la linda y ſabia de Yſabel
   Que ſufre lo que ſienten los auſentes
   Pues fortuna le quiſo ſer cruel.
Laqual tienta alos fuertes como ſientes
   Vienen te a uer con ſobra de razon
   De eſtraños Reynos eſträgeras gétes.
Porque tu ingenio tu conuerſaçion
   Agoras biuas do con hermoſura
   Sale el ſolo do eſta Sententrion,
Deſſeada ſera,que tal uentura
   Es la tuya para en letras y ualor
   Que quererla loar ſera locura
Y mi Muſa buſcarte y a loor
   No puede,ni deue mas al Mantuano
   Heroyco jate Mantua como a flor,

124

Y Betica se huelge con Lucano,
  Y Meonides traiga muy hufana
  Su greçia, mas España a Feliciano
  Contra todos oponga muy loçana.

AL SENNOR DON
LOPE DE GVZMAN.

C on musa triste, de negro uestida,
  Conforme al tiempo, de mi desuentura,
  En los pesares con pesar metida,
A uos buen cauallero doy uentura
  Como puedo, pues que biuo sin ella,
  Y no sin graue concoxa con tristura,
D el feroz Marte, no tengo querella,
  Ni de las amorosas uanidades,
  Ni su tan dulçe pena quiero uella.
R iquezas posseer, o magestades,
  Ser mas galan, o ser mas cortesano,
  No quiero cosas: ya de moçedades.
L a delicada carne, mundo uano,
  El curso de mi uida en mal gouierno,
  De Dios es oluidarnos soberano.
L as regaladas camas, manjar tierno,
  El nunca reformarnos con emmenda,
  Es caminar señor al duro infierno.
B uscar los hombres siempre, la hazienda,
  Andar buscando, en cortes el thesoro,
  A los deleites es soltar la rienda.

N i peno por lo qual señor ni lloro,
  Mas por auellas, sin tiento buscado,
  En desconsuelo de continó moro.

O triste de mi siendo enamorado,
  Y de los regalos, blandos, contento,
  En mundanos plazeres engolfado.

E nellos con tener mi pensamiento,
  Passe ya lo mejor destos mis años,
  Tambien passando assi el breue contento.

A l mundo conoçi y asus engaños,
  Anduue con contino desasossiego,
  Y dexando al bien segui sus daños.

D el final reposo y buen sossiego,
  Y de quien me formo tan oluidado,
  Quanto estaua el sentido ya de ciego.

E n buscar mis locuras enleuado,
  En contino escriuillas muy metido,
  Y de mi alma querida muy quitado,

D el bien ajeno, mi tiempo perdido,
  Buscando algun plazer sin camino,
  Teniendo por mas uil el bien subido.

A me deleites nueuos de contino,
  Gaste tras uil terpeza assi mi uida
  Sin razon orden y sin ningun tino.

O por uana sperança conosçida
  O falso mundo andas enbaucando
  Para saluarse ala gente nasçida.

A ndas con tus mentiras enredando
  Con uil ganar ala humana priuança,
  Del bien eterno muchos apartando.

126

O dichoſo quien puſo ſu ſperança
En la inmortal hermoſura diuina
Sin colocar en ti ſu confiança,
Y ael camino derecho ſiempre atina
Buſcando con ſoßiego algun repoſo
Sin buſcar perlas ni theſoro en mina.
Porque dime traydor mundo engañoſo,
En que para todo lo que tu uendes
Ques duize plazer breue y amargoſo.
P orque o mundo falſo nos offendeſt
O mundo manjar de duros guſanos
Y di porque no ſueltas los que prendes.
Tus queridos regalos ſiempre uanos
Tus galas todas tus cortes penoſas,
Que bien les dan alos triſtes humanos,
Tus altas damas Galanas hermoſas
Se conuierten tambien en dura tierra
Por muy mas lindas o por mas graçioſas.
O mundo uano que contina guerra
Das ſiempre alos que ſiguen tu real
O biuan en poblado,o en agra ſierra.
A unos das un trabajo no mortal
A otros ſiempre das por galardones
Cuidados y ſoſpiros con mas mal.
A otros buelues coſarios y ladrones
En pena de lo qual pierden ſu uida
Por las publicas calles con pregones.
A otros ya ſu renta deſtruyda
O por gaſtalla mal,o por jugalla
Les das como quien eres la cayda

127

En fin que nadie que entra en tu batalla
    Saco fino paßion continuamente
    Que fin uerte pudieran bien dexalla.
Por otra parte dañas a otra gente
    En bufcar parafi conuerfaçiones
    Do corten de las uidas blandamente.
Y a otros a que traten religiones
    Para tratar los amores mundanos
    Con falfo dißimilo en fus fiçiones.
A otros tan robuftos como fanos
    Son con te conuerfar como mugeres
    Y perdiendo fu fefo fon liuianos.
A otros les enfalças con poderes
    Solo para abatillos de alta cumbre,
    Acortando de prefto fus plazeres.
No ay nafçido que con pefadumbre
    No biua mundo por te conuerfar,
    Con oluido de la muy clara lumbre.
Por lo qual te quiero ya dexar
    Llorando de mis ojos cara el çielo
    Y a Dios todas mis culpas co feffar.
A los que habitais en efte fuelo,
    por que no condeneis el alma querida,
    De Dios os conuiene bufcar co ifuelo,
Y pues feñor con mufa tan florida
    Teneis el puro ingenio fublimado,
    En cofa lo emplead que fea fubida,
Y lo que dixe del mundo maluado,
    Fue por que cauallero uos gafteis.
    Con Dios el breue tiempo bien gaftado.

128

L agala quen los uerfos poſeeis,
   A quel ſummo entender con agileza
   Nunca en amores baxos lo empleeis.

P orque no puede ſer otra riqueza,
   De preçio que mas pueda enriqueçer,
   Que contiento biuir en tal baxeza.

Y cumple en la memoria de tener,
   Pues que ſabemos ya ſin duda alguna.
   Quan breue tiene todo el feneçer.

N o ay para que buscar ya ala fortuna,
   Alla en la rica tierra del Oriente,
   Sino ſolo a Dios ques gloria una.

V ueſtro ſaber que cuento tan fulgente,
   Que Dios os dio ſegun que lo moſtrais,
   Tened ſolo en regiros ſabiamente.

Y o tengo entendido que lo obrais,
   Pero no yerro endezillo ſeñor,
   Si lo que digo bien conſiderais.

P ues todo naçe del fiel amor,
   Hatado con uos con nudo herculano,
   Por tanto no curo de daros loor.

B iuid ſeñor contento y muy hufano,
   Que las muſas con uos gran honrra tiené
   Como tuuieron con el Mantuano.

L as letras alos tales bien conuienen,
   Apollo es claro en uos y muy loçano
   Y de uos ſus pyerides ſe ſoſtienen.

FINIS.

129

STANCIAS DE

RVGIER, NVEVAMEN=
TE GLOSADAS.

Rvgier qual siempre fui tal ser yo quiero,
Hasta la muerte y mas si ser pudiere,
O sea amor manso o cruel guerrero,
O la fortuna de lo que quisiere,
Que peñasco mas firme ser yo espero,
Al qual la Mar con fieros uientos hiere,
Con bonança jamas o con tempestad,
No mudare querer, ni mi voluntad.

E scoplo de plomo se ha de uer,
Ymagen en Diamante hazer muy prima
Antes que mudarme jamas de querer
A Rugier que a querello mi se anima,
Y los rios atras tan bien correr
Antes que en mi mudança imprima,
Ni por malos ni buenos mouimientos
Ya no se mudaran mis pensamientos.

COMIENZA LA GLOSA

La bella Bradamante que herida
Esta casi sin sentido con furor
En pensamientos continos metida
En penas y. bires con gran dolor

130

Llorando ausente su muy triste uida,
Escriue a su Rugier con puro amor ,
Diziendo con pesar muy uerdadero,
Rugier qual siepre fui tal ser yo quiero.

La fe que te di tengo con firmeza ,
Comigo biue el contino cuydado ,
Que sufro por ti siempre con tristeza ,
El mismo dolor passo sin mudado
Ser jamas por fortuna ni grandeza.
Que ni por Reinos ni por gran estado
Dexara mi alma de querer como quiere,
Hasta la muerte y mas si ser pudiere.

Jamas igualara a mi querer
Amor ninguno de ningun nascido ,
Las cosas todas mudaran su ser
Antes que de mi Amor punto perdido,
Ni mudança ninguna he de tener,
Para contigo si tengo sentido,
Morire por ti como agora muero ,
O sea amor manso o cruel guerrero.

Agora uista real uestidura,
A ora uestida con sayal me uiesse,
A ora fortuna en la mayor altura
A tu leal Bradamante la pusiesse
Con alteza tan grande que uentura
De sola ella embidia resçibiesse,
Con todo querre,o suerte consintiere,
O la fortuna de lo que quisiere .

1 31·

Si tus cabellos roxos se boluiessen
 Todos blancos por los sobrados años,
 Y tus ojos claros se obscurescçiessen
 Tales qui enel mirar fuessen estraños,
 Y batalla campal contra mi hiziessen
 Causando por quererte brauos daños,
 No mudaria mi querer entero,
 Que peñasco muy firme ser yo espero.

Tendre en te amar mas duro coraçon
 Que la tigre nascçida con brauez̃a,
 Ni que el mas brauo y mas feroz leon
 Quando demuestra mayor fortaleza,
 Que todas las cosas que nascçidas son
 Podran mudarse mas no mi firmeza,
 Pues que ser peñasco uentura quiere
 Al qual la mar con fieros uientos hyere.

En mi sospiros penas son los uientos
 Que al alma hieren muy continuamẽte,
 Y son de tanta fuerça sus tormentos,
 Que por mucho que digo mas se siente,
 Lo qual mas anima mis pensamientos
 Y que quiera mas uentura consiente,
 No dexare querer ni tu soledad,
 Iamas con bonança o con tempestad.

Agora sea la mayor señora
 Del mundo todo desierto y poblado,
 Agora quiças tan baxa pastora
 Que rija por los campos mi ganado,

I ij

132

Agora des de donde Phebo mora
Hasta donde se pone tenga estado
En fin con bien mal ni con aduersidad
No mudare querer, ni mi uoluntad.

Quando a los campos uoy a uer bolar
Las garças que siguen los caçadores
Tus cuidados no puedo alli oluidar
Y junto conellos continos temores
Que no dexan punto jamas descansar
A mi que sufro mortales dolores
A mi que antes que mude querer
Escoplo de plomo se ha de uer.

Escoplo de plomo con lima formar
En biuas peñas alguna figura
Y antes al cielo ueremos baxar
Y dar estrellas la tierra muy dura
Y ardientes llamas antes dar la mar
Que contigo mudar mi fe segura
Y antes hemos de uer pinzel o lima
Ymagen en Diamante hazer muy prima.

A ti el poder mio tengo dado
El alma, lo que soy y la firme fe
Tal que ninguno por Cesar jurado
Soy çierta que mas firme no la posse
Ni que mas tenga seguro su estado
Ni igual amor entre la gentes se ue,
Que qualquier-mudança se podra uer
Antes que mudarme jamas de querer.

133

Mientras que Phebo diere resplandor
Por las verdes campiñas,montes,prados,
Por superbas çiudades , de gran ualor
Por cãpos de la guerra ensangrentados,
Siempre me turara mi firme amor
Sufrido con la fe de mis cuidados
Queriendo por mas que fortuna oprima
A Rugier que a querello mi fe anima.

Veremos los Corderos siempre andar
Entre los lobos por campos pasçiendo
Y por sierras altas las Naos naueger
Las claras aguas los fuegos teniendo
Y Latona Phebal tambien caminar
Quatro cauallos su carro rigiendo
Y todas las cosas contra natura ser
Y los rios atras tambien boluer.

Miran los tristes de las claras fuentes
Y los pastores con sed afligidos
Alos rios dexaran y a sus corrientes
Antes que yo con todos mis sentidos
Dexar de querer mis males presentes
Todos mis bienes alegres perdidos
Y perdere la uida que la prima
Antes que en mi mudança imprima.

No tienes que temer que en forma nueua
Se pueda mudar nunca el coraçon
Ni reyno ni riqueza que lo mueua
Ni todas cosas quantas nasçidas son

134

Que el fuerte amor no sola una prueua
Ha fecho,mas muchas con iusta razon ,
No me mudando sus golpes sangrientos,
Ni por malos ni buenos mouimientos .

El marfil blanco la piedra muy dura
Pueden con fuerças ya desmenuzarse,
Pero no que otra ninguna figura
Pueda en tan duras piedras reformarse,
Mi coraçon que sigue la natura
Conellas todas puede compararse,
Pues con mas males ni descontentos,
No se mudaran mis pensamientos.

FIN.

INDEX